RIDDICK'S
RULES OF
PROCEDURE

FLOYD M. RIDDICK
& MIRIAM H. BUTCHER

RIDDICK'S RULES OF PROCEDURE

*A Modern Guide to Faster
and More Efficient Meetings*

MADISON BOOKS
Lanham • New York • London

Copyright © 1985 by Floyd M. Riddick

Published by Madison Books
4720 Boston Way
Lanham, Maryland 20706

3 Henrietta Street
London WC2E 8LU England

Distributed by National Book Network

This edition was reprinted in 1991 by Madison Books
by arrangement with the authors

Library of Congress Cataloging-in-Publication Data

Riddick, Floyd Millard, 1908-
[Rules of procedure]
Riddick's rules of procedure : a modern guide to faster and more
efficient meetings / Floyd M. Riddick & Miriam H. Butcher.
p.   cm.
Reprint. Originally published: New York : Scribner, © 1985.
Includes index.
1. Meetings—Handbooks, manuals, etc.   2. Parliamentary
practice—Handbooks, manuals, etc.   I. Butcher, Miriam H.
II. Title.
[AS6.R53   1990]
060.4'2—dc20   90–24274 CIP

ISBN 0–8191–8064–5 (paper)

British Cataloging in Publication Information Available

This book is dedicated to our respective spouses, without whose support it might never have been written.

A special thanks to Lucille Place, and to our indexer, Beth Cady.

We would also like to acknowledge all contributors to parliamentary procedure, with the hope that this, our contribution, will add to its rich history.

Contents

Foreword xiii
Introduction xv

Absentee *1*
Absentee Voting *1*
Abstention *2*
Accept, Adopt, Agree To *2*
Acclamation *3*
Addressing the Chair *3*
Adjournment *4*
   Adjourn 4
   Adjourn to a Time Certain 4
   Adjourn Sine Die 5
Administrative Duties of the
   President *6*
Agenda *7*
   Motions That Can Affect the
   Order of Business 8
   Sample Order of Business or
   Agenda 9
Amendments and the
   Amending Process *12*
   Friendly Amendments 12
   Types and Precedence of
   Amendments 13
   Illustrations of the Amending
   Process 15
   Advantages of the Process 19
   Improper Amendments 20
   Amending Motions Previously
   Adopted 20
Announcements *21*
Annual Meeting *21*
Annual Session *22*
Appeal *22*

Assembly *23*
Associate Membership *24*
Assumed or Implied Motions *24*
Attorney *24*
Auditor *25*

Ballot *26*
Ballot to Nominate *27*
Blanks *27*
Boards *27*
Business of Meetings *30*
Bylaws *31*
   Writing Bylaws 31
   Construction of Bylaws 31
   Form of Bylaws 33
   Adoption of Bylaws 33
   Guidelines for Contents of
   Bylaws 34
   Amending Adopted Bylaws 36
   Revision of Bylaws 37
   Interpreting Bylaws 38

Call for the Regular Order *38*
Call Meeting to Order *38*
Call of a Meeting *39*
Call of the House *39*
Candidate *39*
Caucus *39*
Censure *40*
Chairman *40*
   Co-Chairman 41
Changing Previous Decisions *41*
Charter Certificate of
   Incorporation *43*
Charter Members *44*
Classification of Motions *44*

Close Debate 44
Closed Sessions 45
Commit, Recommit, and
    Refer 46
Committees 48
    Ad Hoc or Special Committees
        48
    Standing Committees 48
    Committees to Act 49
    Committees to Investigate 49
    Creation of Committees 49
    Committee Membership 50
    Qualifications of Committee
        Members 51
    Committee Chairman 52
    Conduct in Committee 52
    Conduct of Business in a Small
        Committee 53
    Limitations on Committees 53
    Powers of Committee 53
    Committee of One 54
    Committee Reports 54
    Ex Officio Committee Member
        54
    Discharge a Committee 54
    Committee Minutes 54
Consensus 56
Consent Adjenda 56
Consideration, Question of 56
Consider Informally, Recess to
    Consider Informally 56
Consider Seriatim 57
Consolidation 57
Constitution 58
Consultant 58
Conventions 58
    General Preconvention Business
        60
    Preconvention Committees 61
    Convention Resolutions
        Committee 62
    Opening Ceremonies 63
    Credentials Committee 64
    Rules Committee 65
    Program Committee 65
    Use of Floor Microphones and
        Color Cards 66

Convention Minutes 67
Convention Business Agenda
    68
Courtesy Resolution 69
Counsel 70
Creating a Blank 70
Custom and Precedent 70

Debate 71
    Members' Responsibilities 71
    Rules of Decorum During
        Debate 72
    Presiding Officer's Role During
        Debate 74
    Termination of Debate 75
    Motions That Help Control
        Debate 76
    Legal Interruptions to Debate
        76
    Motions That May Not
        Interrupt the Speaker 77
    Debate Strategy 77
Delegates 79
    Qualifications 80
    Duties 80
    New Delegates 80
    Instructed Delegates 80
    Uninstructed Delegates 80
    Delegates' Reports 80
    Alternates 81
Delegating Duties 81
Deliberative Assemblies 81
Dilatory Motions 82
Directors 82
Discharge a Committee 83
Discipline 83
    Presiding Officer's
        Responsibilities 83
    Members' Responsibilities 85
    Misconduct from the Chair 85
Dissolutions 86
Division of Assembly
    (Verification of a Vote) 87
Division of the Question 88
Documents of Authority 89
    Bylaws 89
    Standing Rules of Procedure 90

Standing Orders 90
Precedents and Practices 91

Elections 92
Emergency Situations 93
En Bloc 93
Executive Board 93
Executive Committee 93
Executive Secretary or Director
    94
Executive Session 94
Ex Officio 94
Expunge 94
Extend Debate 95

Filling Blanks 95
Finance Committee 95
Floor Privileges 96

General Consent 97
Germane 97
Good of the Order 97
Guest Speakers 98

Hearings 99
Honorary Membership 99

Illegal Votes and Votes Not
    Counted 100
Incidental Motions 101
Incorporation 101
Indecorum 101
Informal Consideration 101
Installations 101
Interruptions to Debate 102

Limiting Debate 102
    *Extending the Limit of Debate
    103*

Machine Voting 103
Mail Balloting 103
Main Motion 104
Majority Vote 106
Mass Meeting Requirements 106
Mass Meetings 106
Meeting Requirements 108
Membership 109
    Obligations of Members 110

*Rights of Members at Meetings
    111*

Merger 111
Minority Report 112
Minutes 113
    Contents of Minutes 114
    Sample Form for Minutes 115
Motions 116
    Improper Motions 116
    *Motions That Are In Order
        and Correct 116*
    *Motions That Are Amendable
        117*
    Precedence of Motions 117
    Procedural Motions 119

Nominations 120
Notice of Meetings 124

Oath of Office 124
Obtaining Recognition 124
Officers 124
    President 125
    President-Elect 126
    Vice-President 127
    Secretary 128
    Corresponding Secretary 128
    Directors 128
    Treasurer 129
    Other Officers 129
Opening Ceremonies 130
Order of Business 130
Orders 131
    General Orders 131
    Special Orders 131
Orders of the Day 132
Organizing a Permanent Society
    133

Pairing 135
Parliamentarian 136
    *Parliamentarian at Convention
        138*
Parliamentary Authority 138
Parliamentary Inquiry 138
Past President 140
Plurality Vote 140
Point of Order 140

Policy Statements *141*
Polls *142*
Postpone *143*
Precedents *144*
Preferential Balloting *145*
President *145*
  President's Vote 146
Presiding *146*
  Presiding Skills 146
Presiding by Others Than the
  President *147*
Previous Notice *148*
Privileged Business *149*
Privileged Motions *150*
Procedural Motions *151*
Processing a Main Motion *152*
Protocol *153*
Proviso *154*
Proxy Voting *155*
  Sample Proxy 156
Putting the Question *156*

Question of Consideration *158*
Questions of Privilege *159*
  Privileged Business 161
Quorum *161*

Ratify *163*
Reading Papers *164*
Recess *164*
Recognition *165*
Recommendations *165*
Reconsider *165*
Reference Committees *167*
Regular Order *168*
Renewal of a Motion *168*
Report of Tellers *169*
Reports *169*
  Committee Reports 169
  Report of the President 171
  Treasurer's Report 171
  Report on Finances 172
  Reports of Other Officers 172
Requests—Inquiries *172*
Rescind *173*
Resignations *174*
Resolutions *174*
  Sample Resolution 176

Revote *176*
Rights of an Organization *177*
Rights to Speak *178*
Rules of Order *179*

Secretaries *179*
  Recording Secretary 179
  Corresponding Secretary 181
Sergeant-at-Arms *181*
Seriatim *182*
Session *182*
Social Hour *182*
Slate *183*
Special Committees *183*
Special Meetings *183*
Standing Orders *184*
Standing Rules *184*
Stopping the Clock *186*
Sunshine Laws *187*
  Sunset Clause 188
Suspend the Rules *188*

Table *188*
Tape Recordings *190*
Teleconferences *190*
Tellers and Balloting Procedures
  190
  Recording Ballots 191
  Reporting 191
Terms of Office *192*
Trial and Expulsion of Members
  193

Unanimous Consent Procedure
  194
Undebatable Motions and
  Procedures *195*
Unfinished Business *196*

Vacancy in Office *196*
Verification of a Vote *197*
Vice-President *197*
Votes and Voting Methods *197*
  Method 197
  Requirements 197
  Voting Entitlements 198
  Absentee Voting 198
  Ballot Voting 198

Bullet Vote 199
Computer Voting 199
Consensus 199
Cumulative Voting 200
General Consent 200
Machine Voting 200
Mail Ballot 200
Plurality Vote 201
Preferential Balloting 201
Proxy Voting 202
Revote or Recount 202
Rising or Standing Vote 202
Roll Call Voting 202
Secretary Casting One Vote 203
Show of Hands 203
Telephone Vote 203
Tie Vote 204

Unanimous Vote 204
Unit Rule 204
Voice Vote 205
Write-in Vote 205
Voting Irregularities 205
    Challenging a Vote 205
    Challenging Illegal Votes 205
    Voting Frauds 206
Voting Requirements 206
    Majority Vote 206
    Two-Thirds Vote 207
    *Vote to Elect Committee
        Membership* 207
Voting Rights and Rules 208

Withdrawal of a Motion 208
Index 211

Foreword

A visitor to the gallery of the United States Senate is often surprised to discover that august body being presided over by a relatively unknown junior senator, rather than the Vice-President of the United States. The visitor is impressed by the full command of parliamentary procedures seemingly possessed by the presiding officer. For a quarter century, between 1950 and 1975, the man largely responsible for the illusory parliamentary skill of a succession of junior senators, this writer among them, was Dr. Floyd M. Riddick, now Parliamentarian Emeritus of the Senate.

Dr. Riddick, a mild and softspoken southerner, could lead an untutored presiding officer through complex and heated parliamentary entanglements. His quiet directions, spoken only for the ears of the senator seated directly behind him, and indiscernible in the Senate gallery, or on the Senate floor, would be repeated loud and clear, accompanied by appropriate raps of the gavel. The illusion of command and competence was complete.

As parliamentarian, Dr. Riddick was often at the center of Senate debate. In addition to providing aid and comfort for fledgling senators, Floyd Riddick was known for fair, courteous, and impartial rulings that guided floor leaders and opponents in the preparation and conduct of their debates. His skill and experience admirably fulfilled the purpose for which parliamentarians exist—the framing of issues and questions for orderly debate and resolution.

Dr. Riddick is perhaps the foremost authority on parliamentary procedure in the United States. A product of Duke and Vanderbilt, he has taught courses in political science at a number of colleges and universities, and for years has been active in the work of the American Institute of Parliamentarians. Upon Floyd Riddick's retirement as Senate Parliamentarian, several senators cited his coauthorship of "Senate Procedure" in 1958, and his 1964 and 1974 revisions of that monumental work; he was ranked among "the greatest parliamentarians" with John Hatsel, Parliamentarian of the House of Commons in the eighteenth century, and Thomas Jefferson, whose *Manual* is the original code of rules for the Senate.

Dr. Riddick and his coauthor, Miriam H. Butcher, with contributions and assistance by Lucille Place, have rendered a significant service by combining their unique capabilities in the writing of this new book on parliamentary procedures. These authors, mindful of the changing needs of our society, have blended new concepts of parliamentary process with the traditional, but have eschewed archaic language and unnecessary formalities. These modifications will be helpful to the reader seeking guidance in facilitating business and timely decision making. Moreover, the book is arranged in alphabetical order so that its subject matter is readily accessible.

A new comprehensive work on parliamentary procedure is needed. This volume, in which the rules and information necessary for the conduct of meetings are set forth in orderly fashion, provides easy guidance for presiding officers seeking the means for expeditious decision making. Dr. Riddick and his colleagues have performed a necessary and useful task in presenting modern rules of parliamentary procedure in an understandable and helpful manner.

—WILLIAM B. SPONG, JR.
Dean, and Dudley Woodbridge Professor of Law
Marshall–Wythe School of Law
College of William and Mary

Introduction

The new concepts and innovations to general parliamentary procedure set forth in this book are primarily the ideas and convictions of Dr. Floyd M. Riddick, who has served for twenty-five years as a parliamentarian of the United States Senate. With coauthor Miriam H. Butcher and the assistance of Lucille Place, both former Presidents of the American Institute of Parliamentarians, Dr. Riddick has here set forth a system of rules that is designed to do for meetings of all kinds what his book *Senate Procedure* has done for that august body: to simplify and streamline its procedures without sacrificing the rights of minorities or individuals.

This system of parliamentary rules does not represent a radical departure from the democratic parliamentary tradition; all decisions under the procedures established here are determined by a majority vote except those cases where the rights of the members might be infringed upon, such as in limiting or closing debate. It is, however, the belief of the authors that while the principles of this tradition must be preserved, their practical application must be modified to meet the needs of the society in which they are used. In today's society one such need stands out: to get the business done with dispatch.

Riddick's Rules of Procedure meets this need in two ways. First, the system of parliamentary procedures that it puts forward has been purged of the unnecessary formalities and archaic language that have remained a part of many parliamentary guides. Second, the book itself—in contrast to traditional books of its kind—has been designed for ease of use; its alphabetical format makes it easy to pinpoint specific answers—even in the middle of a meeting—while its extensive index and cross-referencing enable one to quickly trace a topic to its theoretical foundations and to its connections to other areas of procedure.

These features of *Riddick's Rules of Procedure* make it the ideal *parliamentary authority* for organizations of all kinds. The parliamentary authority of an organization is the set of rules on which the presiding officer depends for guidance; it is subordinate to the organization's *documents of authority* (its bylaws, standing rules, etc.) but its sanctity is provided for in these documents. In the past, the selection of an organization's parliamentary authority has been complicated by the fact that traditional guides, while comprehensive enough for this purpose, have been too cumbersome to use in the heat of a parliamentary dispute. *Riddick's Rules of Procedure* is both comprehensive and readily accessible, making it in our opinion the most useful book in its field.

Dr. Riddick sums up well its overall aim:

> The great significance of parliamentary rules of order becomes apparent when a meeting is proceeding improperly and neither can the business be transacted nor the conduct of the assembly tolerated. When such a situation occurs, if there are established rules of order, the assembly has something to fall back on that will bring order out of chaos, when the chair enforces the rules or when a member calls for the regular order, requiring the chair to take over and demand proper procedure. This volume is designed to accommodate such procedure and get the job done after all participants have had their day in court.

—*The Editors*

A

ABSENTEE

Absentee members' rights are protected under common law and the bylaws of the organization. The bylaws should regulate the powers and limitations of the members and the assembly. They cannot be waived or suspended. They protect the adopted order of business, the requirements of a quorum, the right of previous notice, venue, elections, and changes of proposed bylaw amendments. All these protect the absentees.

Absent members do not reduce the quorum requirement but can affect the presence of a quorum. Absent members may not vote in absentia except pursuant to special provisions as provided in the bylaws or articles of incorporation.

Attendance means physical presence. Looking in or casual attendance without taking part in the proceedings, or being present for only a few minutes, does not constitute attendance.

Absent members may be nominated, elected, or appointed to office if prior consent to serve has been obtained.

Members of an assembly not present at a meeting but present at the next meeting are entitled to vote on the approval of the minutes of the previous meeting. Also, members who are absent during the debate and consideration of business of an assembly may vote if they are present when a vote is taken on it. Specific rights and restrictions of absentees are frequently incorporated in the bylaws, which may not be suspended.

ABSENTEE VOTING

It is understood that members should be present in order to vote since, in that way, they can participate in the dicussion and the changes made in the original proposition, and can thus vote more informedly and intelligently. However, the documents of authority may provide for absentee balloting in one of two ways—by proxy or by mail.

See also **Votes and Voting Methods**.

ABSTENTION

Most members of an assembly consider that "I abstain" means one did not vote, but this is not entirely accurate. It is true that by abstaining (abstentions are sometimes called "pass" votes) one does not cast a ballot or does not respond to a call for "aye" or "no," but in a sense a vote is cast. By withholding an opinion, a member automatically casts weight to the prevailing side, since most organizations determine the outcome of a decision by a majority of those present and voting. By not voting, the majority required is reduced by just so many abstentions. If, on the other hand, voting regulations require a majority of those *present*, an abstention is not a neutral position since it now becomes equivalent to a no vote, giving advantage to the negative voters.

Members have an obligation to vote, but cannot be compelled to do so. Abstentions are never counted except to determine the presence of a quorum. However, as an appellate court has decreed, "an abstention is not a vote, but abstainers are bound by the result of those who do vote."

During roll call voting, when not prohibited by the documentary authority, one who wishes to abstain from voting may answer "present," or "here," or "I abstain," but is counted as present at the meeting to assure the presence of a quorum. Members usually abstain from voting when they have a conflict of interest and in some cases are required to do so by the rules. Generally speaking, no member is prohibited from voting for himself or herself in an election for office.

ACCEPT, ADOPT, AGREE TO

To "receive" a report is to "accept" it. To "agree to" a report is to "adopt" it.

A report may be accepted without comment. This means that the report is understood to have been presented and its contents noted. No action, opinion, or endorsement from the assembly is required. No action should be taken. The report is placed on file for reference.

To move to adopt or agree to a report means that the assembly concurs in all the contents of the report and is ready to implement all of its recommendations or policies. Customarily, the assembly acts only on the recommendations or specifics in the report, which are usually placed at the end for the convenience of the assembly. It is possible to adopt only certain sections contained in the report.

ACCLAMATION

Election by acclamation, (or by "general consent") is a voting strategy used to save time. It is used only for elections. When bylaws or standing rules do not require a ballot or roll call vote and there is no nominee other than the one nominated, the bylaws or standing rules can provide this shortcut, if there is no objection, so that the presiding officer may declare a single nominee elected by "acclamation" or by "general consent."

When the required number of nominees, but no more, has been nominated for a committee, the presiding officer may also, with no objection, declare those names as the official committee, since it is assumed that the assembly is content.

Acclamation is not a recommended procedure in some instances since it eliminates any write-in votes, discourages opposition, and implies unanimous consent without any such proof.

ADDRESSING THE CHAIR

Every member is entitled to speak during a business meeting, but the turn to speak must be correctly obtained. When a member desires to speak to the assembly, the member must rise, address the chair by the proper title as Mr. or Madam President, Mr. or Madam Chairman, or by whatever title the organization has chosen. The member then waits to be recognized, that is, acknowledged by the chair as being entitled to speak at that time and to have the right to be listened to with courtesy. It is the chair's duty to protect these rights. No one except the presiding officer has the authority to recognize a speaker. No other officers are addressed during the conduct of business except the chair.

A guest speaker at a banquet or luncheon should address the president first as the official representative of the organization and may address others at the head table or the members collectively.

See also **Rights to Speak**.

ADJOURNMENT

To adjourn means to terminate a meeting. The motions to adjourn take one of the following forms (in order of precedence): adjourn; adjourn to a time certain; and adjourn sine die. These motions have the highest privilege or priority of any motions; they require no second, are not debatable, are adopted by a majority vote, and may not interrupt a speaker. Only the motion to adjourn to a time certain is amendable, and that to time only.

Adjournment usually occurs when the business of a meeting is concluded and no further business is presented. The chair may ask, "Is there any further business?" (pause) "Hearing none, without objection, the chair declares the meeting adjourned." Any member may also move to adjourn; the motion can then be adopted by a majority vote, or, with no objection, by general consent. A meeting may be adjourned at any time during the meeting, as no assembly may be kept in session against its will unless the bylaws require that certain things be done before adjournment. The chair has no power to adjourn a meeting on its own initiative except in case of emergency.

Adjourn

Regardless of how much business remains to be considered or how many motions are pending, any member may move to adjourn when given recognition, unless the documents of authority restrict it. After the motion has been proposed, the chair may briefly point out the consequences of adopting such a motion if the chair believes it to be premature, or any member, with the consent of the assembly, may do likewise. The members, however, must act on the motion.

Adjourn to a Time Certain

The motion to adjourn to a time certain is not in order for a brief interruption of that day's proceedings. To interrupt a meeting for a brief period on the same day requires the motion to recess; the purpose of this motion is to provide continuation of business at a subsequent meeting before the next regularly scheduled meeting. It is, in effect, a recess, called an adjournment because of the length of time involved.

See also **Recess**.

To adjourn to a time certain permits the assembly to move that the current session be adjourned to a specific time, and is designed to permit the assembly to designate when it will come back into session before its next *regularly* scheduled meeting. The motion is amendable as to the date and time for the next (previously un-scheduled) meeting.

Sometimes adjournment to time certain becomes necessary be-fore the agenda has been completed because the room must be vacated, the hour is too late, or for some other reason. On such an occasion, any member who feels that some unfinished business must be completed before the next regularly scheduled meeting (if no motion simply to adjourn is pending) may, after recognition, move to adjourn to a time certain. This means that another day or time that is prior to the next regular meeting may be selected for a meeting in order to continue or complete the necessary business.

The business that may be considered at an adjourned meeting is the continuation of the business scheduled, but not acted on, at the previous meeting from the point where it was interrupted. After the call of a meeting to order, the minutes of the previous meeting are read and disposed of. Adoption of the motion to adjourn to a time certain constitutes previous notice, but the time and place must be included.

All the members need not be notified as in a call to a special meeting. If the business has still not been completed, another ad-journed meeting may be adopted by a majority vote.

See also **Call Meeting to Order**.

Adjourn Sine Die

The motion to adjourn "sine die" (without day) means that no date is set to hold a subsequent meeting. This action terminates the meeting *and* the assembly's right to meet again under the same auspices unless the next meeting is determined by the documents of authority. At an annual, biannual, or biennial meeting or con-vention, at the adjournment sine die the incomplete agenda does not automatically remain the unfinished business. All business must be terminated. If it is to be considered again, it must be reintroduced as new business at the next authorized meeting.

Annual sessions usually consist of a series of meetings, and each day's meeting may better be concluded by recessing (instead of adjourning) until the next day. The final meeting, however, is ad-journed sine die, and the assembly may only reconvene at a sub-sequent date under the authority bestowed in its documentary au-thority.

If an assembly has a membership requiring reelection or redesignation and that time has arrived, it no longer has the authority to act or to legislate for the whole membership, and the meeting must be adjourned sine die. The words *sine die* need not be expressed. In this instance, "sine die" literally means "without day," and is interpreted as "without providing for an opportunity to meet again."

In a convention of delegates whose bylaws provide that the delegates shall serve until new delegates are elected, the present delegates may be called back into session by the president if the bylaws so authorize. The assembly may adjourn as at any regular session or meeting.

Mass meetings, with no plans to meet again, adjourn sine die.

ADMINISTRATIVE DUTIES OF THE PRESIDENT

As administrator, the president is the legal head of the organization. The president is empowered with full authority from the assembly and from the bylaws. To administer is the most sensitive role the president must play—psychologically, perhaps, more important than the ability to preside well. The president speaks for the organization, to the press and at TV interviews, signs documents, observes protocol, greets honored guests, thanks speakers, and so on, unless these powers have been otherwise defined in the organization's documents.

The president needs to be kept informed, involved, and aware of all the activities of the organization. For this, the president is usually made *ex officio* member of committees and can thus supervise and facilitate interrelationships. The president oversees committee work but does not take over. Most of all, the president must be aware of and sensitive to personalities, cliques, stresses, and hidden purposes within an organization. For this, he or she communicates with the members, hears all, sees all, ignores much, but never betrays a confidence.

The president has a proper sense of the dignity of the office and must exercise patience, tact, and common sense. He or she must keep surveillance over rules and regulations as provided in the documents of authority, and should be the first to understand and recognize a need to change a rule to meet a changing situation—but is expected to live by the existing rules until they are officially changed.

AGENDA

With a meeting, as with a play, members are entitled to have a program of the cast and the acts in order of their appearance. An agenda is the blueprint of a meeting; it provides the sequence in which business will be introduced, and may include the hours at which certain items will be presented. Such an adopted agenda provides protection for the membership, assuring them that business will be taken up in that order unless suspended, and enables members to know when they must be present.

If no agenda has been adopted, any member may introduce any subject, when no motion is pending, as soon as recognition is obtained. Agenda should not be confused with an overall schedule or calendar (which includes such proposed items as workshops, speakers, panel discussions, and the like, and is generally called the program of events), though such a schedule may, as at a convention, include the agenda.

Organizations that meet regularly adopt the agenda by a majority vote even if it includes special orders, but it is amendable before adoption and is frequently approved by general consent. The format of an agenda, when it applies to every regular meeting, is best contained in the standing rules.

If a regular order of business has not been adopted in the organization's documents of authority, following the call to order and the determination of a quorum, an agenda is presented to the assembly for approval. (Copies may be made available. If not, it must be read to the members.) The proposed agenda is presented as a main motion; it is debatable and amendable. Usually the proposed agenda is readily accepted, as are its amendments, which are often treated as "friendly" amendments.

The presiding officer may state, "If there is no objection, the agenda is adopted" (or "adopted as amended"). If there is an objection, the adoption of the agenda must be put to a vote.

Once adopted, any changes require a two-thirds vote or general consent. The adopted agenda then becomes the rule of order for that meeting. The presiding officer, however, may request a change in the order of business if there is no objection.

In an organization that meets less often than quarterly, the agenda is prepared by the president, with or without the aid of other officers. Copies should be made available for those in attendance. If an agenda has been included in the bylaws, members have more flexibility if the bylaw states, "The agenda may include . . ."; if it reads, "The agenda shall include . . . ," there is no flexibility, since properly drafted bylaws cannot be suspended except as specifically provided for, and the organization is thus obliged to follow the agenda to the letter. Using the word *may* permits the organization to adopt items in the order that is convenient. Inclusion of an agenda in the bylaws is not recommended; it more properly belongs in the standing rules, where any portion can be suspended by a two-thirds vote when essential. The entire agenda may not be suspended.

When the organization meets regularly, if at one meeting it sets a time for an adjourned meeting or adjourns to a time certain, the motion pending at the time of adjournment is taken up under unfinished business at the next meeting and is followed by other items as scheduled at the previous meeting.

Unimportant items of business should be scheduled at the end of the agenda in order to insure sufficient time for consideration of more important items without delay.

The chair announces each item of business by stating, "The next business in order is . . . ."

See also **Amendments and the Amending Process, Friendly Amendments**.

Motions That Can Affect the Order of Business or Agenda

Adopt Agenda. An agenda may be adopted for each meeting by majority vote. An agenda may also be adopted for all regular meetings by including it in the standing rules. The agenda should never be set forth in the bylaws.

Quorum. If there is no quorum present, there can be no business except a motion to hold an adjourned meeting or to take necessary measures to obtain a quorum.

Amend. A proposed agenda may be amended before adoption by adding other items or changing the order; such amendments can be agreed to by general consent or a majority vote.

Suspend the Rules. A motion may be made to take up an item of business out of the regular or adopted order by a motion to suspend the rules; this motion may be adopted by general consent or a two-thirds vote.

Regular Order. If and when an assembly strays from its authorized agenda, or members proceed contrary to the established rules of procedure, a demand for the regular order returns the assembly to the adopted order of business or the proper rules of procedure. No vote is required.

General Orders.   The order of business is general orders. Business pending at the time of adjournment, items scheduled to be considered but not reached by adjournment, items postponed until the next regular meeting are general orders. A motion may be made to include an item under general orders. No pending business may be interrupted under general orders. They are taken up in the order proposed.

See also **Agenda, General Orders**.

Special Orders.   A motion to set an item of business for consideration at a specified time is a special order. It interrupts business. A two-thirds vote is required to adopt the special order. If a motion is agreed to making a single item of business a special order for that meeting, only that special order may be considered.

See also **Agenda, Special Orders**.

Postpone.   An item of business included in general orders may be postponed until a later time by a majority vote.

Adjourn.   The chair usually adjourns the meeting with general consent when there is no further business or when the time set for ending the meeting has been reached. A motion to adjourn may be made by any member, however, even if business scheduled for the meeting has not been completed.

Sample Order of Business, or Agenda

Such a sample may be employed if not otherwise specified by the organization's documentary authority.

1. **Call to order.**
    The president, standing, at the assigned time, taps the gavel and in a positive but friendly voice says, "The meeting will come to order." The announcement of a quorum establishes that the meeting is legally called, which fact the secretary may enter in the minutes. In addition, opening ceremonies, greetings, introduction of guests, and ceremonial rites may be observed as the custom of the organization provides.

2. **Reading and disposition of the minutes.**
    Chair: "The secretary will read the minutes of the previous meetings." The chair sits. The secretary, standing, reads in a clear, audible voice the contents of the minutes. (Reading at this time may be waived by general consent.) Chair, ris-

ing, asks, "Are there any corrections?" Corrections may be accepted by general consent or by a majority vote. No motion to approve the minutes is necessary since the chair may assume this motion. Chair: "The minutes are approved as read [or as corrected]."

3. **Reports of officers and board.**
Such reports are not always given except at annual meetings with the exception of the treasurer's report, which should always be given. Chair: "The treasurer will present the treasurer's statement." The treasurer's report at regular meetings, as opposed to annual meetings, usually gives only totals, not itemizations, or the amount on hand at the previous meeting, receipts, disbursements, and the amount on hand at the current meeting. A copy is given to the secretary for inclusion in the minutes. This is not a report for action as it has not been verified. Chair (optional): "Are there any questions?"

4. **Reports of standing committees.**
The chair states, "The next business in order is the reports from Standing Committees." The chair may or may not call upon all committees at each meeting. Chairmen are called upon in the order as listed in the bylaws or as created. The report is placed on file. No action is taken on it. Recommendations placed in the report are sometimes immediately taken up for consideration as assumed motions from the committee, but usually they are moved by direction of the committee chairman.

5. **Reports of special or ad hoc committees.**
Special committees are called upon in the order of creation unless the report comes under special orders. They are considered in the same way as Standing Commitee reports.

6. **Unfinished business.**
The chair states, "The next business in order is unfinished business." Unfinished business includes that which was pending at the time of adjournment, that which was postponed until the current meeting, and that which was scheduled for the previous meeting and not reached by the time of adjournment. These are considered and disposed of in the same order if the question of consideration has not been raised and adopted. The chair always announces the unfinished business.

7. **New business.**
    After completion of unfinished business, if there was any, the chair asks, "Is there any new business?" Members are then free to introduce substantive proposals which, if stated by the chair, are disposed of in some procedural manner. Items "understood" to be considered from the previous meeting are brought up under new business by motion.

8. **Good and welfare, or good of the order.**
    This item is optional. It provides for time to be set aside whereby, by use of informal consideration, members may offer constructive criticism or suggestions that could improve the organization. Action on such matters are rarely taken at this time, but if appropriate or viable, they are brought up as new business at a later meeting. An exception is permitted when charges have been implied relating to possible disciplinary action. It is in order for a motion to create a committee to investigate such charges and set a time for a report.
    See also **Discipline**.

9. **Announcements.**
    Announcements are usually (but not necessarily) reserved for a place near the end of the meeting. Correspondence of general interest may be read at this time, but that which is relevant to committee reports may be presented at the time of the report. The chair may call upon the chairman of the program to present the program or introduce the speaker.

10. **Adjournment.**
    If there is no further business, the chair may declare the meeting adjourned or if the hour for adjournment has been reached, or otherwise, by general consent, with no objection. To protect the membership, it might be wise for the presiding officer, whenever practicable, not to adjourn the meeting until the end of the program, if there is to be one. On occasion, there may be a disturbance from audience reaction to some speaker's remarks. The program chairman has no authority to control the situation, but the presiding officer, who has not yet adjourned the meeting, has full authority to restore decorum. The chair may adjourn the meeting after the program or state that, "The meeting will be adjourned at the conclusion of the program."

Any meeting that has been called for special or particular business may not entertain a motion to suspend that business. Only that business as stated in the call may be considered.

AMENDMENTS AND THE AMENDING PROCESS

Amendments, when proposed, are merely suggested changes in the original language of the main motion (or any proposed amendments to the main motion), namely, the addition or elimination of language, or the addition of text to the substance of the proposal. In other words, amendments may propose changes in one of three ways: (1) to add additional text, (2) to strike it out, or (3) to strike out original text and insert new.

The amending process is most important and is perhaps the most complex and difficult portion of parliamentary procedure to explain.

To begin with, only one substantive main motion may be called up and pending at any time. All main motions and amendments are amendable in two degrees, as amendments to the motion and amendments to the amendment. Proposed amendments to the main motion or proposed amendments to amendments to the main motion do not become a part of the main motion until adopted by the assembly.

Any amendment submitted for consideration under general rules of procedure must be germane to the subject to which it is offered unless the documentary authority permits otherwise, as in the case of some legislative bodies. Amendments should be presented in written form when submitted for consideration, and must be so presented upon the demand of any member of the assembly or the chair. Like any other motion, amendments do not require a second.

Friendly Amendments

Much of an assembly's time can be saved by a procedure designated by some as the "friendly amendment" process. By the friendly amendment process, rather than allow the assembly to take possession as soon as the chair states a motion or amendment, another member may suggest to its author certain changes in it which the author might have included on his or her own if he or she had thought of it.

It is in order for the author to accept such a change without a vote. Anyone making a main motion, a motion to amend the main motion, or any other motion or amendment retains the right to modify that motion or amendment until some action is taken on it by the assembly. Such action includes any general consent for the disposition of the issue, adoption of a motion to limit or close debate on that issue, adoption of an amendment thereto, or ordering a vote by ballot. If the author should decline to accept the suggestion, the proposer of the change can move it as an amendment, as long as it is germane, not in the third degree, and not subordinate in precedence to some pending question.

The friendly amendment procedure allows the author to accept modifications or changes, but does not interfere with the majority's rights either to accept or reject the proposal as modified, or to amend it; it does not interfere with the minority's rights to oppose it in debate or to vote no on the modified proposal, or even to propose amendments to the modified version. It does, however, give the author of a motion (or amendment) the opportunity to change any unintelligent words, correct any errors, improve any language, or make some substantive changes to carry out the intent in offering the motion without going through the laborious amending process. This procedure allows any proposers of main motions or amendments the privilege of accepting in lieu of their own other complete substitute motions or amendments.

When the question finally is put to the assembly, if no amendment has been offered and adopted, the chair states, "The question is on the motion (or amendment), to . . . , as modified," so that the members know on what they are voting.

Types and Precedence of Amendments

The order for proposing amendments and for their consideration is dependent upon the situation at the time they are proposed. Some general rules determine the precedence of amendments and whether or not they are in order.

There are two general types of amendments: *perfecting* and *substitute*. Perfecting amendments are just what the name implies—proposals to improve the contents of the language of the original main motion to the satisfaction of at least a majority of the group. A substitute amendment is a proposal offered after a main motion or amendment has been made. Its purpose is to give an acceptable alternative to the assembly by striking out the original language of the proposal and substituting different language and contents (that remain germane). Substitute amendments avoid going through the laborious procedure of presenting and adopting various perfecting amendments only to accomplish the same result. Substitute amendments may be further classified into complete substitutes and less than complete substitutes (discussed below).

Perfecting amendments always take precedence over substitute amendments, and amendments to the language to be stricken out by a substitute amendment always take precedence over amendments to the language to be inserted. This means that if a perfecting amendment is offered to the language to be inserted by a substitute, an amendment to the language to be stricken would also be in order at that time and would, if called up, be considered and acted on before action on the amendment to the language to be inserted, even if the latter were first proposed.

Perfecting amendments include (1) proposals to add additional language to the pending question, (2) proposals to strike out certain language, and (3) proposals to strike out *and* insert. (Note that a proposal to strike out only a portion of a sentence and insert new language is not a complete substitute but, rather, a perfecting amendment.) To illustrate the three forms:

1. "I move we go to the theater." This may be amended by adding the word *tomorrow* after the word *theater*.
2. "I move that we go to the theater tomorrow after school." This may be amended by striking out *after school*.
3. "I move that we go to the theater." This may be amended by striking out *theater* and inserting *movie*.

It should be noted that motions to strike out language and insert new language in its place—commonly referred to as "strike-out-and-insert amendments"—are similar to substitute amendments but are not necessarily *complete* substitutes. For procedural purposes, there is a significant difference between a strike-out-and-insert perfecting amendment and a complete substitute amendment. Anything less than a complete substitute is a perfecting amendment.

Again, perfecting amendments take precedence over substitutes. This gives the membership of an assembly a right to perfect a main motion or a first-degree substitute amendment before a vote is taken to strike out the language of either of them and substitute completely different language in their stead. If a perfecting amendment is offered to a main motion, a substitute for it is not in order until that pending perfecting amendment has been disposed of. Thus, a complete substitute amendment for any proposition is not in order when a perfecting amendment is pending.

If no one proposes to offer a perfecting amendment to a pending main motion, a substitute amendment is in order. After a substitute has been moved and is pending (if no other motion or amendment taking precedence is proposed), perfecting amendments to the language of the main motion proposed to be stricken out by the substitute are in order—as well as amendments to the language proposed to be inserted by the first-degree substitute amendment (i.e., the substitute first proposed). If such perfecting amendments are moved, they should be disposed of before voting on the substitute, with or without amendment. Again, a complete substitute amendment is not a perfecting amendment; it proposes to strike out all of a main motion or all of a first-degree amendment and insert all new language instead.

Finally, amendments to the main motion or amendment cannot be offered in two different places at the same time unless the rules or bylaws of that assembly permit or unless by general or unanimous consent. The language of an amendment must be contiguous, hitting the main motion or amendment in one place at a time. Hence, a second-degree cannot propose to alter a first-degree amendment in two places at the same time; it must be confined to one place. A second-degree amendment cannot touch the text of the main motion; it must be confined to the text of the first-degree amendment to which it is offered. Only the text of the first-degree amendment can be altered by a second-degree amendment.

Illustrations of the Amending Process

Note the following illustration of the amending process discussed above. A main motion is made, and an amendment is proposed to the main motion. Before the main motion is voted on, the first-degree amendment must be disposed of. If a majority of the members vote for the amendment, then the main motion has been changed, and the question then recurs on the main motion as amended or changed.

Likewise, if new language (the amendment) is offered to the main motion and rejected by a majority vote of the members, then the main motion remains the same, and the question recurs on the main motion without amendment.

The following chart explains the procedure: A and B give the order in which the motions would be made, and numbers 1 and 2 set forth the order in which they would be voted on.

The main motion A is made first, and a member then proposes a motion B, a first-degree amendment, to change some of the language in the main motion. The first-degree amendment B must be disposed of first (as indicated by 1, the order of voting), and the

CHART 1

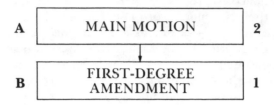

main motion *A* is voted on last, as amended, if amended (*2*). If amendment *B* is agreed to, the question recurs on the main motion *A*, as amended by *B*; if *B* is rejected, the question recurs on the main motion *A*, without amendment.

If, however, the first-degree amendment in Chart 1 did not completely please the members, they have the option of offering amendments to *B* before acting on amendment *B* itself (see Chart 2), in which *A*, *B*, and *C* represent the order of motions made, and *1*, *2*, and *3* the order of voting.

CHART 2

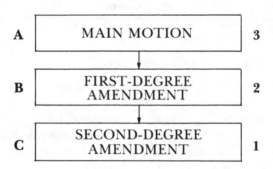

Any members, when recognized, may offer second-degree amendments—either perfecting or substitute amendments—so as to make the first-degree amendment *B* more acceptable (*C* in Chart 2). Such an amendment is a second-degree amendment and is referred to in Chart 2 as amendment *C*. (Third-degree amendments are never in order; second-degree amendments are usually, but not universally, allowed.) As indicated in Chart 2, amendment *C* is voted on first (*1*); then the first-degree amendment (*B*) is voted on (*2*), without amendment or as amended; lastly, the main motion *A* is voted on (*3*), without amendment or as amended.

A, *B*, and *C* are put before the assembly for consideration in that order, and *1*, *2*, and *3* (Chart 2) demonstrate the order for voting on them.

As illustrated, if a second-degree amendment *C* is disposed of, whether it is adopted or not, then Chart 1 again presents the situation; thus, another second-degree amendment, properly drafted, is in order. It should also be pointed out that if a second-degree amendment has been agreed to, another second-degree amendment to the pending first-degree amendment is in order if it does not touch, alter, or eliminate the language inserted by the previously approved second-degree amendment.

Any part of the first-degree amendment which has been amended or rewritten is not amendable, the assembly already having voted to make such change or changes.

If a first-degree amendment is not amended by a second-degree amendment, any part of it remains open to a second-degree amendment until it is amended or disposed of.

After any second-degree amendment is adopted, the question recurs on the first-degree amendment as amended; if all second-degree amendments are rejected, the question recurs on the adoption of the original first-degree amendment without amendment.

Likewise, if both a first-degree and a second-degree amendment to the main motion are adopted, the main motion again is amendable by another first-degree amendment (Chart 1), and by an amendment to the first-degree amendment (Chart 2), if they are properly drafted so as not to involve any part of the main motion already amended.

Another first-degree amendment to the amended main motion is out of order if it is solely to alter the language of the amendment previously agreed to by the assembly. If it proposes to take a bigger bite than the previously adopted language (to strike out and insert), it must accomplish more than just a change in the language or purpose of the perfecting amendments, already added to the main motion, to be in order.

A first degree amendment to strike out and insert that is not a complete substitute for a whole section of a main motion that has been amended can be drafted to be in order if it does more than undo or just change the language previously adopted; it must make other substantial or substantive changes. Such a newly proposed first-degree amendment also is amendable in one degree (see Chart 2).

These procedures of offering first- and second-degree amendments when no like amendment is pending can be repeated as often as the members of the assembly feel it necessary to perfect the main motion—provided, of course, amendments are germane and properly drafted, as explained above.

Motions to strike out a portion or portions of a main motion or a first-degree amendment to it are amendable not only by another motion to strike out a lesser portion, but also by moving to strike out and insert—as long as they are confined to that portion of the language proposed to be stricken, are germane, and are properly drafted. This procedure of proposing to amend a simple motion to strike by inserting language, in effect, turns a simple motion to strike out into a motion to strike out and insert, which is not divisible.

If a motion is made to amend the main motion by striking out a portion of the main motion, this would be a first-degree amendment; a second-degree amendment can then be offered to strike out only a portion of that language in the first-degree amendment; this would be in order. If the motion to strike out the lesser part (the second-degree amendment) is then adopted, that language is stricken out of the main motion and stays out whether or not the first-degree amendment is adopted. The second-degree amendment was to strike out language from the main motion, not just to amend the amendment to strike out.

For example, suppose a main motion has been made that

> the club shall have an outing for its members. Such an outing is to be held at Overton Park on Sunday, June 7, from twelve noon to five P.M., followed by three hours of dancing. The party shall then move to Peabody Hotel at eight P.M. and celebrate until midnight, in the Venetian Dining Room, and each person shall pay $50.00 for the use of the dining room.

A member then makes a motion to amend the main motion by striking out all of the words following the word *dancing*. This is a first-degree amendment to strike out certain language.

Another member then makes a motion to amend the amendment (a second-degree amendment) by striking out of the main motion only the figure *$50.00*. This second-degree amendment, if adopted, leaves in the main motion the residue of the language that the first-degree amendment had proposed be stricken out. If the first-degree amendment is then rejected, that language stays in the main motion and only the figure *$50.00* goes out (unless some other action is taken to eliminate it).

The second-degree amendment having been adopted, the question recurs on the first-degree amendment, as amended, i.e., the amendment to strike out all of the remaining language after the word *dancing*.

The first-degree amendment, as amended (i.e., the figure *$50.00* stricken) is desired by the member offering the second-degree amendment, who only wanted the figure *$50.00* of the main motion stricken out. If the first-degree amendment is now adopted, this does not mean that the figure *$50.00*, stricken out, comes back into the main motion; it does not come back. All of the language after the word *dancing* has been stricken.

How would the main motion sound if the language of the second-degree amendment did come back into the main motion? It would then read: "The club shall have an outing for the members. Such an outing is to be held at Overton Park on Sunday, June 7, from twelve noon to five P.M., followed by three hours of dancing. $50.00."

It would be meaningless. In other words, both parts were stricken out by a majority vote of the assembly, and unless there is a motion to reconsider the votes taken by the assembly and the assembly actually votes to reconsider those votes and reverses its previous decision, both remain out of the main motion.

See also **Germane**.

Advantages of the Process

The procedure of allowing a motion to strike out to be amended by a motion to strike out and insert other language gives a great advantage in the amending process.

First, if a simple motion is made to strike certain language from a main motion, another member of the assembly may propose to amend that motion by inserting certain other language in lieu of the language proposed to be stricken. This motion then, in effect, becomes a motion to strike out and insert.

If the membership does not want this done, they can vote down the motion to strike and insert; if that motion is rejected, the question is then on the adoption of the simple motion to strike out the language proposed to be stricken in the first instance. If, on the other hand, the strike-out-and-insert motion is agreed to, the original language is stricken and the new language inserted. A motion to strike that language is then out of order; thus, the original motion simply to strike becomes academic. The desire of the assembly has been resolved.

It should also be pointed out that this procedure may resolve another problem. If a motion to strike could only be amended by a motion to strike a lesser amount of the language than the original motion, and the first-degree motion to strike should be agreed to, the matter stricken might eliminate all of that subject matter in the main motion. Then any amendment relative to that subject would likely be out of order since it would no longer be germane.

Another procedure usually available for accomplishing the same end, when the desire is only to eliminate paragraphs or sentences but to avoid ending up with meaningless language, is a request for "a division of the question." This procedure can be used in the case of a main motion or an amendment to the main motion.

When an amendment to strike out has two or more independent parts, any one of which could be eliminated without leaving the other part or parts of the amendment meaningless, it is better procedure to demand a division of the question rather than to move to strike part of the amendment to strike.

Since a question is not eligible of division unless each part stands on its own, the rejection of a part does not leave the remaining portion or portions of a main motion or amendment meaningless.

The charts in this entry set forth the procedure usually used by most American organizations: that is, the main motion, an amendment to the main motion, and an amendment to the amendment. Not often is there a need to go beyond the offering of an amendment and an amendment to the amendment; hence, more complex amending procedures than those set forth in Charts 1 and 2 are rarely used except in legislative bodies and large complex organizations.

See also **Division of the Question**.

Improper Amendments

The chair should rule out of order proposed amendments that:

- Are not germane to the pending motion.
- Introduce an independent question.
- Are equivalent to a rejection of the pending motion.
- Are the same as one previously considered by the assembly.
- Will convert the motion to a different motion.
- Are dilatory.

Amending Motions Previously Adopted
See **Changing Previous Decisions**.

ANNOUNCEMENTS

Announcements to be made at meetings should be of interest to the membership at large or of benefit to the organization. The presiding officer should be informed of all proposed announcements ahead of time whenever possible, to insure sufficient time to present them, when there is an agenda. They are usually presented just before adjournment, but officers, committee chairmen, and others may make announcements, when given the floor at the conclusion of their remarks, to say, for example, "The next meeting of the legislative committee will be at International House, Room 9, Thursday, January 17, at 10 A.M."

If an announcement is of concern to only a few members, the presiding officer can usually provide a means for announcing to those few without taking the time of the whole assembly. Any member may seek recognition to ask for general consent to make an announcement.

ANNUAL MEETING

Most ordinary societies provide for an annual meeting in accordance with their documents of authority. Such meetings make provisions for annual reports of the board and officers and of standing and special committees; for the nomination and election of officers; for appointment of committee members; as well as, in some cases, for the selection of delegates to the parent body convention and consideration of any proposed bylaw amendments.

Nominations and elections are special orders and should be provided for rather early in the agenda to allow the necessary time to count ballots, or to reballot in the event that no nominee receives the required vote.

Some annual meetings also take up any business that is normally transacted at a regular meeting—but if the bylaws call for a particular agenda for that meeting, only that business may be presented. Some annual meeting agendas contain a proviso that any other business that properly pertains to the organization may also be considered unless previous notice is required. If any emergency action contrary to the above principles becomes necessary, that action must be ratified at the next regular meeting.

The minutes of the annual meeting may be disposed of at the next regular meeting of the membership if the organization holds any. The minutes should not be held over until the next annual meeting. They may well be corrected and approved by the executive board when so authorized, or by a committee duly created for that purpose by the assembly by a majority vote.

ANNUAL SESSION

Organizations that are widespread geographically in membership or that hold meetings less often than quarterly may hold annual sessions that consist of more than one meeting, as if in convention. An annual session is conducted much as a convention but without delegates. Each individual member attending speaks as a member and is not representative of any group, chapter, or unit as such.

Procedural rules are much the same as those applied to convention. Each meeting recesses until the next meeting on the same or next scheduled meeting day. Minutes are not read if a minutes committee has been appointed, but the report of the credentials committee is presented whenever there has been a change in the attendance.

Although one meeting can be a session, sessions are usually referred to as a series of meetings.

See also **Conventions**.

APPEAL

When a point of order has been ruled upon by the chair, any member may appeal from that ruling. Points of order and appeal result from various procedural circumstances.

A member may appeal from a chair's decision if the member believes the chair has ruled on a matter not within the scope of the organization; that there has been a blatant disregard of the parliamentary rule; that an amendment which the chair ruled in order is not germane to the motion; or that the member thinks the chair has misquoted or misused a rule of procedure. There are all kinds of decisions by the chair from which an appeal may be taken. The chair's decision may be sustained or reversed.

After a point of order has been ruled upon, any member may rise and without recognition, say, "I appeal from the ruling of the chair." An appeal is debatable. When the assembly has heard enough, it may move to limit further debate or to close it. Appeals must be made at the time of the breach. If other business has intervened, it is too late to appeal. No appeal may be taken from facts, or law, or from adopted rules of the body. An appeal is debatable unless the pending question itself is undebatable.

The presiding officer, on his or her own initiative, may rule a procedure not in order, as, for example, by declaring third-degree amendments out of order without waiting for this point to be made from the floor. If the chair's ruling is not challenged, it automatically becomes established procedure. The same is true of any decision made by the assembly, when the point of order is submitted to it for a decision in the first instance or when the assembly reverses a decision of the chair.

Any member taking an appeal has the right and obligation to give the reasons for his appeal. The chair also has the right to explain the reasons for the ruling. This may be done without leaving the chair. Preference is given to the chair to speak first. The chair may speak a second time in rebuttal while the members should speak only once. This rule is to prevent unwarranted use of time on a question that is solely procedural.

The chair should never be hurried in making a ruling even if it should become necessary to recess in order to check all possible available information. When facts are established and discussion reveals that some points have been overlooked, the chair has the opportunity to change the ruling. After an appeal has been taken and debate is closed, or no one cares to speak further, the chair puts the question to vote, always stating it in the affirmative. "Shall the decisions of the chair on . . . stand as the judgment of the assembly?" or "Shall the ruling of the chair on . . . be sustained?" If the ayes have it, the decision of the chair is sustained and the meeting proceeds. If the noes have it, the decision of the chair is reversed or overruled, the situation is corrected, and the assembly proceeds according to their decision. An affirmative vote adopts; a tie vote loses for the lack of a majority, except in the case of taking an appeal from a decision from the chair and that is because of the way the question is put. The chair has a vote, just as on any other question put to the assembly, if the chair wishes to exercise it.

An appeal may be helpful to the chair since it can relieve the chair from the onus of a touchy decision and forces the members to decide. The chair has the right to ask the assembly to make a decision when unsure of the merits of the question or when an appeal has been made.

See also **President, President's Vote**.

ASSEMBLY
See **Deliberative Assemblies**.

ASSOCIATE MEMBERSHIP

Associate membership is subordinate to full membership. In general, an associate member is seen as one not yet qualified to all rights and privileges, or as one interested in the purposes of the organization but who does not desire the responsibilities of full participation.

Associate members hold partial or limited rights as provided in the bylaws. Such rules usually grant permission to attend meetings and to debate but not to vote or hold office. Such members may pay less or greater dues than a regular member depending on associate status in the organization.

ASSUMED OR IMPLIED MOTIONS

As a timesaver, the chair may assume a motion has been made when it is obvious that most, if not all, of the members will vote in the affirmative and that there is no need for debate. Such motions as approval of the minutes and adjournment when there is no further business may be assumed and adopted by general consent, if there is no objection. The chair states, "If there is no objection, the minutes are approved as read," or "Hearing no further nominations, the chair declares the nominations closed." Polls may be closed in like manner once the chair has determined that all have cast a vote who wish to do so. With no business pending, the chair may limit debate by general consent if there is no objection.

Frequently during debate on a pending motion, some member offers a brief one or two word amendment without formally proposing it. When the chair observes that the assembly obviously agrees, the chair may state, "With no objection, the words '. . . . . .' will be inserted [or deleted]." This procedure also applies to editorial changes which, if they do not modify the proposal, may be adopted by general consent and are not considered as motions to amend. If even one member objects to the assumption of a motion to adopt by general consent, the motion, even though it was implied, must be put to a vote.

ATTORNEY

Some organizations, according to their special activities and interests, need a professional consultant on law, hired on a regular or occasional basis. An attorney can help an organization with the legal actions to be undertaken by the group or the legal rights of the members, as distinguished from parliamentary rights or the order of business. The attorney can serve as counsel at conventions to advise on the legality of proposed resolutions and their amendments. This role does not conflict with that of the parliamentarian, who advises on procedural rules.

An attorney is necessary, if the organization wishes to incorporate, to draft the initial and final articles required according to the state's laws for incorporation.

See also **Charter Certificate of Incorporation**.

The attorney can assist an accused member in trials for expulsion from office or from membership and may assist the organization itself should any litigation develop; may serve as chairman of a stockholders' meeting or give advice at that meeting that the corporation has acted in good faith.

The presence of counsel at board or regular meetings is permitted only with majority consent. No individual member should be allowed to bring an attorney into a meeting unless such member is on trial.

See also **Charter Members; Trial and Expulsion of Members**.

AUDITOR

Financial records of an organization should be audited at least annually. A treasurer is responsible for the accuracy of his or her report, but it could be in error and requires verification. An audit provides proof of the correctness of the report or exposes any errors. It is the report of the auditor that is adopted by the assembly, not that of the treasurer.

A treasurer and the organization need to be protected against fraud, misuse, or manipulation of funds. The organization should first seek and secure the proper system of accounting suitable for its needs. The adopted audit provides that protection. When large sums of money are to be exchanged, it is also wise to have the treasurer bonded.

Auditors may or may not be members of the organization, but should possess some knowledge of and qualifications for the job. Appointments to this position should be provided in the documents of authority. If the organization deals with large sums of money, it is best to engage an experienced CPA as auditor, who can usually save the organization time as well as money by auditing the financial records, preparing the tax reports, establishing or reviewing the accounting system, and submitting recommendations for improvement. In very large organizations, a salaried accountant may be retained.

At meetings, after the final report of the treasurer has been presented, the chair asks for the report of the auditor or auditing committee. This report carries with it the report of the treasurer and may be presented by the treasurer. The chair says, "The question is now on the adoption of the auditor's report. Are there any questions?" The motion to adopt the auditor's report may be assumed and need not be offered from the floor. When ready, the chair then says, "Those in favor of adopting the report of the auditor say aye. Those opposed, say no," and then completes the motion by announcing the result, "The ayes [or noes] appear to have it [pause]. The ayes [or noes] have it," and the audit is adopted [or defeated]. That announcement by the chair is final unless reconsidered.

Since an auditor's report is proof of accuracy, the report must be adopted by the assembly as its official acceptance of further responsibility.

If the treasurer's report has not been audited, any member may move to refer it to an auditor with any instructions in regard to it, as when the report is to be made or if to be made to the assembly or board of directors.

B

BALLOT

A ballot is a secret vote that insures protection of privacy to the voter. If bylaws require elections by ballot, no other method of voting is valid. This rule cannot be suspended, even by unanimous consent.

A ballot may be the paper on which the vote is marked or the vote itself. A ballot can be a written vote on paper, a machine vote, or one taken electronically.

Any member desiring a true opinion and an uninfluenced vote may move to have a vote taken by ballot. The motion is undebatable, unamendable, and requires a majority vote. When a vote by ballot has been determined, details for the method used should be decided in advance. If the ballot contains a slate of officers prepared by the nominating committee, ballots should be prepared or printed with adequate space for names of nominees from the floor or for write-ins, unless the documents of authority prohibit it. Instructions as to the correct marking of ballots must be understood before balloting begins. More than one slate or set of nominees may be arranged on a ballot. Paper ballots should be folded as directed and handed to the appointed tellers who deposit them in the ballot box in the presence of the voter, or the voter may place the ballot in the slot provided for that purpose.

It is best to put voting requirements in standing rules instead of in bylaws, so that if a ballot is required and there is only one candidate for an office, the rules could be suspended by a two-thirds vote if the membership so desires.

See also **Acclamation; Votes and Voting Methods, Ballot Voting**.

BALLOT TO NOMINATE
See **Nominations**.

BLANKS
See **Creating a Blank**.

BOARDS

Boards, such as boards of trustees, directors, or management, are created in bylaws or articles of incorporation to act for the society or corporation when its membership or stockholders cannot conveniently convene to act for themselves. Boards are subordinate to the organization or corporation, having no authority to suspend or rescind action taken by the society or stockholders or to act in conflict with its documentary authority.

The organization, however, may rescind, modify, or countermand action taken by the board, if it is not too late to do so (as it may be in such cases as contracts that have been entered into). A board has no power other than that defined in the document that created it.

Authority. The more authority a board is given, the more stringent its regulations should be. Boards can exercise authority only as a collective group. No member has more power than another member and no member may speak for the board unless authorized to do so, as in the case of the president. The president may have special powers and authority, not as a board member but as a president.

Composition.   Boards should be composed of experienced members who will give able, willing, competent input into the organization's business. A board is composed of the elected officials (who usually serve in the same capacity on the board), elected directors, and frequently chairmen of standing committees, as well as any *ex officio* members and such other members for which provisions have been made. All board members are considered officers of the organization.

Executive Committee.   If there is to be an executive committee (a board within a board), it must be provided for in the bylaws.
   See also **Executive Committee**.

Functions of Corporate Boards.   The corporate board has the responsibility to carry out the purposes as adopted in the articles of incorporation; satisfy state and federal laws governing tax status; approve bank and security signatures; authorize contracts and financial deals; enlist services of attorney as required; retain an authorized accountant to prepare the audit; manage all business transactions; and prepare the annual report.

Functions of Unincorporated Boards.   The unincorporated board has the managerial responsibility to formulate policies; control the operating budget; review and act on committee reports; assist in implementing plans and projects; enter contracts and authorize other work assignments; plan for the annual meeting or convention; assist in maintaining good public relations; and submit necessary bylaw amendments.

Meetings.   Board meetings are commonly confidential unless otherwise provided. Members may always be invited to attend to give information or present expert advice. Such members do not necessarily remain for any deliberations.
   See also **Hearings; Sunshine Laws**.

Minutes.   Board minutes are usually confidential and read only to the board. A motion is required for them to be read to the assembly unless otherwise provided. Board minutes often contain the names of those in attendance and a notation concerning whether or not absentees were excused from the meeting.

Procedure of Business at Board Meetings.   Boards are usually permitted to determine their own procedural rules, which may not conflict with or counteract any rules of the parent organization. A quorum of the board is a majority of its members unless otherwise specified. Under common practices, large boards conduct meetings formally, just as in a deliberative assembly. Small boards conduct meetings more informally, as if in committee, with no limit to the number of times a member may speak in debate, although only one member at a time may speak. Members need not rise to be recognized. Debate should not be limited or closed by motion. Informal discussion is permitted without requiring a pending motion. Decisions may be arrived at by consensus or, if there is objection, by majority vote. The chairman need not rise and may speak without leaving the chair and may also propose motions, debate, and vote.

No board may conduct a meeting legally unless all members have been duly notified of the time and place and there is a quorum present. Failure of a board to meet does not cancel the regular meeting of the organization.

Boards do not meet during assembly meetings of the parent body, but may meet between meetings of a session or convention to carry out orders of the assembly or to prepare recommendations. Board members, as the most concerned and most informed, should be present on the floor of the assembly to participate in the debate and the transaction of business.

Reports.   A board reports to the membership. The report does not necessarily include what transpired during the board meeting. It presents the ensuing findings and recommendations, which are drafted at the end of the report. The form of the report is the same as that for committees.

Brief oral progress reports may be presented throughout the year. The final or annual report, often presented in writing, covers the actions taken and the achievements of the administration. The board report should be the responsibility of the president, with or without the aid of other board members, but should be agreed to by at least a majority of the board and signed by the proper authorities, usually the president and the secretary.

Responsibilities.   Boards serve in an advisory capacity, and they administer and manage activities and properties, recommend new ideas and policies, coordinate activities, discover problems, and designate responsibility within their authority. Boards handle jobs too lengthy, tedious, or routine to occupy the time of the assembly. Members can expect their interests to be carefully managed by these entrusted custodians.

Sine Die Adjournment of the Board.   After a sine die adjournment, a new board will have been elected in whole or in part. The outgoing board may not assign obligations to the incoming board, but motions adopted by previous boards are honored unless the new board decides to take action to rescind or change them. Frequently, a convention or annual meeting will refer various items of business to the new board. These are either matters that were not completed at the assembly meeting or business of such importance that it cannot wait until the next regular assembly meeting. The new board, at its first meeting, is not required to consider such items, but in the best interests of the organization usually does so. They are introduced under new business.

No president has the authority to cancel a board meeting unless so authorized in documentary authority.

Teleconferences.   Teleconferences are permitted for use by boards and committees in many organizations, particularly if the membership is widely scattered geographically. Permission must be authorized in the bylaws.

See also **Teleconferences**.

Tenure.   Boards exist for the life of the organization, but its members change. Bylaws should specify the manner of election, size of board membership, terms of office, duties, titles, limitations, authority, provisions for meetings, and how vacancies are filled.

Members are elected to the board at the annual meeting or at special meetings called for that purpose. They hold office for one term or until replaced as specified in the documents of authority. If they are elected to one term, the tenure should be staggered to preserve the continuity of experience on the board. It is recommended that the number of board members be uneven.

Vacancies.   Vacancies on the board must be filled according to the bylaws. A new board takes office with each administration. Replacements of occasional vacancies does not constitute a new board.

BUSINESS OF MEETINGS

The business of an organization to be set before the assembly for consideration comes from introduction of new business by a substantive main motion or resolution; reports of committees recommending certain actions, or motions postponed or made a general or special order.

Unfinished Business   is that which was pending, but not completed, at the time of adjournment; motions that were postponed or made a general or special order; reports out of committee on a motion previously referred to them; or items scheduled on the agenda but not reached at the time of adjournment. They are taken up in that order.

New Business.   Near the end of an agenda, a place is reserved for the introduction of new business. Any member may propose any business related to the purposes of the organization that has not been previously disposed of in some other manner, if not prohibited by documentary authority. The chair will announce when new business is in order, whereupon any member, upon obtaining recognition, may propose a motion to take action or to adopt an opinion, to create a committee, or to establish a policy.

See also **Order of Business; Agenda**.

BYLAWS

Other than the corporate charter, the bylaws of an organization are its most important document. The use of a constitution, which properly belongs to governmental documents, is superfluous to deliberative societies; it contains nothing that cannot be properly contained in the bylaws.

Bylaws are the vital document that protect the members and their organization. They relate to the fundamental structure of the organization, its composition, and its functions. They include the rights and obligations of members and officers whether present or absent and the rights of the minority as well as the majority. The provisions are of such importance that they cannot be suspended even by unanimous consent unless the documents provide for their own suspension.

Bylaws should not contain procedural rules on how to transact business; such rules properly belong in standing rules. Bylaws contain the structural framework designed to fit a particular organization.

Bylaws, by common practice, are presumed to be valid as permanent law of the organization. (Members are entitled to copies, but even without them, they are presumed to know the contents and are legally bound by them.) However, bylaws that have been disregarded over a period of years, without protest, should not suddenly be enforced without the adoption of a motion that they again be observed. Likewise, a practice observed over a period of years attains the force of a bylaw until the society takes some proper action to the contrary.

Writing Bylaws

Well-written bylaws prevent confusion and inequity, and provide guidelines for continuity and permanence. The most common causes of trouble in any organization are poorly written bylaws or the failure to adhere to them. Bylaws should never be written haphazardly. To compose or to revise bylaws, a committee should be created of members who can write well and who will research patiently and accurately. A qualified parliamentarian is essential to assist such a committee, and if the organization intends to incorporate, the advice of an attorney is required.

The committee should determine the kind of bylaws its organization needs to protect it if it is to be corporate, incorporate, religious, social, civic, profit or nonprofit, and the like. It must find out if there are any restrictions to be imposed by its parent body, or if there are any other restrictive laws. It should study bylaws of comparable organizations and note the differences required. Only then should the committee determine the contents of its bylaws.

Construction of Bylaws

Bylaws should be written article by article after the general plan has been determined. There are certain fundamental articles required: Name, Object, Officers, Membership, Meetings, and Provisions for Amendment. Many organizations include the adopted Parliamentary Authority in the bylaws, but this would be more properly placed in the standing rules since the authority is referred to only when there is no bylaw or other adopted rules (the document of authority) that cover the situation. Likewise, if the parliamentary authority is designated in the standing rules, it may be suspended if the situation should require it.

Besides the required articles, the committee may include one or all of the following articles or add others especially designed to fit the organization's needs: Board, Standing Committees, Duties of Board and Officers, and Nominations and Elections. Because of IRS regulations, an article on Dissolution should be included as a protection. The committee should bear in mind that too many unnecessary provisions, repetition, and verbosity contribute nothing of value and tend to confuse.

See also **Dissolutions**.

Form of Bylaws

Outline form should be used throughout, and the writing should be uniform in style. The use of the word *may* is preferable to the word *shall* in many cases, for greater flexibility. Abbreviations are never used. Numbers are spelled out except for dates and money. Articles are listed under Roman numerals with a separate heading. Sections are listed under Arabic capitals. Subsections are listed under small *a, b, c* or *1, 2, 3.* Pronouns should not be used. Each sentence should require no reference to another, but should stand alone.

At the final draft, a careful study should be given to language, grammar, punctuation, all of which can affect the meaning. As few words as possible should be used. The formula for writing bylaws is that they must be definable, clearly understandable, not ambiguous, enforceable, and within the jurisdiction of the parent body.

Each article should be checked for inconsistencies, contradictions, and repetitions so that the meanings are clear, precise, and have only one possible interpretion, and so that there is no confusion as to the lines of authority. Privileges granted in bylaws should be specific and may not be assumed.

Adoption of Bylaws

When the committee on bylaws is ready to report, the chairman states, "By direction of the committee (which was agreed to and signed by at least a majority of its members), I move the adoption of the bylaws as proposed." The presiding officer says, "It has been moved that this organization adopt the proposed bylaws. Will the Bylaws Chairman read the proposals, article by article." As the chairman reads each article, the president calls for discussion. At that time, amendments may be offered, if germane, and the amendments are then voted upon. After this process has been completed, the chair then says, "Are there any further amendments to be offered at this time?" Amendments, when in order, may be proposed to any articles already considered, or new articles may be proposed. When no one rises to debate further or offer amendments, the presiding officer, under the generally accepted procedure, puts the set of bylaws to a vote. They are adopted by a majority (unless a greater majority has been previously agreed upon), to become effective immediately unless otherwise stipulated.

When members, with or without previous notice of the proposals, are considering adoption, time may be saved if there is no objection by considering only those articles that need discussion or amendment and then voting on the package as a whole.

Once bylaws have been adopted, there should be little reason for continual tampering, but as time goes on and situations change, there may come a need to amend.

If the assembly has no bylaws, it may create guidelines of its own, provided they do not conflict with any superior authority.

See also **Proviso**.

Guidelines for Contents of Bylaws

Articles in bylaws denote separate provisions. Some are fundamental. Others are added to meet the changing needs of the society.

ARTICLE I
Name

The name must be spelled out in full, properly punctuated.

ARTICLE II
Object or Purpose

This should be concise, exact, in a single sentence, unless there is more than one purpose.

ARTICLE III
Membership

Classes of membership should be named (Active, Associate, Honorary, Life, Nonresident, and so on) with the distinction among them as to rights, dues, qualifications, eligibility, application, and acceptance procedures, voting rights, initiation fees, when dues are payable, penalty for nonpayment of dues, method for reinstatement, and dual membership requirements in national, state, or parent society. Not all of these requirements will apply in every case.

ARTICLE IV
Officers

Include how many officers there shall be, the titles, qualifications for office, duties, honorary officers (if any), and position of President-Elect if there is to be one. It is recommended that for easy reference all data on accession to office be under a separate article. It may, however, be included under the article on officers (see Article VI).

ARTICLE V
Meetings

The day should be specified for regular meetings, but not the time or place. A provision should always include "unless otherwise ordered by the society." This provides for necessary changes in an emergency. The quorum should be specified. Provisions for calling special meetings, and for the annual meeting, should be included.

ARTICLE VI
Nominations and Elections
(May be placed elsewhere)

The process whereby nominations may be made should be specified. Included in this article are terms of office, whether positions are reelectable, qualifications for office, how vacancies in office are to be filled, provisions for removal from office, and method for submitting resignations.

If the office of president is vacated, the position is automatically filled by the first vice-president, then the second, and so on. The vacancy finally occurs in the lowest office.

The term of office should specify "to serve for a term of . . . years OR until a successor is elected." This provides for a continuation in office and also permits a recision of election should that become necessary. Include also the number of offices a member may hold at the same time (only one office at a time is recommended, since each office should require full-time attention).

Placing nominations and certain specifics on election (such as time for the election and officers to be elected) in the bylaws is important to the continuity and life of the organization. Otherwise, these vital decisions would be at the whim of each administration.

ARTICLE VII
Board

The title of the board should be specified: Executive Board, Board of Trustees, Board of Directors, or Managers; name as well as composition, powers (authority) and limitations, meeting dates, qualifications for membership, how elected or appointed, special duties (if any), and its quorum.

ARTICLE VIII
Standing Committees

Specify the names and composition of standing committees, the manner of selection to membership, duties or jurisdiction, and authorization for creating new standing committees. Also, specify how special committees may be created other than by adopted motion from the floor.

ARTICLE IX
Amending Bylaws

Include provisions for amending, how much previous notice should be required, what vote should be required, when and how the provisions for amending may be proposed, and so on.

ARTICLE X
Parliamentary Authority

This provision should be placed in standing rules.

ARTICLE XI
Dissolution

Specify the method to be used, particularly if the society is for profit.
See also **Dissolutions; Vacancy in Office**.

Amending Adopted Bylaws

If one or more articles need amending, or new articles need to be added, it is best to have a bylaws committee appointed to write them. The bylaw amendments can then be prepared in the correct form before they are submitted to the membership for approval—saving time. The bylaws should provide when and how amendments may be proposed. If they do not, any member, having given previous notice, may propose an amendment at any regular meeting. Most organizations provide for the amending process to take place only at the annual meeting or convention. Except as otherwise stipulated in the bylaws or rules, the regular amending process is followed in amending bylaws.

Previous notice, together with a copy of the proposed amendment, should be required. No amendment is in order that exceeds the scope of what was stated in the notice. Amendments must be germane. After an amendment has been prepared, the committee chairman states, "By direction of the committee, I move the adoption of the following bylaw amendment(s)." The presiding officer then states, "The following amendment, which proposes that . . . , is now before you for consideration and adoption." The reasons for the amendment may be explained by the chairman before the debate begins. After discussion and possible amendments to the proposed bylaw amendment, which are disposed of by majority vote, the vote is taken on the adoption of the new amendment as amended (two-thirds vote is usually stipulated in the bylaws of most organizations). Each amendment to the bylaws is voted on separately unless it has been agreed to consider them en bloc. An amendment, if adopted, goes into effect immediately unless it specifies otherwise.

See also **En Bloc**.

Revision of Bylaws

Revision is authorized at the discretion of the assembly. Bylaws are not static, and changes are required from time to time. If a revision has been ordered, any or all portions may be altered, and even an entirely new set of bylaws may be submitted. A bylaw committee prepares a revision with the same careful attention to details as for writing a new set of bylaws. This committee is authorized to proceed after a motion to do so has been adopted by majority vote or general consent. This motion is considered previous notice. The preparation of the revision does not require previous notice of each individual amendment.

The revision committee may hold hearings so that members may present suggestions and have an opportunity to justify them. After completion of the revision, copies are distributed to each member, together with the date for consideration. The revision is introduced by the committee chairman: "By order of the committee, I move that the following revision be adopted." The presiding officer instructs the chairman to read the revision, article by article, and explain the difference from the old bylaw to the revised bylaw, including the reason for and effect of any change. Each revision may be amended from the floor, the amendment limited only to being germane. Such amendments are debated and adopted by majority vote. When all the articles have been considered, the presiding officer puts the vote on the revision as a whole. Bylaws are a "sacred" document that protects the organization as specified in that document. Adoption of a revision becomes effective immediately upon approval by a two-thirds vote (the same as for amending bylaws) unless otherwise provided for. It is possible for a revision committee to report that "no changes are recommended in the bylaws at this time."

While revision is under consideration, the original bylaws remain in effect but are not open to consideration or amendment. Any change in any bylaw adopted by the assembly becomes binding upon the entire membership.

Interpreting Bylaws

It is of importance how and by whom bylaws may be interpreted. Bylaws are a contract written to protect the members as well as the organization, and that organization should have final determination of what is the meaning and intent of any bylaws. If it should occur that there are two possible meanings, the more absurd of the two should be disregarded. Any generalized bylaw yields to a specific bylaw.

Interpretation includes understanding of why the bylaw was written, if it can be affected by the parent organization (or other higher authority), if it is in harmony with other bylaws, and if it is in accord with the intent of the bylaw at the time of adoption. The chair will interpret bylaws subject to appeal, an *ad hoc* committee could be appointed to submit a report on the interpretation, or the chair may submit the interpretation to the assembly for a vote.

See also **Documents of Authority**.

C

CALL FOR THE REGULAR ORDER
See **Orders of the Day.**

CALL MEETING TO ORDER

At the scheduled time, with a quorum present, a meeting is called to order by the presiding officer. This may be the president, or in his absence, the vice-president or some other authorized officer. If none of these officers are present, the secretary will call the meeting to order and call for nominations for and election of a presiding officer pro-tem, who presides until the authorized presiding officer arrives. Election is by voice vote. A reasonable time—about ten to fifteen minutes—is long enough to wait for the arrival of the presiding officer.

See also **Presiding.**

CALL OF A MEETING
See **Mass Meeting Requirements; Meeting Requirements; Special Meetings.**

CALL OF THE HOUSE
See **Votes and Voting Methods, Roll Call Voting.**

CANDIDATE

A candidate is a member seeking nomination to office. After nomination, the member becomes a nominee. If a candidate is not nominated but is eligible for office, election to office is still possible by a write-in vote—unless the bylaws prohibit it.

See also **Votes and Voting Methods, Write-in Vote.**

CAUCUS

Caucus is a good method to use for a preliminary screening of the candidates. Usually conducted by well-informed, experienced members during convention, annual sessions, or special meetings, a caucus may be for the purpose of determining support for a particular nominee, or for or against policies or propositions scheduled to come before the assembly. A well-conducted caucus is invaluable. It helps members to become better informed, and it saves considerable time and confusion on the assembly floor.

A caucus is conducted informally if the group is small, more formally if the group is large. A chairman, whether selected by rank or casually, directs the proceedings and discussion so that some decorum in debate is preserved. Members have more opportunities to speak freely, ask questions, or propose resolves and amendments. This helps to clarify and relax situations that might otherwise take up too much time on the assembly floor. In a caucus, significant strategy can be determined for resolving problems confronting the assembly. The information gained in caucus may prompt further action. Members who attend a caucus are expected to support the decisions made there, but are not compelled to do so.

Any small group can, and usually does, talk freely over issues during lunch, recess, whatever. This is not a caucus since there is no chairman or rules of procedure.

CENSURE

The motion to censure is a main motion, debatable, amendable, and requiring a majority vote.

Censure is a form of reprimand, a warning that the assembly uses to voice displeasure or indignation at the acts or words of a member or officer. It permits the person being reprimanded the opportunity to heed the warning.

A member may be censured for using unacceptable language, attacking the motives of another member, disregarding of the rules, disturbing the members or disrupting proceedings by acts of indecorum, or disobeying the legitimate orders of the presiding officer.

In addition to the above, an officer may also be censured for neglect of duty, for showing partiality, or for misconduct in office. If the president is about to be censured, the vice-president or other authorized officer should take the chair. If the chair refuses to recognize a member entitled to the floor who wishes to move for censure, the presiding officer should leave the chair, allowing another authorized officer to preside and recognize properly the motion to censure. The motion to censure may not be reconsidered. Adopted motions to censure are included in the minutes.

See also **Discipline**.

CHAIRMAN

The chairman is the presiding officer (who may be called a president or chairman of a committee). A presiding officer is essential if a meeting is to be conducted properly. If no special title has been assigned to the presiding officer, that person is properly referred to as the chairman.

A chairman of a committee may take an active role as a participant in debate, making motions and voting, unless the documents of authority provide otherwise. A president of an assembly does not participate while presiding. This avoids any display of opinion while acting as an umpire during debate.

If the president is not authorized to appoint a committee, the chairman of that committee may be designated in the motion to create the committee. If no specific designation is made, it is customary for the person first named to serve as chairman, or the committee itself may be authorized to select its own chairman. The chairman and the committee membership may be appointed by the president of the assembly or by some other authorized authority when so specified in the motion or documentary authority.

The origin of the word *chairman* comes from early English history. In 959 A.D., castles were poorly furnished, and the only chair was reserved for the presiding officer, usually the king or the king's spokesman. The rest of the group sat on benches. Because the presiding officer must sit before others and alone, this person has become the "chairman." *Man* is a generic term meaning mankind, and *manus* is the Latin word for "hand." Thus, the chairman is one who handles the meeting.

Co-Chairman

Co-chairman is a term used frequently, but to have co-chairmen is often impractical. The only reasonable purpose for co-chairmen is to allow one to preside when the other is absent. When both are present, there must be a determination as to which member is authorized to preside. There can be no situation that properly permits two persons to preside at the same time, since trouble would obviously ensue if co-chairmen made contrary decisions.

The member chosen to be the chairman must possess the authority to preside.

If a committee has a divided responsibility, there may be a chairman chosen for each division, but only one of them becomes the official chairman. Selection of a vice-chairman provides a better solution.

CHANGING PREVIOUS DECISIONS
(Amending Motions Previously Adopted)

Frequently, decisions made in a deliberative body must be referred to again. Members sometimes need to review a decision made too hastily, or when a changed situation, new developments, or additional information prompts the need to reexamine the adopted issue.

Main motions, once adopted, remain in effect until action is taken to the contrary, or until the life of the motion expires. There is more than one way to change or modify adopted motions. They are to amend, reconsider, rescind, or adopt another revised (*de novo*) resolution as a renewal related to the original motion. These motions are debatable and amendable, and previous notice should be required to protect those members who might otherwise be absent. A majority vote adopts. Each of these motions is introduced as a main motion.

The change can affect all or part of an adopted proposal, or become a substitute for it. If a contract or binding committal has been entered into, it is too late to alter it, but one can move to change only that part of a decision not yet implemented or put into contractual effect.

If the approval of the adopted motion occurred within the time limit of the same or next day, only the motion to reconsider the vote is in order. After the period for reconsideration has expired, the procedure to be used is different. The methods to rescind or change (amend) action may be used. They are nearly equivalent and are disposed of in the same manner. Rescind countermands the entire motion, while amend adopted action alters some part of the previous decision or that part not yet implemented. The parties involved shall have been notified by previous notice. A new motion offered as a substitute must also be made under the same conditions.

The following illustrates this procedure. Let's assume that a 500-page multimillion-dollar school board budget was adopted at a September meeting of a board of education. Later, it became apparent that changes or adjustments had to be made in the portion of the budget providing funds for fuel.

At the January meeting, a motion is made to change (amend by substitution) the portion of the budget relating to fuel. Instead of changing a page here and another there, the entire section is rewritten and presented as follows: "Mr. Chairman, as stated in the previous notice, I move that the following proposal be made and on its adoption will replace pages 35 through 110 of the school budget." This procedure keeps the entire section intact; nothing is lost in the shuffle. The newly adopted proposal supersedes all of the previously adopted portion of the budget pertaining to fuel. One entire section has simply been substituted for another by amending or changing a previous decision.

Bylaws are binding orders, but they may also be amended, since bylaws themselves should make provision for this. In the case of amending bylaws, previous notice is also required. The proposed changes may not be increased or reduced below the existing provisions as greater or less than that given in the prior notice. Debate in all instances may include discussion on the original action it proposes to change.

CHARTER CERTIFICATE OF INCORPORATION
(Articles of Incorporation)

Charters supersede all other documents of authority which, like bylaws, may not be suspended or altered without adhering to the procedure for change.

A corporation is established pursuant to law. Corporations derive their existence from their creator, the state or federal government as the case may be. Bylaws are created by the organization members themselves and are subordinate to a charter. Corporate organizations share a contract of rights with the concerned state or government that exceeds the contract of rights between bylaws and members. A charter helps to protect members from personal liability for obligations incurred by a member in serving the organization. The charter becomes the "person" to be dealt with instead of the member.

Charter rules are structural. The charter should contain as few rules as possible to permit more flexibility in the use of any documentary authority. They contain title, objects, membership, voting rights, and other articles as may be necessary. If these articles are entered in the charter, they need not be repeated in the bylaws but are frequently included for the sake of convenience.

There are advantages in incorporation. It provides for perpetual succession. Corporations may sue and be sued, but members may not be sued as individuals when executing duties for the organization. It provides the power to enter contracts of real or personal property, to receive or give grants, and to own an official seal, and provides the organization with a legally recognized status.

Any changes to be made in a corporate charter must be done so pursuant to the law that created it.

An incorporated society is a legal entity. No member of the corporation may act for the corporation unless empowered to do so by the corporate law.

If an established organization wishes to become incorporated, it should engage a local attorney (local because of familiarity with the laws of incorporation for that state). If the society is seeking a federal incorporation, the appropriate attorney should be engaged. When an organization desires to incorporate, that organization's board or designated committee prepares for the attorney all necessary data:

title, purpose, documents of authority, officers, membership, meetings, and whether profit or nonprofit.

From these facts, the attorney prepares a first draft and submits it to the membership for approval or amendment. Once the draft proves satisfactory, the attorney prepares the final draft. The membership signs this draft before the secretary of state's office (of the concerned state) is contacted to complete the processing and final acts of incorporating.

If a group has not previously been organized and is planning to be incorporated, it prepares in writing for submission to the secretary of state the statistics containing title, purpose, qualification for membership, manner of admission, whether profit or nonprofit, term for which the corporation is to exist, names of resident subscribers, officers and time they will be elected or appointed to office, names of pro tem officers to serve until the first election, number of board members serving pro tem, and by whom the bylaws are to be written, amended, and rescinded. This application must be signed by those competent to contract, as acknowledged by all subscribers, before a notary.

Charter amendments are subject to the requirements of law as well as to any limitations placed within the charter itself. No organization may amend its charter rules by its own decision unless the charter permits this.

CHARTER MEMBERS

Charter members are those members who adopted the original charter, paid their dues, and attested to this by signature. If the organization is unincorporated, the original members' names, after dues are paid, are entered in the minutes as charter members after a motion to that effect has been adopted.

CLASSIFICATION OF MOTIONS
See **Motions, Precedence of Motions.**

CLOSE DEBATE

The purpose of this motion is to stop debate at once on the pending motion and to vote on it immediately. Its adoption prevents any further action on the motion except the motion to table.

The motion to close debate may be proposed at any time after the chair has stated that the main motion to which it applies is pending. The maker of the main motion should not move to close debate on it until at least one other member has spoken.

The motion applies to the immediately pending question. If a member wishes to close debate on all pending questions, the motion must be stated "to close debate on all pending questions." This will include all pending motions in the succession as they stand as well as the immediate pending question.

A proposal to close debate is not debatable or amendable, as that would defeat the purpose of the motion. A motion to reconsider a losing vote is not in order, but the motion to close debate may be renewed after any business has taken place. It requires a two-thirds vote since it suspends the rules of debate. The motion may be withdrawn by general consent prior to a vote.

Motions to close debate should be used with great caution. Much good time can be wasted by this procedure, and if the debate and amending process are proceeding smoothly, the purpose of a deliberative assembly is being accomplished. Shortcuts can be expensive, and minority rights can be abused.

CLOSED SESSIONS

Meeting in "executive session" has come to mean that the group or assembly resolves itself into a closed session for the transaction of confidential, personal, or executive business. The use of the term *executive session* no doubt grew out of the use of the phrase by the Senate of the United States. The Senate acts on treaties and nominations in executive session, and until 1929, when the rule on that subject was changed, these proceedings were behind closed doors unless the Senate ordered them open. The rules of the Senate referred to the meetings as "executive sessions" not solely because they were secret sessions but also because the business transacted was executive business, namely, nominations and treaties that are submitted to the Senate by the president, the executive.

All references in the Senate rules to "secret sessions" now refer to such sessions as "closed sessions."

It would be wise for any organization now to use the term "closed session" instead of "executive session," because the latter does not necessarily mean a "closed" or "secret" session. The use of the term *executive session* gives no concept of being closed; the expression is archaic.

The motion to go into closed session is privileged and not debatable; otherwise the purpose of the motion could be lost by exposing what was proposed to be done before going behind closed doors; the motion is not amendable and requires a majority vote, or general consent.

Only members of the group are allowed to attend a closed session, unless nonmembers are invited to remain because of the need for their assistance. The proceedings are kept secret unless the assembly votes to make them public; otherwise, only actions taken are entered in the regular minute book.

The purpose of closed sessions is to transact business without telling your opponents, the public, or other organizations what was being discussed or what business was being transacted. For example, if the board of directors of a corporation meets to discuss plans for taking over another corporation, that board would not want their plans or actions exposed to the rest of the world.

There is seldom need for closed sessions in most organizations except to consider matters dealing with improprieties of its members, such as preferring charges or conducting a trial. Closed meetings may be called for the consideration of the qualifications of applicants for office, salaries of employees as well as promotions, and for granting charitable aid to a member or for planning an award.

Anyone advising an organization as to their rights and privileges in avoiding the divulgence of the information on what was done in a closed meeting should be well-informed about the so-called Sunshine Laws of the state having jurisdiction over the closed meeting.

The procedure for closed meetings for all practical purposes should be much the same as that for transacting any business. Any organization should be free to alter its procedure for closed meetings to meet its needs, but under all circumstances minutes should be kept, even if they have to be kept under lock and key after the meeting.

Any group meeting in closed session must determine if and when the proceedings should be released for public information. The government, at state and local as well as federal levels, might under certain circumstances demand access to the records of such closed meetings. If ever such a demand is made, it would be wise to consult an attorney.

See also **Sunshine Laws.**

COMMIT, RECOMMIT, AND REFER

These three motions, when adopted, have the effect of taking the motion or resolution from the assembly and referring it to committee or a designated group for consideration. Each differs in certain respects, but all are designed to accomplish the same end— that is, delay consideration of the proposal by the assembly until a committee has studied it and reported back.

Each of the motions is open to amendment by adding instructions to the committee concerned (for example, when to hold hearings or to report). They are all debatable and in order when the business is pending before the assembly for action and no motion of higher precedence is pending (namely, all other motions on the ladder of precedence above *refer*).

The two motions, to commit and to refer, are much the same in concept. The motion to refer a matter to a committee is generally the first action taken by the assembly on a proposition that has been submitted to it on which it is not ready to act but desires study by a smaller group of the membership (a committee) prior to further consideration.

When no motion of higher precedence than refer is pending, a motion may be made to refer a pending proposal to a committee, with or without instructions to study, to report, or to make recommendations to aid the assembly in making a decision.

The motion to commit is a bit broader in scope than the motion to refer. When an assembly has already given the matter some consideration but has concluded that the matter is not ready for approval or disapproval, it may commit the matter. The commit motion implies the assembly prefers to have the matter committed to a standing or newly created (by motion from the floor) ad hoc committee, for study and recommendation. A motion to commit may be to gain information and recommendations to assist the assembly in reaching a decision, or it may possibly be an indirect way on the part of the mover to kill the proposition.

At any rate, both motions, when adopted, take the proposal away from the assembly and place it in committee.

The motion to recommit is more restricted; it sends the proposal back to the same commitee for further consideration; that is, the committee has already considered the proposition once, it has been before the assembly for action, but the assembly thought it was not ready to act on approval or disapproval. Thus, the assembly votes to put the proposal back into committee for whatever reason.

The following is the form for a motion to create an ad hoc committee when one is needed so that a matter can be referred to it:

"I move that a committee of . . . be formed, to be appointed by the chair, to [act or investigate] and to report to the assembly at the next regular meeting."

Or, "I move that Mr. X, Miss Y, Mr. Z be named to a committee to . . ."

Or, "I move that Mr. X, Miss Y, Mr. Z, with Miss Y as chairman, be named to a committee to . . ."

Or, "I move that a committee of three be elected from the floor to . . ."

COMMITTEES

Committees are the workhorses of the organization. And since they do the bulk of the work that keeps the organization functioning, their importance cannot be overestimated. Committees can take the time and care to explore all sides or options, with more exchange of opinions, whereas the general assembly must operate within a controlled time frame. And since committees can work more efficiently and represent a group of members, their recommendations have clout.

Yet no committee should be created without a real need for it. To create a committee that has no real job to do leaves its members disgruntled and dissatisfied.

There are three kinds of committees: *ad hoc* or special, standing, and executive.

See also **Executive Committee.**

Ad Hoc or Special Committees

These committees are created pursuant to the bylaws or as authorized by the adoption of a motion from the assembly. Members are selected to perform a particular assignment. As soon as the assignment is completed and the final report presented, the committee ceases to exist.

Standing Committees

These committees should be stipulated in the bylaws, which usually designate their title, composition, jurisdiction, and duties. New standing committees, created from time to time, must be created according to the document of authority.

Standing committees are permanent and, as integral parts of the organizational structure, are assigned certain areas of work on a continuing basis. At the end of each administration, the committee continues but the membership is subject to change. The term of membership usually coincides with that of the administration.

Standing committees are not subordinate to the board of directors unless the bylaws so specify. They report to the board and to the assembly as required. The chairman of a standing committee frequently serves as a member of the board.

Standing committees carry out the functions necessary to preserve the organization, such as membership, finance, publications, and the like. They prepare an annual report, as the bylaws require.

An annual meeting does not necessarily discontinue the work of a special committee, but if the committee gives no report at a convention, it may be discharged by order of assembly.

See also **Discharge a Committee.**

Committees are created for three purposes: to act, to investigate, and to recommend. Special committees and standing committees consider motions and resolutions to be reported to the general assembly with or without recommendations for action.

Committees to Act

Frequently, the assembly decides to assign to a committee the duty of administering certain provisions of a motion previously adopted by the assembly. The committee may be directed "with power" to act before or after fully investigating the situation. These committees should be small in size and composed of those favorable to or in accord with the action to be taken.

Committees to Investigate

These committees should be somewhat larger than a committee to act and be composed of members representing the various factions within the organization. An odd number of members helps prevent a tie vote. The responsibility for these committees is to gather information as fact finders, to deliberate, to prepare reports containing facts, and to recommend any action that might be taken by the assembly.

Creation of Committees

Committees may be created in several ways. Standing committees are usually named in bylaws. Methods for creating special committees may also be provided in bylaws.

Committees may be created by motion from the floor. Such motions may include the names of the chairman and members of the committee, or may specify the number of members and how they are to be appointed or elected. If there is no provision for appointing a chairman, the committee may choose its own, or, by custom, the first-named serves as chairman.

Some bylaws authorize the president or the board of directors to create and even name the members of a committee. The motion to create a committee is a main motion, amendable and debatable, and requires a majority vote.

Committee Membership

Membership to committee is determined in several ways:

1. *Appointment by the president.* This power is granted in document of authority or by motion from the floor. Such appointments are final. No vote is taken.

   The president should announce to the assembly the names of those appointed before the committee can take any official action. If the president is not given a specific time in which to make the appointment and must appoint immediately, the chair may ask for a brief recess to confer with certain members as to their willingness to serve. Or the chair may ask the assembly for its approval—by general consent or a majority vote—for the appointment of committee members during the intermission between meetings, so as to obtain those members most suitable to serve, and the announcement of the names at the next regular meeting.

2. *Nomination by the president.* This method allows the assembly veto power over the nominations. Any nomination disapproved must be replaced by further nominations by the president until approval is reached. Members may not nominate, but may vote to accept the names presented by the president. This method protects the society from any indiscretion of the president.

3. *Nominations from the floor.* A motion may be made to select a committee from the assembly. The motion states: "I move that a committee of . . . be nominated and elected from the assembly." Nominations are then named—up to the required number (the slate). If no more names are offered, the chair may declare such nominees elected to membership by acclamation. The members have tacitly voted consent.

   If more than enough names have been submitted, the nominees are voted on in the order presented. Those first receiving the required majority vote are declared elected.

Those nominees not yet voted on are ignored because the slate has been completed. Election is usually by voice vote. No more than one nomination at a time may be made by any member except by permission granted by general consent.

4. *Election by ballot.* This method is used when protection is needed from partisan-dominated organizations. It is used when the selection of a committee is of vital or critical importance. The motion is: "I move that members of this committee be elected by ballot." Should there be confusion as to who could best serve, the problem could be resolved by moving for a recess to work out an agreement. The names of committee members are nominated until the required number is reached. The assembly may then amend the list of nominees by moving to strike out and insert. The final vote on nominees is determined by ballot.

   See also **Nominations.**

5. *Appointment by board of managers or directors.* Some organizations authorize in their documentary authority that the board of directors may create standing committees, *ad hoc* committees, or both, and name their members. This too burdensome procedure tends to perpetuate the same members in key positions and deprives the membership of the democratic opportunity to select their own committee members. It is not recommended unless selection by the general assembly would be too burdensome or unless the organization is a widely scattered one.

Qualifications of Committee Members

It is frequently beneficial to an organization, particularly when action is to be taken, to select only the chairman and to permit that chairman a voice in selecting the committee members, members with whom he can work in harmony.

Members of a committee should not be selected for popularity alone. Such a selection does not always produce the most competent and can result in those who will only support the majority point of view. Members who volunteer are usually too few or too many and often lack the necessary qualifications for that particular assignment.

Appointed members should be named after careful, thoughtful selection from the field of their expertise.

When asked to serve, members should either promptly accept or decline.

Committee Chairman

A good chairman should be qualified for the job. Any good chairman knows that the chairman alone does not constitute *the* committee, but is only an integral part of it.

The chairman should be dynamic and positive, forceful, and make positive contributions to the conduct of the committee. The chairman should have knowledge of how to conduct a meeting informally but correctly, how to handle personal relationships, and be able to keep an open mind.

The chairman takes an active part, participating fully, making motions, debating, and voting. It is the responsibility of the chairman to obtain copies of assignments and any pertinent records, and to clearly understand instructions, any powers of the committee, and the date to report.

If a chairman fails to call a meeting promptly, a majority of the committee after proper notice may call the meeting on its own.

Conduct in Committee

A comfortable meeting room should be provided, as this is conducive to harmony. Each member should have the names and phone numbers of the other committee members. If any members are not known to each other, proper introductions should be made before the meeting begins.

Meetings should be held regularly, and as many should be called as needed. They should begin at the appointed time. Members should not be kept late unless by general consent. It is better to schedule another meeting.

Committees should meet at a time most convenient for the majority. If more than one meeting is required, a meeting may adjourn at the call of the chairman, or the next meeting may be prearranged by the committee.

Meetings are generally conducted informally, but if the committee is large—over fifteen, say—the formality increases in proportion to the size. Since a committee is of itself a deliberative body it may make its own rules, if these are not in conflict with the rules of the parent body. Rules of debate require that only one member may speak at a time; that speakers get as many turns to speak as requested, if recognized by the chairman; that all discussions be germane; that a motion is not required before a subject may be discussed; that decisions are reached by consensus or majority vote; that a motion to reconsider is in order by any member; and that all input be courteously received. A majority of the committee constitutes the quorum unless otherwise stipulated. Meetings are closed to nonmembers unless the committee decides it may be public, or unless stipulated otherwise in the documents of authority.

The committee should preserve all records referred to it and return them in good condition after the assignment has been completed or when they are no longer needed.

A committee may appoint from among its own members, subcommittees, which are answerable only to the committee.

When a special or *ad hoc* committee has completed its work, it votes to report. This adjourns, or ends, the committee meetings for that business. A report is prepared for submission to the parent body.

A special or *ad hoc* committee may continue its work until it presents its final report or until discharged by the organization. The assembly may, at any time, give instructions to a committee.

See also **Discharge a Committee; Consider Informally.**

Conduct of Business in a Small Committee

Committees conduct business as if in informal consideration. There is no limit to the number of turns a member may speak, but only one may speak at a time. Members need not rise to be recognized. Debate is not limited or closed by motion. Informal discussions may be permitted without requiring a pending motion. Decisions may be made by consensus or, if there is objection, by majority vote.

Limitations on Committees

Only members of the organization may serve on committees. Commitees cannot fill vacancies or add to or subtract from their membership except through the parent body. A committee, in its reports, should confine itself to material that falls within its jurisdiction and is in accordance with any instructions.

Powers of Committee

No committee powers are inherent. Powers are granted by the bylaws or motions adopted by the assembly and may be full or limited. With full power, the committee may act independently without board or assembly approval, spend money, or do whatever it is authorized to carry out its responsibilities. The assembly can alter or rescind these powers.

Committee of One

A committee of one is legitimate. One member may be assigned to a particular responsibility as authorized.

Committee Reports
See **Reports, Committee Reports.**

Ex Officio **Committee Member**
See ***Ex Officio*.**

Discharge a Committee
See **Discharge a Committee.**

Vote to Elect Committee Membership

Vote to Elect Committee Membership in small groups is used when selecting a committee by election where more than the required number for the committee have been named. The chair calls each name in the order of nomination. Hands are counted. Those nominees who first receive a majority vote are declared elected. The rest of the names are ignored. This vote can also be taken by a rising vote.

Committee Minutes

Committee minutes are usually more detailed than assembly minutes and are really a flow chart used as a reference of progress. Minutes may list ideas proposed, points made during discussion, what was postponed, reconsidered, decided upon. Such minutes are the property of the committee and are usually destroyed after the final report. The chairman often acts as secretary, but may appoint some member to serve as a recorder or secretary. Minutes of an assembly meeting should be made available to a committee if it needs them.

Format for Committee Minutes: A Record of Proceedings
Post sheets before meeting starts
Number of meetings depends on the assignment

1	2	3
NAME OF COMMITTEE (IF ONE) NAME OF CHAIRMAN PHONE: _____ NAMES OF COM. MEMBERS DATE OF ASSIGNMENT __ DATE TO REPORT _____ ASSIGNMENT _____ INSTRUCTIONS _____ POWERS _____	DATES FOR MEETINGS _____ _____ _____ DISCUSSION _____ _____ IDEAS _____ _____ _____ BENEFITS _____ DEFECTS _____	SUB-COMMITTEE ASSIGNMENTS 1 _____ TO: _____ 2 _____ TO: _____ 3 _____ TO: _____

4	5
FINDINGS _____ _____ _____ DECISIONS _____ _____ _____ _____	RECOMMENDATIONS _____ _____ _____ PREPARE REPORT

Secretary-Recorder:

1. Write large, legibly, fast—important words, basic ideas, not every word, abbreviate

2. Use symbols, circle key words, star important decisions, use numbers, arrows

3. If decisions or ideas come too rapidly ask committee to pause a minute

CONSENSUS

Consensus is a collective opinion, a general agreement. The regular method for the chair to use is to ask the members, "Is it the consensus of this meeting that . . . is agreed to?" or, "Is it the will of the assembly that . . . is agreed to?" or, "Is there an objection?" Consensus has been used successfully throughout the years by Quakers, Indians, New England town meetings, and others as a decision-making procedure. It permits compromise. In small groups where less formality is required, it is a simple method for making decisions.

General consent is an equivalent to consensus, when done without objection. Otherwise, a formal vote must be taken.

CONSENT AGENDA

An assembly with a large number of routine or noncontroversial matters on its agenda may find it not only convenient but expeditious to consider these matters under unanimous consent procedure. This gives every member an opportunity to object. At the same time, it gives the presiding officer an opportunity to dispose of a great deal of the agenda confronting the assembly quickly and efficiently, particularly when it would be most helpful to the assembly to get its job done. This can even be done by taking en bloc action (that is, disposing of various items at the same time without taking separate consideration of them) when matters are not controversial or are of minor importance to the assembly, though every member has the right to object.

CONSIDERATION, QUESTION OF
See **Question of Consideration.**

CONSIDER INFORMALLY, RECESS TO
CONSIDER INFORMALLY

It is often helpful to consider a proposition informally, such as a need to determine whether or not a society wants to undertake a new responsibility, adopt a new policy, or find the correct wording in order to avoid time spent amending a poorly worded motion. At such times, correct decisions can be arrived at more effectively when formal rules of debate are not used. When there is a long list from which a selection must be made, it saves time over the lengthy process of creating a blank.

Any member, after recognition, may state, "I move that the assembly recess for . . . minutes [or recess subject to the call of the chair, if the time needed is indeterminate] so that we may discuss this matter informally." The motion is not debatable and is amendable only as to time. As soon as the motion is adopted, the chair continues to preside. If for any reason the chair declines to do so, the maker of the motion may designate a temporary presiding officer by general consent or majority vote. The chair may also, by general consent, state that the assembly will recess to consider a proposition informally.

Regular rules of debate are observed except that there is no time limit imposed on debate and no limit as to the number of times a member may speak after having obtained recognition.

Such consideration permits discussion of a subject before a motion has been prepared. When the members are satisfied, by consensus or majority vote, that a properly worded motion has been provided, a member states that motion. This terminates the informal consideration, and the assembly reconvenes. The same is true when members feel that a list has been satisfactorily filled. A member then moves to adopt the list as prepared. When the assembly reconvenes, the motion is processed under the regular rules of debate.

The motion to recess for informal consideration generally applies to main motions, amendments, and for preparing lists.

CONSIDER SERIATIM
See **Seriatim.**

CONSOLIDATION

A consolidation occurs when two or more organizations combine to form a new organization. Each loses its identity and independent existence. Each organization adopts a resolution to authorize this action, prepared in the same manner as for a merger, except that in this case both prepare and adopt the same resolutions. After each organization has adopted the resolutions, a joint meeting is called for the purpose of organizing the new entity with a new set of bylaws, new officers, and new name. The resolutions are so worded that the new organization comes into existence simultaneously with the demise of the discontinued organizations.

See **Merger.**

CONSTITUTION

Parliamentary authorities, today, generally agree that constitution and bylaws should be one document. No real purpose is served by separating them. The word *constitution* properly applies to the governing of a sovereign state or nation.

A constitution, if adopted as a separate document, contains the fundamental provisions that relate to the preservation of the life of the organization. They are: name, objective, members, officers, and meetings. Such rules, since they are basic and essential to the perpetuity of the organization, should require a higher vote to amend than bylaws if there are to be both a constitution and bylaws. Because of their vital importance, they have been set aside in a constitution, but there is no real need to separate them from the bylaws.

In the case of a corporation, a constitution contains the basics found in the charter. Besides, both the constitution and bylaws are subordinate to the charter.

CONSULTANT

Consultants may be such persons as the parliamentarian, the executive secretary, the attorney, the accountant, the executive committee, or others whose skills and expertise are essential to the organization. A consultant may or may not be a member of the society. The consultant may be called upon to advise on bylaws, policies, finance, membership, and the like, and is expected to help find solutions to problems.

A consultant to an ordinary deliberative body should be familiar with its bylaws and other documents of authority, its procedural rules, developments in similar organizations, local, state, and national laws that pertain to the organization, and the rules of the parent body.

CONVENTIONS

Conventions provide a showcase for members to display their parliamentary talents, achievements, and enterprise. Organizations of any size hold annual or biennial conventions. They may consist of one meeting or a series of connected meetings. Each convention is independent of any other, although procedural rules are usually much the same with occasional minor adjustments. Conventions provide a convenient way for all constituent units or chapters to meet, deliberate together, and address problems common to the entire membership.

Conventions are a meeting of delegates, elected or appointed, to represent their constituent unit, chapters, or groups of members in accordance with the parent organization's documents of authority. Delegates are the voting members in attendance. Other members may attend but hold no voting privileges.

There are three important aspects of a convention, business, education, and entertainment. Adequate time should be provided for each.

1. *Business.* The primary function of any convention is its business, the adopted agenda. At convention time, review of past activities and plans for the future become most important. The business usually consists of acting on propositions as recommended in progress reports, or as stated in the call to convention; hearing reports that will increase the delegates' knowledge and information about the scope of activities of the parent organization; and electing officers and directors and other board members.

    During the conducting of business the delegates have an opportunity for input through debate on the issues presented. It is necessary that procedural rules be well understood and that the presiding officer be competent. Employment of a qualified professional parliamentarian is essential.

2. *Education.* Programs should be prepared to advance the knowledge of new as well as experienced delegates. Workshops, panel discussions, displays, books, and pamphlets should be provided.

3. *Entertainment.* Supplementary activities add to the knowledge and social development of conventioneers. Good fellowship draws members together in closer harmony. Social contacts promote solidarity. Political disagreements can often be solved amicably during social hours. Acquaintances are made or renewed to the mutual benefit of all. There should be advance publicity for tours, special events, and programs designed to induce good attendance (always specifying required fees, if any).

See also **Agenda; Delegates.**

General Preconvention Preparation

The bylaws of an organization should include a section on conventions, specifying: when and how often such meetings should convene; the powers and duties of the convention governing body; the convention's quorum (usually a majority of the registered delegates whether or not they are in attendance); qualifications of delegates and alternates and the number from each unit allowed; and the method for selection of delegates and alternates.

Conventions begin with the selection of the proper site, which is usually made by the board. After selection of a site, a general convention coordinator is appointed by the board as early as possible. Usually this coordinator lives in the site area so as to handily establish rapport with hotels, convention centers, the chamber of commerce, available entertainment, and educational facilities. Thus, plans can be readily escalated. The coordinator prepares contracts for submission to the board for approval and selects committee members from nearby resident members in order to facilitate ease and speed in developing plans. The coordinator will often need an assistant coordinator as well, whose job is to be available with advice and aid at all times and who can communicate rapidly with the coordinator during the convention session in the event of breakdowns in planning, equipment problems, and other sudden emergencies. The operations of a convention require near clockwork precision; to this end, the assistant coordinator can give immediate attention to changes in arrangements and accommodations. Kits of materials and information for each delegate, alternate, and member to receive upon registration can also be prepared through the assistant coordinator's supervision. Obviously, the assistant needs to work closely with the program and protocol committees.

The treasurer for the convention, usually appointed by the coordinator, establishes a local bank account in the name of the convention committee. All fees should be deposited there by the treasurer and expenses paid from signed vouchers. Accurate financial records must be kept for inclusion in the final report to the governing body. Provisions should be made for bonding the convention treasurer, the same as provided for the organization's treasurer. The two officers may frequently work closely together.

The registrar is responsible for the preparation of a record of the delegates, members, and guests expected to attend the convention. He or she also takes care of special requests for room reservations, special dietary meals, orders for tickets for special events, and the like. Room reservations are usually made by the delegation dealing directly with the hotel management, but the registrar may assist the delegates in arranging for room sharing. The registrar works in cooperation with the credentials committee, sometimes serving as its chairman.

Preconvention Committees

Convention committees should be appointed as early as possible in the preconvention process, since most of their work involves pre-planning. The chairman of each committee reports regularly to the general convention coordinator and, at the end of the preconvention process, gives a final report on the committee's progress.

In addition to the pivotal resolutions committee (dealt with below), the usual convention committees include:

1. *Hospitality committee.* This committee's chairman arranges for local members to serve as hosts to the conventioneers: they welcome delegates arriving in the hotel lobby, arrange to meet planes, buses, and trains, and so on. A hospitality room should be provided for the convenience of arriving delegates and guests to meet informally. This committee should supply an information desk, a lost-and-found service, and first aid provisions.
2. *Protocol committee. See* **Protocol.**
3. *Decorations committee.* This committee plans for flowers, decorations, flags, and the like, and is responsible for signs and placards to be used during the convention.
4. *Public relations committee.* This committee is usually composed of a chairman and one or two assistants. They arrange for news releases, press and TV interviews, and so on, checking in advance for local media instructions.

Publicity is important. Prominent speakers and guests should be publicized. Important decisions or positions taken during the business session on legislative, political, religious, or other matters of public concern should be given prompt notice to the media.

In order to control a lengthy schedule in a specific limit of time, promptness is important. The presiding officer must be assured that all is in readiness—and in well-organized order—before the convention is called to order.

There are, in many large cities, professional convention bureaus. For the right fee, they organize all or part of any proposed convention program. While use of professionals reduces the work and anxiety for the convention members, it also reduces, and may even eliminate, the opportunity for members to work closely together on a major project that can produce benefits of loyalty, friendship, and interrelationships among the entire membership.

The *call to convention* should be issued, in writing, according to the documents of authority requirements, at least thirty to forty days prior to the event. It includes the theme for the convention (if any), dates, time, place, and the proposed procedural rules and the proposed program. To fulfill the requirements of previous notice, any bylaw amendments to be proposed are included. The report of the nominating committee (if any) is added. Copies of resolutions that may be controversial are usually supplied. The call to convention also includes pertinent information on hotel reservations, expenses, meals, and transportation.

The *preconvention board meeting* should precede every convention. During this meeting, every detail of preparation should be checked and rehearsed. The parliamentarian is the key consultant and is necessarily present at this meeting. Here he may speak rather freely in offering advice, helping to formulate resolutions, and advising on strategy techniques and procedural rules.

See **Parliamentarian.**

Convention Resolutions Committee

During a convention or annual meeting, the resolutions committee, sometimes called the platform committee, is of paramount importance, for a great proportion of the business undertaken at a convention is the consideration of the resolutions submitted to the assembly.

All resolutions to be presented to the assembly should first be submitted to the resolutions committee by a specified time, which should be far enough in advance to permit copies of the resolutions to be prepared. The authorship of the resolutions and required signatures should accompany the copies of the resolution.

Resolutions involving a legislative bill or other legal document should be accompanied with a copy of the bill or document, the name of the proposer, and the date of its publication.

The resolutions committee should meet at a specified time to screen and review all resolutions submitted to it. This committee is empowered to rule out of order any resolutions whose subject matter is in violation of any national, state, or local laws or organizational rules.

Some organizations also empower the committee to rule out resolutions that engender or provoke racial or religious dissension.

Early screening permits the committee to edit resolutions for language, grammar, punctuation, and clarity, to confer with the sponsors, and, subject to their consent, to rewrite a resolution in correct or better form before its submission to the delegates.

The resolutions committee, unless otherwise specified, has no power to reject (not to report) resolutions that meet the requirements of bylaws, charter, and adopted rules. At the plenary meeting, the committee may propose each resolution with or without recommendations from the committee. The committee may or may not explain their reasons.

Prior to submission to the assembly, the committee will hold a hearing. This permits the sponsors to explain their resolutions and to answer questions. It gives the delegates an opportunity to ask questions, participate in discussion, and suggest amendments. A parliamentarian in attendance is helpful. After the hearing, the committee meets again to consider the findings, to reconsider its recommendations (or its lack of them) and to prepare to offer amendments.

In conventions where many resolutions may be presented for consideration, such resolutions may only be brought to the floor after the recommended resolutions have been disposed of first. Depending on the adopted rules, a member may or may not be permitted to propose a resolution from the floor.

The resolutions committee may prepare resolutions of its own, in particular those referring to policy statements. This committee also prepares a courtesy resolution.

The chairman, when presenting resolutions, states, "By direction of the resolutions committee, I move the adoption of the following resolutions." They are then considered seriatim, but may be adopted en bloc if the situation warrants it.

See also **Hearings; Resolutions.**

Opening Ceremonies

Opening ceremonies, such as welcoming speeches, introductions, and patriotic or religious observances, may be conducted after the call to order. These are hospitality and courtesy rites in observance of protocol and need no legal authorization.

Convention business cannot begin until the convention is legally ready, that is, duly organized by the adoption of three committee reports presented in the following order: credentials, rules, and program. The chairmen of these committees are usually appointed by the president.

Credentials Committee

This committee supervises the registration of delegates, alternates, and other voting members. Much of this should be done prior to the convention; so, early appointments to this committee are necessary. It must distribute to the member units the requirements for eligibility for delegates and alternates, and information about the manner of their election as specified in parent bylaws. It must also distribute credential blanks, with instructions for filling them out before returning them to the credentials committee. From the information received, the committee compiles an official list of the number of delegates and alternates each unit is entitled to, and of the voting officers.

The committee arranges for a time and place for registration. As delegates arrive to register, their credentials are verified, and appropriate badges are issued. The committee checks on any irregularities and makes replacements as required. In the event of a contested delegate, it determines their authenticity—unless it wishes to refer the final decision to the assembly.

Alternates, officers, members, and guests are also registered and issued appropriate badges. Ushers should require all persons to show their credentials before they are seated in their assigned seating sections.

A duplicate list of delegates and alternates is prepared for use by the election committee.

If proxy votes have been authorized, the committee counts and verifies those entitled to proxies and their number.

The enrollment list should be separated into categories: the total number present; the number of delegates and voting officers present; and the number of alternates, members, and guests in attendance.

After the call to order, before any business can begin, the presiding officer calls for the report from the credentials chairman, who reads the report as prepared. The chairman says, "By direction of the credentials committee, I move that this report be the official roll for the convention." The presiding officer then announces that the quorum (a majority of the registered delegates, regardless of their presence or absence from the floor) has been established, and the report is adopted by a majority vote. Subsequent supplementary reports are presented at the beginning of each meeting, or whenever a change in quorum and registration requires it. It is necessary that these reports be accurate.

The committee continues to function until registration ceases.

Rules Committee

The rules committee prepares a set of rules under which the convention is to operate, unless it submits previously adopted standing rules with little or no changes. Standing rules adopted for the organization's regular meetings may be utilized. It is also possible to use the adopted standing rules used in board meetings of a national or large association.

These standing rules should become the rules for the convention, unless changes are adopted by a majority vote. These rules may deviate from the adopted parliamentary authority, but may not conflict with the bylaws of the parent organization. The rules should be designed to provide the most effective means for the greatest achievement in the minimum of time. Proposals to suspend the rules, with or without notice, require a two-thirds vote.

Since the rules are basically the same from year to year and must be presented to the voting body prior to their adoption, they are usually printed in the call to convention or distributed at the time of registration. Or, a rule may be adopted that the convention shall be conducted according to the rules in the printed program—subject to such modification as the convention body may make from time to time. Since copies have been distributed, the rules are seldom read aloud. When the rules are presented for adoption, the chairman states, "By direction of the rules committee, I move that the standing rules, as printed, be adopted." Or, if the documentary authority has so provided, the presiding officer may state, "The standing rules as adopted by this organization shall serve as the standing rules for this convention, with the following changes." Only the changes would then be voted on.

The following are examples of typical rules for a convention:

A delegate may speak only once on a proposition.
A speaker may speak no longer than three minutes.
No hats may be worn on the assembly floor.

Program Committee

After the adoption of the rules committee report, the president calls upon the program committee chairman to present the program committee report. The program committee is responsible for providing a stimulating program that enables delegates to leave with a positive evaluation of the convention. The program should not become too crowded: when time is so vital, substantial deviations in the program can unfairly deprive the next speaker or business of rightful time. The planners should be able to juggle essential time, providing for flexibility in the program, and should allow provisions for sudden change. This committee should keep in close touch with the president to avoid springing surprises that could impair his scheduled responsibilities.

A program can consist of workshops, speakers, tours, demonstrations, banquets, and other events as well as the agenda. The chair states, "By direction of the program committee, I move the adoption of the printed program with such changes as may become necessary." It is adopted by majority vote even if it contains special orders. It is amendable. Once adopted, it takes a two-thirds vote to suspend any portion of it.

To be successful, a program should be carefully prepared so as to avoid conflicts and contain something of interest to stimulate each member. Events should be carefully fitted around the business agenda and in no way conflict with it. The business agenda normally is the real business and purpose for the convention and must have priority at all times in the program schedule.

The program chairman usually introduces the speaker, panel members, or participants in the program, and in consultation with the president, arranges for opening ceremonies.

It is possible for the program to include the business agenda, or it may be adopted separately. A separate adoption of the agenda is recommended procedure since it may be amended and because of its importance to the convention business.

See also **Order of Business, Orders, Special Orders.**

Use of Floor Microphones and Color Cards

When an assembly is so large that the use of microphones is required, the microphones should be placed strategically about the floor. However, decorum can still become difficult to maintain if too many delegates gather around the microphones. In such large assemblies, the chair could rule that only those wishing to speak on the pending question are allowed to line up, one at a time at the microphone, and that those preparing to ask for recognition on the next proposition refrain from getting in line. Since the would-be speakers come from all over the floor (or even a balcony), this method becomes too time consuming. The parliamentary rule is that only the speaker should be standing. Therefore, a row of empty chairs should be kept behind the microphone for those seeking a turn. Seating the waiting delegates clears the floor and provides for better visibility.

Standing at the front of the line does not insure the delegate the right to the next turn. The chair decides who is entitled to be recognized next.

Using color cards provides an additional aid to help those delegates seeking to be recognized. "Mike" monitors, members who are knowledgeable and experienced in the use of motions, should be appointed to distribute color cards to the waiting delegates according to their purposes. The color cards may be green for those who wish to speak for motion, red for those who wish to speak against it, yellow for those who wish to make a subsidiary motion, and white for those who have priority requests, such as points of order, division, and personal privilege. Each monitor should have at hand a list of precedence of motions—motions that would properly interrupt and motions that would be out of order. Thus, the monitor can readily assign positions to the delegates as they approach the microphone. Special microphones may be assigned for particular purposes, but in a large assembly this becomes cumbersome.

Monitors can even assist a delegate with suggestions as to which motion the delegate is seeking to use. No color cards are used for main motions or resolutions, as they are already provided for in the adopted agenda.

Convention Minutes

Bylaws or standing rules should authorize a committee or the board to approve convention minutes, and if such is authorized, all decisions or determinations should be entered in the minutes of the board.

Minutes of a convention are best assigned to a minutes committee, appointed by the president at the beginning of the session. These committee members should then take careful notes of the proceedings.

Too much unnecessary time is consumed when minutes are read and approved at the beginning of each meeting, particularly since delegates from the previous meeting are not always in attendance to vouch for accuracy. However, approving the minutes should not be held over to the next convention. So, at the end of the proceedings, the minutes committee should review, correct, and approve the minutes of the secretary. Each member should then sign his or her name to the minutes (as amended, if required), which signifies that the minutes have been officially approved. Convention minutes are placed on file with the secretary, the board of directors, or the executive secretary as specified in the bylaws.

See also **Minutes**.

Convention Business Agenda

The business agenda of a convention is a proposed program for action by the convention for the transition of its business. It is adopted by the assembly after the adoption of any amendments to the agenda. Such amendments are acted on by majority vote.

The business agenda usually consists of the reports of officers, the board, the executive director, and the standing and special committees (*ad hoc*), with or without recommendations. These reports present information on the activities of the organization, its officers, managers, and staff. Also included are any resolutions to be considered and any nominations and elections as provided for in the documentary authority. Resolutions relating to policy or legislation must have ample time provided for their consideration.

The business agenda is usually prepared by the executive director in consultation with the president and, on occasion, with the board of directors. The president announces the printed agenda and asks for its approval by majority vote if it is not presented by the program committee and adopted by the assembly. The motion for its adoption may be assumed.

If the order of business (the agenda) is to be amended after adoption or items moved to be taken up out of their adopted order, general consent is usually used; otherwise, to amend the order of business or to suspend the rules requires a two-thirds vote.

SAMPLE AGENDA FOR CONVENTION, ANNUAL SESSION

Call to Order
Opening Ceremonies: invocation, pledge of allegiance to the flag of the United States of America, welcoming speeches, introductions, music, etc.
Appointments: parliamentarian, tellers, timekeeper, minutes committee, others as required. The president makes the appointments. If a parliamentarian has been engaged on a regular basis, the assembly is introduced to that person. Appointment of auditors is made sometime prior to convention. The president announces their names.

Adoption of the Credentials Report: this is an initial report to establish the quorum.

Adoption of the Rules Committee Report: it may be amended at this time.

Adoption of the Program Committee Report: often includes the business agenda, which may be adopted as a separate item.

Reports of Officers: according to rank, with the president first, who does not leave the chair to report.

Reports of Board of Directors, Executive Director: officers and board reports may be printed and distributed so that only additional comments are made.

Reports of Standing Committees: usually according to the list as stated in the bylaws, or in alphabetical order, or as specially selected, such as the bylaws committee first. Action may be taken on committee recommendations as they are presented.

Reports of *Ad Hoc* Committees: action is taken on reports as required.

Nominations and Elections of Officers: in an election year, these are provided according to the method adopted by the organization. This item should be inserted early in the proceedings to provide for reballot time, if necessary. In most instances, reports and business can continue throughout the election proceedings with a brief recess to ballot, or by balloting before, between, or after a meeting.

Announcements: special remarks, such as congratulations and necessary information not presented in reports.

Presentation and Adoption of Courtesy Resolution: and other acknowledgments.

Installation of Officers: this is optional and usually done at a later ceremony.

Adjournment Sine Die: all unfinished business is terminated, but may be introduced under new business at the next convention.

Courtesy Resolution

A special committee or the resolutions committee itself often prepares a courtesy resolution—more appropriately called an appreciation resolution—for those who have contributed to the success of the convention in some way.

Near the time of adjournment, the chairman of the committee reads the resolution and moves for its adoption. The presiding officer sometimes takes only the affirmative vote, unless a negative vote has been called for. The chair directs that copies of the adopted resolution be sent to the appropriate recipients.

COUNSEL
See **Attorney.**

CREATING A BLANK

Creating a blank, a procedure for selecting a choice or choices from multiple proposals—e.g., a date for a meeting or place of meeting—authorized by the adoption of a motion by majority vote, while favored by some parliamentary authorities, can be a cumbersome procedure. The normal amending process, by striking out and inserting, can accomplish the same end without adding further complicating procedures.

A simpler method would be to recess and consider informally. *See also* **Consider Informally**.

CUSTOM AND PRECEDENT

Many organizations develop certain habits or customs through the years that have not been challenged. Many customs are good and become prized traditions. These customs may be written or unwritten. They do not need to be recorded to become authoritative, and have the force of law unless they violate any laws.

Since they have been pursued for some time without objection, it would take a point of order and a ruling by the chair (which is appealable) or the adoption of a motion to change them. Such a motion would be debatable and amendable and would require a majority vote for passage.

If a bylaw has been disregarded over a period of time, the same procedure would have to be utilized to bring that bylaw back into practice.

Customs cannot excuse officials of an organization from any dereliction of duties or responsibilities.

See also **Precedents**.

D

DEBATE

John Stuart Mill defined debate as "the clash of opposing ideas that gives truth a chance to emerge."

An organization conducts meetings primarily to provide an opportunity to consider proposals and make concurrent decisions about the proposition under consideration. The basic principle of parliamentary procedure is that such consideration, called debate, be free, full, and vigorous. Debate permits oral communication—during which opinions and facts, pro and con, can be presented by the members with the intent to persuade the listeners to adopt the debater's point of view and to help decide the proposition accordingly.

Debate is intentional thinking. The speakers present their case to support their advocacy.

Discussion is reflective thinking. Facts are presented, weighed, and evaluated; compromise often results.

Both methods are used in consideration of a proposition. In a general meeting, debate is more practical, whereas discussion is more suitable for committees. In any case, no proper solutions can be achieved until the assembly has identified the problem and understood the purpose.

Debate follows a pattern of formality to preserve an objective, impersonal interchange of thought, as well as to help maintain order. Formal debate provides for order and courtesy. In small meetings, such as in a committee, members may remain seated during debate. In large meetings, formality increases with the size of the meeting; at a convention, for example, those wishing to speak may move to a microphone rather than address the assembly from their seats.

See **Rights to Speak**.

Members' Responsibilities

Members should learn the rules of debate and the use of parliamentary motions in order to exercise their rights, to participate effectively, and to assist in forming a well-considered conclusion. Too many members rise to speak, presumably to gain attention,

without contributing new information. A wise chairman will tact-
fully forestall this by asking, "Is there anything new to add to the
discussion?" If the chair suspects dilatory delays, it may discourage
recognition of a troublemaker. All members should use:

Rules of Decorum During Debate

1. All main motions are fully debatable. Other motions have
   limited debate. Some motions are not debatable, since any
   debate would defeat the purpose of the motion. Brief comments, a clarification, or a question made before the statement of a motion is sometimes permissible but must not be
   abused. They are not considered as debate but as informal
   consultation.
2. Every member is entitled to speak in debate, but only when
   recognized by the presiding officer. All members share equally
   in the discussion.
3. No debate may begin until a motion is pending before the
   assembly. During debate on a motion, members may obtain
   recognition to offer amendments or other motions relating
   to the disposition of that pending main motion, or to raise
   some questions as to procedure. These motions must be
   solved before action on the pending main motion, and when
   offered, they immediately become the pending question.
4. Every member, after recognition, may speak with impunity
   as long as the rules of debate are observed. No member
   may use a turn to speak in order to incite to riot or violence,
   or to impugn the reputation of the society or any of its
   members.
5. Each speaker is entitled to be listened to with courtesy and
   may demand that the chair enforce this courtesy.
6. No member has privileges in debate in excess of other members unless granted by the assembly—except that the maker
   of the motion should have first right to speak on the motion.
7. All debate must relate directly to the pending proposition
   (be germane). If the speaker departs from this, the chair
   may call that person to order, or any member may do so
   by rising to a point of order or by a call for the regular
   order.
8. All remarks are addressed directly to the chair, using the
   correct title of the presiding officer.
9. No member may speak longer than the established time
   limit. If none has been established, custom provides that

ten minutes shall be the extent of time allowed for speaking. Time for debate may be limited or extended by the assembly.

10. No member may speak more than twice on the same pending question on the same day except by general consent or adoption of a motion to that effect. No member should have a second turn to speak until all who wish a first turn have spoken. No member has the right to monopolize the debate.

11. A member has the right to speak twice on any debatable motions that have been applied to the main motion.

12. The proposer of a motion should not speak against it, unless it has been greatly amended against the will of the mover, as that would be considered dilatory, but may vote against it.

13. Names of members are not to be used by the speaker, nor may the speaker attack the motives or character of another member. It is the issue, not the member, that is being considered.

14. In debate, it is not in order to introduce past or future actions. Past decisions may be used only as references.

15. If a member wishes to reply to a question from the floor, with the consent of the assembly and the speaker, the time is deducted from that speaker's time.

16. Members may read papers only by general consent. Brief pertinent quotes or reports are allowed, but they are included in the speaker's time allotment.

17. All members except the recognized speaker should be seated so that attention may properly be directed to him or her. Even the presiding officer sits, unless the comments will be very brief. The chair can gauge this in most cases, from the nature of the proposition.

18. A brief explanation as to why a motion is to be proposed may be permitted occasionally—and only when it is necessary.

19. No member may reserve an unexpired part of speaking time until later except by general consent.

20. The recognized member may not transfer or yield time for debate to another except by general consent; the speaker may yield for questions, with such time consumed to be charged to the speaker.

21. After a member has been recognized but has not yet spoken, it is out of order for any member to move to table or adjourn.

22. If there is difficulty in wording a motion properly, the chair

may offer assistance if the speaker desires it. A member may ask for this.

23. No member should use dilatory tactics during debate with the intent to delay, disturb, or confuse the assembly. The chair should call the member to order, ignore a later call for recognition, or otherwise reprimand the person. Any member may, on a point of order, demand that the chair restore decorum.

24. Rules for debate may be included in an organization's standing rules.

25. Comments between members during debate must be addressed through the chair.

See also **Limiting Debate; Consider Informally; Discipline.**

Presiding Officer's Role During Debate

The presiding officer is responsible for supervising the debate efficiently and accurately, in observance with the rules of decorum. His or her primary responsibilites are (1) to control and expedite, (2) to protect the rights of the members, and (3) to maintain order and keep the debate germane.

1. The chair should not participate in debate, in speech or manner, in order to preserve impartiality. The chair only directs the traffic of debate.

2. However, if the chair believes strongly in the merits or demerits of a proposition, the presiding officer should not hestitate to participate as a member—as the most concerned, most informed member in any situation that can affect the reputation of the organization. To do so, the presiding officer is expected to leave the chair, and the vice-president or some other authorized member presides. The president is given priority in being recognized to speak. The president should not resume the chair until the issue has been resolved.

3. The chair may clarify issues, or offer obscure or additional facts without bias to help debaters. The chair might say, "If you vote yes on the motion, the result will be. . . . If you vote no, the following situation will result. . . ."

4. The chair is the only member with the authority to recognize those entitled to speak, so the chair must carefully provide equal opportunity to both sides. If the chair is in doubt as to whom to assign the floor, the chair may seek assistance from members of the assembly.

5. The chair should take the vote accurately, both pro and con, and announce the vote so all may hear. If the proposition requires action, the chair will announce who is to implement the action.

6. If "division" is called for in taking the vote, the chair will not permit any further debate except by general consent.

7. If a vote requires a two-thirds majority, the chair should announce the count first, before announcing the result of the vote. Two-thirds vote should not be taken by voice.

8. The chair may comment on an appeal or explain a ruling on a point of order without leaving the chair. Assignment to the floor may not be appealed in a mass meeting. Large conventions frequently adopt a rule that no appeal may be made from the chair's recognition of assignment to the floor.

9. The chair has the responsibility to protect members from any indecorum, disturbance, or interruption during debate, and must deal firmly and promptly with such infractions. The speaker may demand that order be preserved, although there are some cases where an interruption is legitimate.

10. The chair should use the correct language and procedure of debate to avoid confusion among the members.

Termination of Debate

Debate may be terminated in several ways:

1. If no one rises to debate after a motion has been stated by the chair, after a sufficient pause, the chair may put the motion to a vote or state, "If there is no objection, the motion is adopted," or, "The motion is adopted by general consent."

2. After the chair states the pending question, if no one wishes to speak further or rises to claim the floor, after a sufficient pause, the chair puts the question to a vote.

3. If a time limit for debate has been set and that time has arrived, the chair puts the question to a vote.

4. If the motion to close debate has been adopted, the chair is required to put the question immediately to a vote.

5. Certain motions, when adopted, may be used to delay temporarily decisions such as to refer to committee, to postpone, to recess, to adjourn, or to move for an adjourned meeting.

6. The chair may not close debate on its own initiative.

7. If the chair puts a question to a vote too hastily, that is, without sufficient pause for a member who desired and sought recognition, the chair should back up and permit resumption of debate even if the result of the vote has been announced.

Motions That Help Control Debate

Adjourn:	closes debate and the meeting.
Close debate:	stops debate entirely and prohibits any further motion except to table, recess, or adjourn.
Commit or refer:	refers the matter to a committee temporarily until reported back to the assembly.
Extend debate:	expands the time allowed for debate as specified in the motion.
Limit debate:	sets a time for duration of debate or number or length of speeches.
Postpone:	sets another time for consideration of the question.
Question of consideration:	prevents any further discussion whatever on the pending motion if the members vote to refuse its consideration.
Recess:	suspends debate temporarily.
Table:	disposes of the motion by killing it.

Legal Interruptions to Debate

Interruptions are usually made by the presiding officer when the speaker fails to observe the rules of debate or to restore order. Such remarks from the chair may be:

"Your remarks are no longer germane. Please confine them to the subject."

"Your speaking time has expired. Kindly be seated."

"Comments attacking the members' motives will not be tolerated. Please refrain."

"There will be order and quiet in this assembly."

If the chair fails to interrupt any indecorum during debate, any member may take the initiative to do so by rising to a point of order or calling for the regular order.

Motions that may interrupt the speaker or call for the regular order follow.

Point of Order. The member will rise and address the chair, saying, "Mr. Chairman [or Madam President, etc.], I rise to a point of order." The chair will ask the member to state the point. If the chair determines the point is valid, the error will be corrected immediately.

Question for Speaking Member.   If a member wishes to question a speaker, the member will rise, address the chair, and ask through the chair if the speaker will yield for a question. The chair will then inquire if the speaker is willing to yield for a question. If the speaker replies in the affirmative, the question is directed through the chair. The time to reply is included in the allotted speaking time.

Question of Privilege.   The member will rise and address the chair, saying, "Mr. [or Madam] President [or Chairman], I rise to a question of privilege." The chair asks the member to state the question and then determines if the question merits a privileged status; if so, the member proceeds accordingly. Such questions might be to ask the speaker to use the microphone, to repeat a total of figures, to ask for order, or to request more heat in the room. If the question of privilege is not an emergency, the chair will so rule and then resolve the question of privilege at the first opportunity.

Motions That May Not Interrupt the Speaker

No member has the right to move a privileged motion (such as to adjourn, recess, or table) while another member has the floor.

Yielding for Interruption.   When interrupted by the chair because of an emergency, the speaker stands aside until the problem has been resolved. Then the chair directs the speaker to proceed. The time for such interruptions is not deducted from the speaker's time. If the speaking member indulges an interruption by another member and replies to it, the time is counted against the alloted speaking time. A speaker may be interrupted against his or her will only when the matter is urgent and must be resolved before the speaker continues. The chair determines the urgency; otherwise interruptions occur after the speaker has yielded the floor.

Debate Strategy

The purpose of debate is to persuade and convince others to the speaker's point of view. There are certain psychological factors and debate techniques that help secure a positive reaction. Use of such strategy is acceptable and legal procedure. The following suggestions are simple and workable:

- Provide for comfortable surroundings before the meeting begins. Discomfort provokes irritability.
- Close the doors to shut out distractions. Enclosure promotes a sense of solidarity.
- Keep the meeting moving. It needs to be paced, but never hurried. This is largely the responsibility of the presiding officer, but members can use parliamentary rules to expedite.
- Ensure that the discussion is confined to the same subject and its purpose is understood.
- When debate becomes heated or extensive, members become tired; they will be uncooperative and think less clearly. Move for a recess, for an adjourned meeting, or even for adjournment.
- Use of humor provides an outlet for reducing tensions. However, sarcasm or barbs aimed at other members should never be permitted.

Effective techniques to use when debating:

- Make the motion psychologically attractive, well-worded, in the affirmative, and well-organized. The proposer should believe in it.
- The speech should be planned, brief, germane, without repetition.
- Only facts and provable statements should be used. Never generalize.
- Speak audibly, pleasantly, understandably, enthusiastically.
- Get support. Ask members of prestige or authority to speak for the motion. Cite convincing quotes, but have proof with you.
- Never underestimate the opponents. Listen to them attentively. Note data to be used in rebuttal. Ask for proof of the opponent's valid points when they seem obscure.
- Know more than the opponents. Never be caught short with factual information. Insufficient evidence dooms one to failure.
- Disagree agreeably. Avoid emotionalism, which beclouds the issue. Keep cool and calm.
- Be ready to compromise. Offer amendments to save the situation. Only a majority has to be convinced. If in danger of losing, move to delay a decision by use of certain parliamentary motions.
- Get down to business. Move to limit debate.
- Remember to win graciously and to lose gracefully.

Members' responsibilities during debate:

- Contribute opinions at open meetings.
- State facts; guesses waste time.
- Debate briefly, concisely keeping remarks germane.
- Address all remarks to the chair.
- Remain seated during debate; rise when floor has been yielded.
- Confine remarks to issues, not motives or persons.
- Present motions in the correct forms.
- Observe decorum of debate.
- Accept the will of the majority gracefully.
- Vote. Abstentions prove nothing.

Strategies for the presiding officer:

- Anticipate trouble.
- Keep cool, patient, tactful.
- Be firm when ruling, and defend ruling on appeal.
- Observe formality.
- Adhere strictly to rules.
- Accept only legitimate motions or interruptions.

DELEGATES

Delegates are those members whom an organization selects to represent it at a convention. They are elected or appointed according to the document of authority of the parent organization. While every member has the right to attend a convention, only delegates, officers, and others as provided in the documentary authority may debate and vote. The number of delegates is usually in ratio to the unit membership. They are elected to represent their respective membership as determined by the parent body.

Qualifications

Delegates should be chosen for their concern in organizational affairs and should be faithful to their obligations. They should be selected not only for their intelligence but for their ability to listen to debate and participate effectively, making judgments based on facts, not emotions. It is preferable to select delegates who have some knowledge of parliamentary procedures.

Duties

Delegates, on arriving at a convention, should check with the credentials committee to receive their badges and information kits, which they should study to equip themselves by learning the rules, resolutions, and information they contain. Delegates should arrive promptly at all business meetings and remain until the meetings end. They should listen objectively to speeches, take notes, attend workshops and other programs. They should be friendly with other delegates, responsible, and courteous.

All delegates should use proper decorum in debate, when recognized by the presiding officer, by giving name and unit represented. All remarks must be addressed to the chair. The floor should be yielded promptly when speaking time has expired.

New Delegates

Delegates should acquaint themselves with the parliamentary rules and the issues to be presented, in advance of the meetings. Some convention bodies hold orientation meetings conducted by the parliamentarian to instruct them as to the procedures they may anticipate during the transaction of business during the meetings.

Instructed Delegates

Delegates may be instructed by their home units as to how they are to vote on one or all issues. Unless a computerized voting record is kept, however, each delegate is trusted and expected to comply with the instructions. Instructing delegates is not recommended since debate and amendments may materially alter the proposition.

Uninstructed Delegates

If delegates are not instructed but selected because of the home unit's faith in their good judgment, they may vote as their conscience determines, always keeping in mind the wishes or opinions of their own units and supporting them whenever they do not conflict with the desires of the whole group.

Delegates' Reports

Delegates should report to their own unit on returning home. The report should be brief but interesting, noting positive and constructive points. The report should include all essential information on who presided along with a summary of the business transacted, with elaborate reports on items that would be of particular interest to the home unit. It should contain ideas gained, especially if they are adaptable to home use. Speakers should be quoted only briefly, for noteworthy remarks.

Alternates

Alternates replace delegates during their absences. They should possess the same qualifications as delegates. Alternates, too, must register with the credentials committee and obtain identifying badges. Until an alternate officially replaces a delegate whose badge has been surrendered to the credentials committee and the alternate has received his delegate's credentials, the alternate may not participate in debate or vote. Temporary absence of a delegate does not qualify an alternate to actively replace him. If a delegate returns before the voting has been completed, he or she may reverse the alternate's vote unless the vote has been by ballot.

Alternates elected in a designated order will serve in that order as vacancies occur. An alternate who replaces a delegate who holds an office is not entitled to the office.

See also **Conventions.**

DELEGATING DUTIES

The duties of officers and standing committees and their chairmen are usually stated in bylaws or standing rules—or the group may refer to the adopted parliamentary authority.

A board or committee may appoint a subcommittee to carry out an assignment. These subcommittees are selected from the board's or committee's membership and answer only to their appointing power, which is responsible for the acts of the subcommittees.

Definitive powers or duties cannot be delegated. Duties assigned to officers and members of the board in their documents of authority must be conducted by those to whom the responsibility has been designated.

DELIBERATIVE ASSEMBLIES

An assembly is a meeting of persons who come together to transact business for a definite purpose. This body meets to deliberate (to discuss, debate, expose facts, sift evidence, ask questions, persuade, and convince) in order to come to concurrent decisions arrived at by majority vote. The vote is usually a majority of all those present and voting.

Sometimes the assembly does not come to a definite yes or no decision. It then uses a motion to gain more time or to conclude the matter temporarily without voting on it, such as to refer to a committee or to postpone.

To meet legally as an assembly requires proper notice to all members; the presence of a quorum, a presiding officer, and a secretary; an adopted order of business; proper decorum; strict adherence to all adopted rules; and all actions taken at the meeting should be accurately recorded in the minutes.

Any recognized parliamentary manual may be used as a guide for rules and be adopted as a procedural authority (a procedural authority is one which is used whenever the assembly has no adopted rules of its own sufficient to take care of the parliamentary situation). Bylaws, a charter, and standing and special rules outrank any adopted parliamentary authority as do any applicable local, state, or national laws.

DILATORY MOTIONS

Dilatory motions are those that have no real purpose or meaning to the business of the meeting, that conflict with the purposes of the society, or that deliberately are moved, to obstruct business. Such motions, if adopted, might not be enforceable. When they are made, the chair may immediately rule them out of order. The chair's duty is to protect the membership from malicious, unreasonable, mischievous, and unnecessary motions that appear to be made for ulterior purposes. Such motions include persistent requests for division, motions to adjourn made early in the meeting (for no apparent reason), and rising continually to a point of order or to a parliamentary inquiry.

The chair, in ruling the motions out of order, may or may not give reasons for doing so. If the chair is in doubt whether the motion is dilatory, he or she should give the maker the benefit of the doubt or refer the decision to the assembly. Once a ruling has been made, it is subject to appeal.

See also **Appeal.**

DIRECTORS
See **Boards.**

DISCHARGE A COMMITTEE

When an assembly has referred a question to a committee, the assembly cannot take any action on the matter until the committee has made its report, nor may it consider like motions.

If the committee fails to report or take any action, or delays in the assumption of its responsibilities, the assembly may wish to take the matter into its own hands and discharge the committee, refer the matter to another committee, or drop the matter altogether.

If any of these actions or delays occur, a motion is in order to discharge the committee. It requires a majority vote, and previous notice ought to be given. The motion is debatable and can be amended to the extent of setting a specific time for a report or changing its previous instructions. Any of the procedural motions may be applied to it. A negative vote may be reconsidered.

After a committee has presented its final report, there is no need to move to discharge the committee. A special committee is automatically terminated. A standing committee remains intact, but the members are discharged from any further action on the question referred to it.

DISCIPLINE

Every association has an inherent right to expect members to conduct themselves in a manner that will be a credit to the organization and to perform at meetings so that the assembly may transact its business in an orderly fashion. The right of assembly and the right to an orderly meeting are intrinsic protections for an organization. The whole membership also has an inherent right to discipline any of its members for cause, even to the point of expelling them from membership.

Presiding Officer's Responsibilities

The presiding officer has a compelling duty of leadership to maintain order and enforce decorum. His responsibility is to protect the members from improprieties, abuses, and disturbances, and to do so promptly. At such a time, the advice and assurance of a good parliamentarian is invaluable.

The presiding officer has the responsibility to know that prevention is the best medicine and that tact, common sense, firmness, and patience are the best requisites. The chair has the right to reprimand any member for small infractions of rules and has the right to stop the meeting if it gets out of hand. To do so, the presiding officer never pounds the gavel in an effort to drown out noise. The chair stops, waits, taps the gavel once so as to be heard, and says firmly, "Your chairman will not let the meeting continue until you are quiet and in your seats." The chairman then waits for order to be restored. If disruption continues, the chair can recess or even adjourn the meeting. The chair has authority to withhold recognition to the floor for cause. The chair has the duty to enforce rules rigidly when debate "heats up." She or he has the responsibility to know the rules and how to use them and has the responsibility to anticipate trouble. If a meeting is about to consider controversial issues, the chair should consult in advance with the parliamentarian to determine salutary methods for handling the situation.

Conduct by members that is subject to disciplinary action includes:

- Continuous violation of assembly rules.
- Intemperate remarks during debate.
- Disobedience to legitimate orders from the chair.
- Defrauding or cheating.
- Conduct inimical to the society or organization.
- Any act that jeopardizes the good name of the society.

The chair has no authority to punish members except to call them to order and, if that fails, to cite them by name, stating the offense. This publicizes the offender, as the "naming" is entered in the minutes for the permanent record.

The presiding officer may order nonmembers to leave. If a nonmember does not leave as ordered, the chair may assign the sergeant-at-arms (if there is one) or at least two other members to escort the disturber from the assembly. The chair is also careful to appoint two members as witnesses to the eviction as a protection to the organization in the event of a later suit that undue force was used to evict.

If a member continues to disrupt a meeting, any member may move to have that member evicted; and by a majority vote, the chair would take the same procedure as for nonmembers.

Since the chair cannot determine punishment, when indecorum continues, the chair may ask the assembly, "What action shall be taken against this member?" By motion, members may decide to demand a public apology, suspend privileges to the floor, remove the disturber from the meeting, or adopt some other deprivation. Members may not move to fine another member unless so authorized in the documentary authority; that is a prerogative of the courts.

By tradition, members are expected to obey the legitimate orders of the presiding officer. In fact, certain deliberate disturbance can be an indictable offense.

See also **Censure**.

Members' Responsibilities

When members join an organization, they are expected to obey all rules and regulations. There can be no exceptions. These rules are designed to protect as well as regulate the behavior of the members. No member has the right to interfere with orderly conduct or the rights and dignity of other members by word or action. If a member thinks an order from the president is unfair, a point of order may be made, followed by an appeal from that ruling. If the ruling is upheld, it becomes binding. No member may refuse to cooperate with the decision of the assembly.

Members have the responsibility to preserve decorum in debate and to assist the presiding officer in preserving order by such actions as to raise a point of order, to table, recess, refer to committee, or adjourn; or to make a question of privilege.

Members have the responsibility to know the proper use of motions. They may seek a vote to test their confidence in the chair by moving for a vote of confidence. While this motion has no parliamentary significance, its adoption can improve a situation psychologically.

Members have the responsibility to determine punishment for offenders, including that of censure. Members should express disapproval in a legitimate manner.

See also **Censure; Trial and Expulsion of Members**.

Misconduct from the Chair

No organization has to endure misconduct from the presiding officer and may take steps to rectify the situation. If the chair, while presiding, refuses to recognize members entitled to the floor, accept an appropriate appeal, rule on a point of order, or state a motion and put it to a vote, any member may rise to a point of order, citing the transgression. If the chair does not correct the error, a member may appeal. If the chair ignores the point of order, any member, after repeating the citation, and with the consent of the members, should be permitted to put the issue to a vote.

If the chair willfully withholds information, fails to preserve order, fails to recognize members impartially, enters into debate while in the chair, or neglects his duties, any member may move to censure the chair or to suspend the presiding officer. Both motions are debatable, amendable, and require a majority vote. In such a case, the presiding officer next in rank should preside to put the question to a vote and announce the result.

If the chair should continue in willful misconduct or neglect of duty in office—such as by misusing funds, misrepresenting the offices of the organization, being convicted of a felony, or being a member of a subversive organization—any member may move to appoint a committee to investigate the charges and report to the assembly. If the charges are found to be in the affirmative, a motion may be made to hold a trial, which should be held in closed session.

The power to appoint carries with it the power to remove unless the documents of authority stipulate otherwise. An elected officer can only be removed by a vote of those who put him in office as provided in the documentary authority.

See also **Trial and Expulsion of Members.**

DISSOLUTIONS

When a meeting adjourns (sine die) without provision for its recall, this adjournment dissolves that assembly, but not necessarily the organization. When this motion is used and the chair feels that there is reason for another meeting before dissolution, the chair should so inform the membership so that a motion for adjournment for another meeting may be provided for in the adjournment motion. This occurs frequently in mass meetings.

When an organization is no longer viable and needs to disband, it is necessary that this be done properly so as to avoid a possible future law suit. If the organization is incorporated, an article providing for its dissolution should be included in its charter. Incorporated organizations must dissolve according to the laws of incorporation. Their attorney is advised; he or she prepares the necessary papers. The corporation then surrenders its charter and terminates its existence. The board of directors (or whatever) may continue to meet until all obligations of the society are concluded.

If the organization is unincorporated, after its meeting of the membership to consider dissolution, the board, as authorized, prepares a resolution such as the following:

Whereas, The . . . Club can no longer fill its membership
(or for whatever reasons);
Resolved, That the . . . Club will be dissolved of . . . (date).

As a second resolve or as a separate resolution, the board prepares
a statement informing members of the plan to dispose of its assets.
If the organization is tax-exempt, having received this status from
state or federal action, all assets must be disposed of according to
tax laws. Not-for-profit organizations cannot dispense remaining
assets to any personal gain. Assets must go to the parent body or
to some other organization, such as a charity, church, or school.
Since to disband is to rescind the bylaws, it should require previous
notice and a vote of a majority of the then-existing total membership. Copies of the resolutions must be sent to all recorded members
remaining on the roster. A mail vote may be used to determine the
results.

If the resolutions are adopted, no more meetings may be held,
but the board of directors (or whatever) may continue to meet until
it has concluded all of the affairs of the organization.

DIVISION OF ASSEMBLY
(Verification of a Vote)

As soon as the chair has taken a vote, both pro and con, but before
the chair has announced the result of the vote, any member may
call for a "division" of the assembly. This is an incidental motion
that requires no vote and is not debatable or amendable. It is, in
fact, a demand, and the chair will comply.

A call for division can interrupt, since it must be given immediate
attention. Division alerts the chair that the result of a vote may be
in doubt. The chair states, "All those in favor, please rise." (Pause.)
"Be seated. All those opposed, please rise." (Pause.) "Be seated."
The chair then announces the result of the vote as was visible to
all members. In small groups where all members can be seen, a
show of hands will suffice. The chair can, on his own, call for a
division vote when it appears that the result is uncertain. If division
has been called for after the vote is in process, debate may be
resumed only by general consent.

If doubt still prevails, the chair may order a counted vote. Also,
any member may move to take a counted vote; this motion must
be adopted by general consent or a majority vote. The chair will
appoint a sufficient number of tellers or order a count-off (serpen-

tine vote). The chair calls for members from each side—first the proponents and then the opponents—to rise as the vote is called for and to remain standing until counted. The tellers bring the results of the count together to compile the final results. The final tally is presented to the chair, who announces the results.

The chair may rule, subject to appeal, that a motion for a counted vote is dilatory if he believes it was intended merely to consume time and was unnecessary since the previous result was apparent. A counted vote leaves no doubt as to which side prevails.

After division of assembly has been taken, a member may move to reconsider the vote. If this is agreed to, a member may move to use another method of voting, such as a ballot.

DIVISION OF THE QUESTION

Any pending question before an assembly that is divisible may be divided upon demand of any member, without motion or a vote. Otherwise, any pending question would not be divisible even on motion. The presiding officer is charged with the sole responsibility of deciding upon the divisibility of a question, subject to an appeal of the decision of the chair, which is debatable.

To be divisible, each part of a question on which a separate vote is requested must be totally independent of all other parts. Each part on which a division is demanded must present a separate and independent question to the assembly for action, even if any or none of the other parts should be adopted. For example, if an office is proposed and the duties of that office are set forth along with the name of the office, the two would not be divisible, for if the latter part—assigning the duties—were to be adopted, it would be meaningless if the creation of the office were to be rejected.

To demand a division of the question, a member need not wait for recognition by the chair. However, the request for division must occur before any action is taken by the assembly on the parts of the question that would be involved. Any member desiring a division of a question merely addresses the chair, even when another has the floor. The member states, for example: Mr. President, I call for a division of the pending question, with a separate vote to be taken on each part as follows . . .

The debate and votes on each question, unless otherwise ordered, occur in the order the questions appear in the motion, resolution, question, or amendment, as the case might be.

See also **Seriatim.**

DOCUMENTS OF AUTHORITY

Under modern practices, most organizations combine their constitution and bylaws into a single document and designate it "bylaws." Since most formal or sophisticated organizations are incorporated under a state law, the body of law under which they are incorporated—the corporate charter—could well be considered their constitution.

If an organization wishes to have a constitution and a set of bylaws separately, it certainly has the right to do so. Such a decision would not be in conflict with any of the parliamentary authorities, even though a constitution is not usually recommended. The contents of a constitution, if thus utilized, could well include the basics of an organization, partly lifted from the law of incorporation, particularly the legal provisions applicable to that organization. Other basics could include the organizational setup, name, purpose, and structure—including the regions and chapters or clubs, seal and insignia, and the amending process for the constitution, the bylaws, the standing rules, or whatever.

If the organization prefers only one instead of two documents, it should be designated or named the constitution and bylaws, or just "bylaws." It is also a good idea for each organization to compile the provisions of law, if any, under which it was incorporated or created and to attach them to its documents of authority.

The documents of authority should always include at least:

1. Bylaws.
2. Standing rules of procedure for conducting meetings.
3. Standing orders of the organization.
4. A compilation of customs, precedents, and practices of the organization.

Bylaws

The first document, unless there is a constitution, is designated the bylaws.

Since under various parliamentary authorities there is confusion as to whether certain provisions of the bylaws can be suspended, it is proposed here to simplify that matter. Some authorities specify that a provision of a bylaw concerned only with procedure may be suspended; all other parts may not. This places more authority at the discretion of the chair and allows for far more confusion and delay of proceedings.

The bylaws of all organizations should be confined to contents dealing with the functions and structure of the organization; nothing should be included in the bylaws dealing with the procedure of meetings of the organization. To illustrate: the bylaws should create and establish the officers of the organization and define their respective terms of office and their duties, while the procedure to be utilized in the election of such officers should be set forth in the standing rules of procedure. In this way, you could not eliminate an office by suspending the bylaws, but by a two-thirds vote you could suspend the rules setting up the procedure for electing the officers. Think what it would mean if the bylaws were to provide the procedure for the election of officers by ballot—meaning that the election could not be suspended—and only one candidate was nominated. Why not put such a proviso in the standing rules of procedure, which could easily be suspended by a two-thirds vote or by general consent, and then vote on the nomination by voice vote when there is no significant opposition, without wasting the time of the organization in balloting when there is only one candidate? If there is expected to be a significant write-in vote, a two-thirds vote to suspend the rules would not likely be forthcoming.

See also **Bylaws.**

Standing Rules of Procedure

The second document is the standing rules of procedure for conducting meetings.

In the standing rules of procedure for conducting meetings, nothing should be included that deals with the functions and structure of the organization; only matters concerned with the procedure for conducting meetings should be set forth. Under this concept, any standing rules could be suspended by a two-thirds vote, and such decision would not be subjected to the discretion of the chair.

See also **Standing Rules.**

Standing Orders

The third document in rank is the standing orders of the organization. Such rules or regulations, adopted or amended from time to time by the organization, are usually related to its policies, customs, and administrative details. They may not be in conflict or in opposition to its standing rules or bylaws, both of which embody higher authority.

Standing orders of an organization are not concerned with the organization's functions and structures nor with the rules of procedure for conducting meetings. This portion of the documentary authority is confined to matters that are significant to the organization but that can be suspended, changed, or repealed by a majority vote without notice. The standing orders are concerned with regulations, limitations, or stipulations of conditions of such nature that they should not be included in the bylaws or standing rules. They may need frequent changes or alterations. They may well include matters such as the time for daily meetings, the printing of reports, a code of ethics, publication regulations, official emblems, and stipulations for entries and awards. For example: "There shall be printed an annual report of the treasury," or "Each meeting of the general assembly shall begin at 12:00 noon." This latter order is important, but it should not take a two-thirds vote to suspend the rule in order to meet at a different hour—as it would if it were a standing rule.

Precedents and Practices

The fourth document consists of a compilation of precedents, customs, and practices of the organization. Each organization should collect and compile these data for attachment to its documents of authority. There is no better guide to an organization's procedure in the conduct of its business than the decisions of the chair on points of order, or the decisions of the assembly when a point of order is submitted to it—whether initially or when appeals are taken to the chair's ruling. Such decisions become the established procedure for the said organization. Equally helpful to an organization in its operation is the knowledge of the way that organization has performed in the past. This can be accomplished if the parliamentarian, the secretary, the historian, or any other officer designated by the organization compiles and keeps up to date their precedents, established customs, traditions, and practices. A complete compilation of such information is not only helpful but essential to the smooth and efficient conduct of business of an assembly. Such information is invaluable to a presiding officer.

While the precedents, customs, and practices more or less become the established procedure for the said organization, if the members later wish to discontinue any such procedure they can do so by adopting by majority vote a motion to that effect. Likewise, when the chair rules at a subsequent date on a point of order raised against a procedure so established, the membership could take an appeal from the decision of the chair and reverse that procedure.

See also **Bylaws; Charter Certificate of Incorporation; Standing Orders; Standing Rules.**

E

ELECTIONS

Each organization determines its own method of elections to office. This method should be decided with care. Nominations and elections are vital to the continued well-being of any organization. Most organizations include nominations and elections in their bylaws or standing rules, considering them too important to be left to the whim of each administration.

Bylaws, preferably the standing rules, may provide that if only one member is a nominee for office, the chair may state that the nominee is "elected by general consent" (or "elected unanimously") if there is no objection. If there is an objection, the chair puts the election (question) to a vote. General consent or voice vote is a time-saver but is not always acceptable to every organization.

There are certain general rules for elections:

Members may vote for themselves, if eligible.

Members who were absent or abstained in the first ballot may vote on the second or any subsequent balloting.

Members who are in arrears for dues may vote unless the documents of authority prohibit them.

"One man, one vote" is the general rule for all elections unless otherwise provided.

If the standing rules require a ballot vote, this method can be suspended by unanimous consent or a two-thirds vote.

Serving more than half a term is considered a full term.

Elections take effect immediately unless the documents of authority provide otherwise.

Installations are not necessary as a condition to assume office, but may be required in some organizations.

If a ballot or roll call vote is interrupted by adjournment because of some necessity, the voting will be resumed at the next meeting. Necessary precautions must be taken to preserve the secrecy of the ballots that have already been cast.

Majority vote elects unless otherwise provided. If no majority is reached on the first ballot, voting continues until a majority is obtained—unless the documents of authority have provided another solution.

All eligible members of an organization are entitled to vote, including tellers.

Elections to fill a vacancy may be held at any regular meeting, or as determined in documents of authority.

If voting by ballot is not included in the documents of authority, any member may move to adopt such a method.

Balloting procedure should secure secrecy, preventing any exposure of how one votes. Otherwise, the purpose is defeated.

See also **Ballot; Tellers and Balloting Procedures.**

EMERGENCY SITUATIONS

In larger organizations, the documents of authority should provide for a continuance of the incumbent administration in the event of an emergency, such as natural disaster, war, or gas shortages, so that if the annual meeting cannot be held the incumbent officers continue until an election can be conducted. In such circumstances, a provision could be included in the bylaws to authorize conducting an election by mail.

EN BLOC

En bloc means that a group of resolutions, amendments, or propositions are voted on simultaneously. This is sometimes called *en grosse.*

EXECUTIVE BOARD
See **Boards.**

EXECUTIVE COMMITTEE

The creation of an executive committee must be provided for in the bylaws. It is composed of members of the executive board, usually the officers and such other board members as deemed necessary. The committee should be small so that it can take prompt action between meetings of the executive board as needed. Its duties, functions, and powers are defined in the bylaws. The executive committee operates on behalf of the total membership but is directly responsible to the board it reports to for any action it takes. Its actions are entered into the board minutes.

The executive committee's role is often consultative, but it may also be authorized to negotiate contracts on property and take direct administrative action on personnel problems. It usually meets in closed session, with or without consultants as the committee wishes. Minutes are usually kept, but are not usually circulated.

EXECUTIVE SECRETARY OR DIRECTOR

A competent executive secretary, executive director, administrative manager, or whatever title used is an invaluable asset to an organization. Whereas officers are temporary, an executive secretary provides continuity. The documentary authority should provide the qualifications for employment, conditions of tenure, and duties. The salaried employment of a secretary is usually approved by the board. Some business experience is preferable, since this position requires management of the business office, employment of personnel, and negotiation of their salaries, as well as helping to plan the organization's business. The executive secretary should relieve the president of many administrative details, such as preparing agendas and reports, and doing research. This person performs duties assigned by the membership though he or she takes directions from the board and the president. The executive secretary has no vote on the board unless elected to it as a member, but may vote at regular meetings of the assembly if he or she is a member of the organization.

EXECUTIVE SESSION
See **Closed Sessions.**

EX OFFICIO

Documentary authorities often provide that certain officers are *ex officio* members of certain boards or committees by virtue of their office. This establishes them to full-fledged membership without obligations, unless otherwise stipulated. The position ceases when the tenure of office terminates. *Ex officio* members are not counted in the quorum.

EXPUNGE

When an organization has done something it later wishes it had not done, and the action was recorded in the minutes, the motion to rescind may be made and adopted, but the action that was taken may not be deleted from the minutes. The record of action, once taken, cannot be obliterated. Nothing contained in the minutes can be eradicated or defaced.

A motion to expunge is in order when no other motion is pending or no other motion blocks its consideration. It is adopted by a majority vote.

When a motion to expunge is adopted, the secretary draws a line through or a circle around the part to be expunged and writes in the margin, "Expunged by order of the assembly on . . . [date]" and then initials it. This action is entered in the current minutes without stating what was expunged.

The motion to expunge is debatable and amendable, and previous notice is required since the parties involved have a right to be informed. A negative vote can be reconsidered. If the minutes are to be published or distributed, the expunged portion is omitted. It is not read to the assembly in future references to those minutes.

In rare situations, when the board or assembly unanimously agrees that certain actions or procedures should never be exposed or put in the minutes, they may agree to expunge completely every reference to some of these actions or procedures—if done immediately so as to clear the slate, forget completely, and start anew. Of course this is not orthodox procedure for expunging records, but it has been done by groups known to the authors to avoid the exposure of situations that would be helpful to no one and embarrassing to everyone involved. This action has been referred to, on some occasions, as "cutting the Gordian knot" before the situation reaches a stage beyond solution.

EXTEND DEBATE
See **Limiting Debate.**

F

FILLING BLANKS
See **Creating a Blank.**

FINANCE COMMITTEE

If the organization is large or handles a considerable cash flow, the establishment of a finance committee is a must. The treasurer should be a member of the committee. Others may be appointed as provided in bylaws.

The finance committee prepares a budget, studies and provides means for financing undertakings, and projects for the organization as provided by bylaws. It cannot levy or execute money transactions, unless so authorized in the documentary authority, but makes recommendations to the board or membership. The organization will usually adopt the proposed budget, with or without amendments, and authorize the proposed expenditures.

See also **Committees.**

FLOOR PRIVILEGES

The floor is the part of the meeting room of the assembly where debate takes place. Only the members entitled to speak and participate in the transaction of business, and certain persons such as the parliamentarian, secretary, and sergeant-at-arms, are entitled to the privileges of being seated and to move around in the section reserved for the membership of the assembly. Others are entitled to observe from other sections of the room. A member obtains a right to the floor to speak when recognized by the chair. Only the chair has the authority to recognize and should do so with impartiality.

To obtain the floor, a member must rise and address the presiding officer by the official title: Mr. or Madam President, Madam or Mr. Chairman. In large meetings or conventions, the members when recognized are usually required to state their name and what group they represent, before they proceed to speak.

A member should not rise for recognition until the previous speaker appears ready to conclude his or her remarks or has yielded the floor.

The chair will recognize the member by name or some other form of recognition: "The Chair recognizes the gentleman in the fifth row," or "Standing at microphone number three." In a very small group, the chair might be considerably less formal.

The member then has the privilege of the floor and may speak. This also entitles the member to expect courteous attention, to be heard and to be listened to without interruption as long as the rules of decorum of debate are observed. It is the chair's responsibility to maintain order and protect the speaking member's rights. Should the chair fail to do so, the member may demand that the chair maintain order and protect his or her right.

By unanimous consent agreements, the chair may be partly denied the privilege of recognition when a motion stipulates who may be recognized, such as "I move that Mr. A and Mrs. B be given the next opportunities to speak on this matter."

See also **Rights to Speak.**

G

GENERAL CONSENT

Motions that appear to have no opposition because they are relatively unimportant, uncontroversial, or because approval is obvious, permit the chair to say, "The motion, without objection, is adopted" (or agreed to), without putting the motion to a formal vote. General consent implies that no one cared enough to oppose the motion or proposition. Unanimous consent implies that everyone was in agreement. If there is even one objection, the request is denied and the question must be put to a vote for adoption.

See also **Unanimous Consent Procedure.**

GERMANE

The requirement that debate be germane implies that the speaker must speak to the pending subject or question. Members are expected to know this. If they do not comply, the chair may interrupt and request the speaker to confine the remarks to the subject, or any member may rise to a point of order and demand that the speaker confine the remarks to the subject under discussion.

The requirement that debate be germane saves the assembly from wasting time. It protects members against any devious strategy that might affect the result of the vote.

The requirements that amendments be germane limits the subject matter of the amendment to be relevant to the pending question. The amendment may not be germane if it introduces new subject matter. If amendments are not germane, the chair may rule them out of order. This ruling may be appealed.

See also **Amendments and the Amending Process; Debate.**

GOOD OF THE ORDER

Some organizations make provisions, in their agenda near the close of a meeting, which are considered to be of benefit to the members and are known as "good of the order" or some other comparable

name. At such time, members may offer new suggestions or constructive criticisms that propose to improve established procedures,
or proposals to enhance the name of the organization. These comments are considered to be offered in good faith. Often, particular
members or committees are complimented at such a time.

No official motions or actions are taken at this time. Some of the
suggestions may later be proposed as motions under new business.
It is possible to place formal disciplinary charges and procedures
under this agenda item.

See also **Agenda, Sample Order of Business.**

GUEST SPEAKERS

The program chairman usually engages and introduces the speaker,
who should be engaged well in advance. The speaker should be
informed of the subject material she or he is expected to cover, the
length of time for the speech, whether there will be a question and
answer period, the time scheduled for the introduction, and the
time the meeting is to begin.

At least a day before the scheduled speaker is to arrive, the program chairman should check with the speaker to be sure of the
engagement. This can help prevent last-minute panic or cancella-
tion with no time to seek a replacement.

On the day of the meeting, the program chairman should arrive
early enough to check that the lights, ventilation, water pitcher and
glass, required audiovisual aids (if any), and microphone are all in
readiness.

Every courtesy should be extended to the speaker because of his
or her importance and personal schedule. The speaker is presented
as scheduled in the adopted program or whenever it is appropriate,
but should never be kept waiting unduly. If business is pending, a
motion to postpone it until after the speaker has completed her or
his remarks is in order. If an important speaker must hurry on to
meet a plane schedule or other assignment, business can be interrupted. Careful prescheduling by the program chairman can usually prevent this.

The president calls upon the program chairman to introduce the
program. Introductions should be brief, to the point, and never
infringe upon the speaker's time. If the speaker is not well-known,
a few comments as to his qualifications are in order. The better
known the speaker, the less said: for example, "Ladies and Gentle-
men, the President of the United States."

The speaker's title should be included in the introduction. If the speaker is already waiting on the platform, the program chairman should half-turn when introducing him by name, then by title. The program chairman should never turn his back to the assembly to make the introduction.

If the speaker is to be presented after a banquet, he or she should never be asked to begin until dishes are cleared unless this is agreed upon.

Speakers should seldom be interrupted. If the speaker continues substantially longer than the time allowed, the presiding officer may surreptitiously slip him a note or say quietly, "You have two more minutes." If he continues, the presiding officer may rise and state, "Regrettably, your time has expired."

The president thanks the speaker on behalf of the organization, tying the remarks in with the subject.

After the meeting, the speaker should be escorted to the door. His check, if any, should be presented as he leaves. A note from the program chairman expressing appreciation is always welcome. It gives the speaker an idea of the satisfaction given.

See also **Protocol.**

H

HEARINGS

A hearing refers to a proceeding by a committee taking testimony from "witnesses" for or against a subject or proposition falling within its jurisdiction, which it has under consideration. A committee assigned to investigate a matter may invite certain members or nonmembers to appear before it to present their views or give information on the subject. The persons invited are usually those with particular expertise or experience, or who sponsor the proposition.

After all the witnesses have presented their information pro and con, and any other pertinent data, the committee meets, generally in closed session, to consider the data received and determine its recommendations to be made to the parent body.

See also **Committees.**

HONORARY MEMBERSHIP

Honorary member is a title of respect, a complimentary title, bestowed upon members or officers, even nonmembers who have made some significant contribution to the organization. Bylaws should specify the requirements and the procedures for granting honorary membership to members or officers. Such a title is perpetual unless otherwise restricted or rescinded. If the title is given to an officer, the officer becomes an honorary officer of the same title.

Becoming an honorary member entitles one to attend all meetings of the organization and to participate to the extent allowed by the document of authority and the generally accepted practices of the organization. The right to vote or to propose motions is usually denied unless the member pays dues. No duties are imposed by this title.

Bylaws sometimes provide for an honorary life membership, in which case full membership rights may be extended.

Honorary members are not counted in a quorum unless otherwise authorized.

I

ILLEGAL VOTES AND VOTES NOT COUNTED

Legal voters sometimes cast votes illegally, usually because they have not followed instructions. Illegal votes should not be used when determining a majority vote.

Illegal votes are:

- Votes cast by persons not entitled to vote. If the number could affect the result, the balloting is voided and a reballot must be taken.
- Votes cast for those ineligible to serve.
- Two ballots, filled out, that have been folded together.
- Votes for too many nominees in a multiple choice ballot, making it impossible to determine which nominees were selected.
- Violation of secrecy when balloting. If this affects a substantial number of voters, the ballots are voided and a reballot is ordered.

Illegal votes are of little significance unless they can affect the results. The following votes are not necessarily illegal, but are not always tabulated:

- Blank votes are not credited to any nominee.
- Omission of a choice or a mistake in the choice when a ballot provides for multiple choices does not void the ballot for those votes cast legally—but if the choices exceed the number to be elected, the vote is void.

- Unintelligible votes, if they can affect the result, are reported to the chair, who immediately asks the assembly to decide on them.

  Votes where the intent is clear but the names are misspelled or there is some other irregularity are not counted as illegal ballots.

See also **Votes and Voting Methods.**

INCIDENTAL MOTIONS
See **Motions.**

INCORPORATION
See **Charter Certificate of Incorporation.**

INDECORUM
See **Debate; Rights to Speak.**

INFORMAL CONSIDERATION
See **Consider Informally.**

INSTALLATIONS

Installation is an inducting ceremony wherein the newly elected officers take an oath of office, swearing to discharge their duties under the documentary authority to the best of their ability. The ceremony may be simple or elaborate and done with humor or with dignity. A good installing officer can make this ritual a pleasant activity rather than a stale performance.

Officers may assume their duties immediately after the results of the election have been announced, providing that they are present, or as soon as they have been notified, if the rules and regulations permit. A person should not be nominated for office without the assurance that the nominee will serve if elected.

Bylaws may determine when officers shall assume duties to provide for a smooth transfer from an incumbent officer to a new one, as at the adjournment of the annual meeting or convention or even after installation. Installations do not affect the time officers assume office unless the bylaws so designate.

It is, at time of installation, a good practice to include a charge to the membership to support the new officers loyally and in good faith, and to uphold their responsibilities to the organization.

INTERRUPTIONS TO DEBATE

Once speakers have been recognized, they may not be interrupted as long as they conform to the rules of decorum in debate. There are times, however, when interruptions may be legally made: motions that are urgent because they involve the rights of the members and cannot wait, such as points of order; a question of privilege may also interrupt a speaker because it pertains to the rights of the membership or the comfort and welfare of any or all members.

The motions to reconsider, appeal, or division of assembly may interrupt the business pending, but not the speaker, since these motions must have prompt attention because of their specified time limits.

See also **Debate, Legal Interruptions to Debate.**

L

LIMITING DEBATE

This motion is used to curtail or extend the time limit of debate to be devoted to the pending questions. It may be adopted to apply to one motion or to a series of motions. It is used to define the time for which a question may be discussed. The motion may be applied to all debatable questions.

It is a motion of high rank in the precedence of motions. It is not debatable. It can be amended as to time or number of turns the speaker may be granted. It can be reconsidered when defeated. Because it is a suspension of the rules and deprives members of their rights to debate, the motion takes a two-thirds vote.

Limit Debate.   This motion is used when there is a definite need to transact business within a specified time. Any member may move, upon recognition, by stating, "Mr. Chairman, I move to limit debate to three minutes per speaker." Other forms of limiting debate may be: to limit the overall time to debate; to limit the number of speakers from each side, pro and con; or to stop debate at a preset hour. The presiding officer should be cautious of misuse of this motion and warn members when suspicious that it is being used as a parliamentary strategy to prevent exposing significant facts.

The chair may suggest the use of this motion, which may be adopted by general consent if there is no objection. If there is, the motion must be put to a vote.

When adopted, the motion is in force only for that pending business. Any such limitation in debate is applicable to the main motion or any amendment to the main motion to which it is directed.

The motion to close debate may be made after a limitation has been adopted, and it takes precedence.

The motion to limit debate is not used in committees.

Extending the Limit of Debate

The motion to extend debate is used to remove a previous limitation placed on debate. When the debate time has been exhausted and members wish to hear more facts or get more information, any member, after recognition, may state, "Mr. Chairman, I move that the debate be extended for another . . . minutes." He may also move to hear two more speakers, one from each side; to debate until a set time; or to have the speaker continue for an additional three minutes.

The motion is not debatable and may be amended only as to time, or length or number of speeches.

The chair may ask for general consent to extend time for debate, especially when it appears obvious that members are not ready to make a decision. The motion requires a two-thirds vote to adopt.

MACHINE VOTING

Only very large organizations such as unions, political parties, or legislative bodies use machine voting. Various types of voting machines include computers, electrical button pushing, and manual.

The cost of such machines for most organizations is prohibitive. Machine operators require particular and detailed instruction in their use of the machines.

MAIL BALLOTING

Mail voting is a form of absentee balloting and may be used only if provided for in documents of authority. It is used mainly where membership is widely scattered over a large area.

Ballots are mailed to each member whose name appears on the

currently official roll of membership. Tellers will check all ballots against this list to certify the legality of the ballot.

Ballots are sent to the members with the printed names of the candidates or the list of items to be voted on. Sometimes, information as to the qualifications of the candidates or facts about the issues are supplied on a separate sheet.

Members check X before each vote selection (or as otherwise instructed) and sign their names on a line reserved for their signature. They should return the ballot to the tellers as instructed by the required date.

If the ballot is to be secret, the marked voting ballot, containing no signature, should be folded and then inserted in an inner envelope. This envelope should then be sealed and enclosed in a self-addressed envelope on which the voter's name is placed, and mailed to the tellers as instructed. After the names of the voter on all of the outer envelopes have been checked against the accurate and current roster list, the envelopes are opened, the inner envelopes are removed, and the ballots are extracted, still folded, and deposited in the ballot box. When this step is completed, the tellers proceed to count the ballots. Tellers need to take great care to preserve the secrecy of the ballot and to assure accuracy in counting the votes.

See also **Votes and Voting Methods, Mail Ballot.**

MAIN MOTION

A main motion is a proposition that introduces business to the assembly for discussion and decision.

It may be proposed when no other business is pending. Only one main motion may be considered at a time, but other motions may be applied to it, becoming in succession the immediately pending question to be disposed of before acting on the main motion or next pending motion. A main motion is always debatable, amendable, and can have any other appropriate motions applied to it. It requires a majority vote and may be reconsidered.

There are three types of main motions:

1. The new main motion that brings new substantive questions upon which action is desired.
2. Motions that reintroduce business that has already been acted upon in which the assembly has been involved. These motions are to rescind, reconsider, change adopted motion, ratify, and discharge a committee. These motions may be introduced when no business is pending.

3. Other procedural motions may be acted on in the same manner as main motions when no other business is pending. They are to adjourn, recess, and limit debate.

A good main motion requires thoughtful preparation if it is to promote positive results. It should be:

1. Affirmative. To avoid confusion in the voting, avoid negative statements. It is incorrect to move not to do something, which is the same as making no motion at all. For example: "I move that we do not approve this bond issue." (Wrong: Its adoption expresses no opinion.) "I move that we go on record in opposition to this bond issue." (Right: Its adoption expresses a particular opinion.)
2. Clear and definite. The purpose is understood with one possible interpretation.
3. Concise and neatly worded with the best possible vocabulary, to make it comprehensive.
4. Administratively possible to execute.
5. Pertinent. Motions are not in order that conflict with the objectives and purposes of the organization or of the government—local, state, or national.
6. Constructive. Motions are not in order that entail jurisdiction beyond the powers of the organization, that reflect on the motives of members, or that intend deliberately to obstruct business.
7. Incisive. A main motion yields to all other motions in the ladder of motions. Its position is at the bottom of the ladder. When postponed, it carries with it all other pending motions. When referred to a committee, it carries with it all amendments already adopted or pending.
8. Supported by its proposer. The maker of a motion may vote against the motion, but should not speak against it unless amendments have materially altered the motion.
9. Submitted in writing to assure exactness. This is especially true when motions are long or complex.
10. Prepared in advance. The secretary is not empowered to paraphrase a motion. A thoughtful member prepares at least three copies of lengthy motions in advance—one for the secretary, one for the chair, and one for the proposer.
11. Proposed exclusively. No member may propose two motions at the same time, unless the assembly gives such permission.

See also **Dilatory Motions; Suspend the Rules.**

MAJORITY VOTE

Jefferson's *Manual* states, "The voice of the majority decides . . . when not otherwise provided for." Courts have ruled that "a majority may impose control and that a minority must accept it as long as it remains a minority."

Every organization should define the vote required for election of officers, for certain decisions affecting the rights of members, and for other important matters. For decisions made during the ordinary conduct of business, the majority vote is understood to be over half the votes cast, a quorum being present.

Each organization should define how a majority is to be determined. It may be a majority of a quorum; a majority of those present and voting; a majority of those present, voting or not; a majority of the membership, present or absent. There are often rules that require a greater vote than a majority (two-thirds, unanimous, and so on), which must be clearly defined in the documents of authority, or for less than a majority (plurality), which may not be used except as properly authorized.

See also **Plurality Vote; Voting Requirements, Two-Thirds Vote.**

MASS MEETING REQUIREMENTS

Deliberative meetings and the establishment of organizations cannot occur without a desire or need that should result from some careful planning. To be legally organized, any group that assembles must conform to the following parliamentary requirements: (1) previous notice of the meeting, (2) presence of the required quorum, (3) presence of a chairman and a secretary, (4) conducting of the meeting under some parliamentary rules for decorum, and (5) arriving at decisions by a majority vote of those present, by general consent, or some premium vote (more than a majority) previously agreed upon.

Mass Meetings

A mass meeting is a gathering by an unorganized group. It may be called for a variety of reasons. The call may be for one meeting, or the assembly may vote to continue with an adjourned meeting if the business has not been completed, or even decide to form a permanent society.

Mass meetings are generally open to the public, although some are called by special interest groups whose call to meeting may be restricted to an invited attendance. Such a call may specify the class of persons invited to attend while others are excluded by the sponsors, who have paid all expenses for the meeting and who may also control what business is to be considered. Otherwise, a mass meeting is open to anyone interested in the purpose of the meeting as stated in the call.

Those in attendance are considered members who may participate and vote. The quorum is the number in attendance, which is an indeterminate number of members.

Those who attend to oppose, disrupt, or abolish the intended purpose of the meeting may be excluded as nonmembers, and the chair may demand their expulsion. To prevent this, sponsors sometimes appoint a doorkeeper or issue tickets to the desired attendees.

The call to the meeting must specify which persons are eligible to attend; the date, time, and place; the purpose for the call; and must be signed by the sponsors. Sponsors of the meeting should determine, in advance, who shall call the meeting to order, who shall be nominated for chairman and secretary, what rules (if any) should be adopted, and who can best explain the purposes of the meeting.

If procedural rules are not adopted, the meeting will proceed according to accepted procedure, such as that a majority vote decides and only one member may speak at a time. If no time limit is adopted for speeches, the common practice is to permit a ten-minute duration. In a mass meeting, there is no appeal from the decision of the chair as to who is entitled to the floor. Any motions contrary to the purpose of the meeting should be ruled out of order.

At the appointed time, the meeting is called to order by the selected sponsor, who may nominate someone to serve as chairman for the meeting. Nominations are allowed from the floor. The election is taken by voice vote of the majority. The new chairman takes the chair immediately and calls for nominations for secretary. There may have been a preselection for nomination for this office as well, since the officers chosen should be competent and have a sincere interest in the purpose of the meeting. The secretary is also elected by voice vote.

The secretary is called upon to read the call, which serves as the bylaws for the meeting. The chair then calls upon the person selected to explain the purposes, the action to be desired, or the policy to be adopted. The sponsors should be ready to answer questions and give further information.

Usually, a predrafted resolution has been prepared, or after discussion, a committee may be appointed by the chair to draft one. While the committee retires to do so, discussion may continue, or the meeting may recess. As soon as the resolution is ready, the chairman of the committee or the secretary reads it and moves its adoption. The resolution is then open for debate and may be amended, even substituted, provided the material is germane and does not reject the purpose of the call.

After the resolution has been adopted, the members may:

1. Move to adjourn, or the chairman may declare the meeting adjourned (sine die), which dissolves the assembly.
2. Move to hold another meeting (move to hold an adjourned meeting) or to hold a series of meetings.
3. Move to become a permanent society.

The call of a mass meeting should include the following information:

> To whom concerned.
> Date, time, and place.
> Purpose of the call.
> Signature of sponsors.

The order of business at a mass meeting:

> Call to order at appointed time.
> Election of a chairman.
> Election of a secretary.
> Reading of the call.
> Explanation of the purpose.
> Proposal of a resolution and its adoption.
> Adjournment.

See also **Organizing a Permanent Society.**

MEETING REQUIREMENTS

Meetings are called by persons interested in certain subjects who wish to study, pursue, and take concurrent action on them. Such business in deliberative societies is transacted at a meeting, which is an assembly of persons. There are several kinds of meetings. They are: regular, special, annual, adjourned or special, mass meeting, and closed session. Board and convention committee meetings are part of their respective organizations.

Meetings of organizations are convened according to their documents of authority. In an unorganized group, they are convened under accepted parliamentary rules or procedures commonly referred to as general parliamentary procedure.

There are certain general accepted parliamentary requirements for calling meetings of a deliberative organization in order to transact official business, such as:

1. *Previous notice.* This is a notice to all members as to time, place, and date. Any meeting held without adequate previous notice to all members is invalid. No part of a meeting is legal that begins before the scheduled time. If a member fails to attend, after proper notice, that member forfeits any rights to decision making during the meeting. Notice of meetings as adopted in bylaws and standing rules is considered adequate previous notice.

2. *Presence of a quorum.* As long as a quorum is in attendance, no member can claim that the meeting was illegal or unrepresentative. The number of members required to be in attendance to make a quorum is set forth in the bylaws.

3. *Presence of a presiding officer and a secretary.* The presiding officer conducts the meeting, and the secretary or clerk takes a record of the proceedings. Their presence validates the meeting. The two officers are counted in the quorum. Bylaws may prescribe other officers who may initiate a meeting. In an unorganized group, the person in charge or the management of the proposed meeting may call the meeting to order.

   Worthwhile meetings are conducted by leaders who know how to use time effectively and use rules efficiently.

   Both the presiding officer and the membership have responsibilities. The presiding officer is the catalyst who steers the debate according to the rules of decorum. The members play the essential role of intelligent decision making.

Order, structure, and rules protect and promote good meeting procedures. Knowledgeable participants using courtesy and fair play promote satisfactory accomplishment.

See also **Quorum.**

MEMBERSHIP

Members are essential to any organization. They provide the officers, workers, money, ideas, and source of achievements.

1. Applicants, after fulfilling requirements, may be voted into membership according to the bylaws. If any applicant is dis-

qualified, the membership chairman may care to explain to the applicant the reason for disqualification. If the reason is valid, the chairman may be direct; for example, "I am sorry, but you do not reside within the ascribed territory." If it is for some other reason, the chairman will use tact and not explain, other than to say, "I am sorry, but you did not receive the required number of votes." It should never be revealed who voted against the applicant.

2. There are classes of membership, such as associative, regular, life, honorary, *ex officio*. Rights and obligations will vary with the class of membership.

3. Qualifications for membership should be contained in the bylaws. Sponsoring members have a distinct responsibility to acquaint prospective members with the society's program, activities, personnel, even bylaws, so as to enable them to decide where they can serve in the capacity best suited to their abilities.

4. A letter of resignation goes into effect when received unless an effective date has been supplied. No one can be forced to remain a member. Resignations are accepted with regret or with hope for reconsideration, or a member is dropped if in bad standing.

Obligations of Members

Members should:

1. Become familiar with bylaws, policies, protocol.
2. Pay dues promptly.
3. Protect the good name of the society and be loyal to its objectives.
4. Attend meetings on time and remain until adjournment.
5. Be attentive, open minded, and fair.
6. Participate in activities and serve on committees.
7. As members, respect the chair's opinion and obey legitimate orders.
8. Nominate and vote for well-qualified officers, then support them.
9. Insist on law and order during meetings.
10. Support the rules, regulations, and bylaws; treat customs and protocols of the organization with respect.

Rights of Members at Meetings

Members have the right:

1. To introduce business and to speak in support of it.
2. To receive all notices and have a copy of the bylaws.
3. To speak without interruption except as authorized by parliamentary practices.
4. To attend meetings.
5. To use all parliamentary motions and request certain privileges.
6. To speak twice, within the legal time limit, on all debatable motions.
7. To vote, to vote for oneself if not for personal gain, to abstain.
8. To nominate and to be eligible for nomination.
9. To appeal from the chair's ruling.
10. To change one's vote before the result is announced (except by ballot).
11. To inspect records of the meeting.
12. To resign at one's own time.
13. To insist upon compliance with bylaws and parliamentary rules.
14. To hold office, if qualified according to bylaws.
15. To trial, if accused.
16. To enjoy all the fellowship and activities the society provides.

If a member's rights are violated during business meetings, in the functions of the organization or use of its property, legal action against the organization may be taken only after all rights as provided by the organization have been exhausted.

MERGER

A merger is the combination of two organizations in which one of them loses its identity and ceases to exist as such; it becomes absorbed into the other organization.

In the event of a merger between two corporate societies, consultation is required with an attorney, who prepares the necessary papers.

If the organizations are not incorporated, each prepares a resolution. Both organizations include how the assets, properties, liabilities, and transition of officers (if any) will be disposed of. Both resolutions require previous notice to the membership and the required vote determined by the two organizations for adoption. Careful preparation is required to avoid later complications. The absorbing organization only may retain its title or a new one may be chosen. The merging organization, which will lose its identity, prepares a resolve stating that it will hereby become merged into the other organization as of . . . (date) and by what method, and that the other organization has agreed to accept it. The absorbing organization prepares a resolve to accept the merger under the conditions as cited in the first resolve.

MINORITY REPORT

Although the majority decides in a democratic society, the minority has rights that must be protected. Courts and bylaws make such provisions. Yet when a two-thirds vote is required, the power of decisions favors the minority, as one-third plus one defeats the proposal of the majority to act.

A majority should never withdraw from the assembly to destroy a quorum required for a legal meeting, nor should a minority do the same to reduce the attendance so as to break a quorum.

Minority members, as such, have the same rights individually as majority members. They may express their views in debate and vote. They may propose motions.

Minority views or opinions may be expressed after a committee report, but such views are merely received for information and filed. No action is taken on them. In many instances, minority reports from a committee are unnecessary, since the minority always has the opportunity to change opinion through debate and to propose amendments and vote against the recommendations.

If the minority moves to substitute the recommendations in the committee report with the recommendations from the minority report, then the recommendations are treated as a substitute motion and action can be taken on the motion to substitute. Action is not taken on a report but is taken on the recommendations to the report, when so moved.

A minority opinion must be made immediately after the report of the committee (majority report). The chair should be informed, in advance, that the minority will seek this opportunity so that the chair is prepared to recognize the reporting member. A minority may recommend rejection of certain parts of a report's recommendations, or that the recommendations be amended, or propose a substitute for all of the recommendations of the majority report. Any member may move to adopt such recommendations.

A committee member sometimes signs a committee report, but notes any exception to concurrence with the full report.

If the documentary authority authorizes minority reports, they may be filed just like a majority report, and a motion is in order to act upon the recommendations.

MINUTES

Minutes are the official record of action taken in a deliberative society—the proceedings of the business, what was done but not what was said.

Minutes must be accurate, clear, concise, up-to-date, intelligible, and presented in an orderly format. They are the legal documents of the society that can be impounded during court proceedings.

Verbatim records—stenotype or tape recordings—are not acceptable as minutes. They contain debate, do not always identify the speakers, and have extraneous remarks that make them voluminous. Also, they can easily be spliced and altered.

The secretary's job is to keep track of the parliamentary situation, to determine what is action and what is dialogue, and then put together an accurate account of the action. Minutes should be kept in a bound book; looseleaf books are vulnerable to change. The secretary keeps the minutes in a safe place. Members may examine the minutes at the convenience of the secretary.

Minutes should be written on the right-hand side of the book. The left side is kept for noting corrections or for marking expunged material.

Minutes that are typed triple-space permit room to mark for corrections or comments, (which may be put in the left margin instead of the left-hand page). The right-hand margin contains the title of each paragraph. Each new subject is entered in a new paragraph, including the name of the reporting committee. The result of action taken may be noted in the right margin for ready reference. All lines should be numbered in the left margin.

Minutes written in essay form make rapid referral difficult. Any good outline form is preferable.

Minutes are presented near the beginning of a meeting as a review of action taken at the previous meeting, to refresh memories, to bring those who were absent up to date, and to remind of any postponed business.

The minutes are read for approval and corrections though minutes may be corrected by motion at any time if an error can be verified. Minutes may be corrected by a majority vote or approved by general consent. The motion to approve may be assumed by the chair.

If minutes have been prepared and distributed, oral reading is not necessarily required. The chair may say, "You have received your copy of the minutes. Are there any corrections to the minutes as circulated?" (Pause.) "If not, they stand approved."

Published minutes contain all action taken. The signature of the president is required along with that of the secretary. Since the presence of the presiding officer and the secretary is required in order to hold a legal meeting, the notation (name and title of who presided and the signature of the secretary) offer proof.

The president may instruct an inexperienced secretary in the proper method for writing minutes and require the secretary to submit an advance copy for early review.

Minutes of conventions and annual sessions may be reviewed by bodies other than the regular assembly.

See also **Annual Session; Conventions, Convention Minutes; Expunge; Secretaries, Recording Secretary.**

Contents of Minutes (with a Separate Paragraph for Each Subject)

1. Kind of meeting, name of society, date (including the year), and time of meeting. If held other than the regular place, the place also is entered.
2. The name and title of the presiding officer is noted in full.
3. The presence of a quorum is entered as stated by the chair, as proof of the legality of the meeting.
4. The disposition of the minutes of the previous meeting.
5. Names of reporting officers, if any.
6. Treasurer's statement, in totals only. Amount on hand at the previous meeting, receipts, disbursements, amount on hand at the current meeting.
7. Names of all reporting chairmen and names of the committees, both standing and special committees.
8. All main motions in the exact words intended and approved by the mover. The secretary may temporarily interrupt business to get the accurate wording. The chair may require that the motion be put into writing. The name of the maker is usually included with the motion, if the society requires one.

Sample Form for Minutes

1 The regular meeting of the Astor Civic Association was called to   Call to
2 order by the president John Silver, on September 10, 1982, at 8:00 P.M. Order
3 in the Town Hall. Mary Gold, the secretary, took the minutes.

Robert Blue not present

4   Members present were: Mike Green, Joe Black, Robert Blue, Sally   Attendance
5 Brown, Mary Orchid, [etc.].
6   The minutes of the previous meeting were approved as corrected.   Approval
7   Report of the board was read for information only and placed on file.   Board
8   The treasurer's statement is: Report

9 Amount on hand at previous meeting $879.21   Treasurer's
10 Receipts   42.20   Report

correct total = #843.41

11 Disbursements   78.00
12 Amount on hand, current meeting   840.41
13 Reports of standing committes were read and filed.

10 new members: total=38

14 Holly Wood, Ch. Membership, reported ten new members increasing   Membership
15 membership from 28 to 40.
16 Sandy Gravel, Ch. Building Maintenance, reported that the new flag pole Flag
17 was to be installed by Oct. 1, 1982.
18 Report from the special committee: Bylaws, Mary Goodhope, Ch.,   Bylaw
19 recommended that a new Standing Committee be created on Public Relations, Amend.
20 members to be elected from the floor. Previous notice having been given, Art. V   Adopted
21 the motion was adopted by a two-thirds vote.
22   New Business: Jack Webb moved that we request police protection   Police
23 be increased in the Westbank Shopping area after 5 P.M. Motion Adopted. Protection
                                                                           Adopted
24   Mary Orchid moved that we send a committee of three, appointed by   Parking
25 the chair, to request special parking permits for this association   Committee
26 when meetings are held. Motion adopted.
27   The chair appointed Mike Green, Joe Black, Mary Orchid to the committee Comm.
28 to contact the Police Dept. for parking permits.   Appointed
29   His Honor, Mayor Perkins explained to us the problems of government   Mayor on
30 by the people as The Indirect Initiative.   Government
31   There being no further business, the chair adjourned the meeting at   Adjournment
32 10:45 P.M.

                              Mary Gold, Recording Secretary

9. All motions on which a vote is taken. Also points of order and appeals.
10. All counted votes.
11. Results of action taken in informal consideration, if any.
12. Results of action taken on recommendation from reporting committees. Reports themselves are placed on file unless a motion has been adopted to attach them to the minutes or to spread them on the minutes.
13. *Optional.* Each society may decide if it wishes to include the names of the guest speakers or the program and the title of the speech or the subject of the program as a record. If a salient point or two is added, the secretary takes great care to avoid a personal observation of bias.
14. All previous notices to meet requirements.
15. Time of adjournment.

Minutes are signed by the recording secretary including his or her title. After approval, they are frequently initialed by the president as further proof of their accuracy.

See also **Agenda.**

MOTIONS

Motions are proposals to bring business before the assembly and to dispose of them. Under the entry *Motions* in the index is a list of the numerous kinds of specific motions discussed in this book.

Improper Motions—motions that are not in order—are those that:

- Conflict with any laws or with rules of the organization.
- Propose action beyond the scope or authority of the organization or its objectives.
- Present the same question previously rejected at the same meeting.
- Conflict with a question temporarily disposed of by some procedural action.
- Conflict with previously adopted action still in force.

Motions That Are in Order and Correct must be:

- Worded concisely and accurately.
- Complete.
- Worded in acceptable language.
- Stated in the affirmative.

Motions That Are Amendable:

- Adjourn to a time certain.
- Amendments in the first degree.
- Division of the question—on demand, if divisible.
- Limit or extend debate—only as to time.
- Main motions and resolutions.
- Motions that affect election procedures.
- Motions that affect nominating procedures.
- Postpone—only as to time.
- Recess—only as to time.
- Refer to committee—as to instructions.

For other groupings, see also **Debate, Legal Interruptions to Debate; Privileged Motions; Undebatable Motions and Procedures.**

Precedence of Motions

Parliamentary motions fall into three general categories:

1. Main motions (substantive motions).
2. Amendments to the main motions.
3. Procedural motions, including privileged.

Before any item of business can come before an assembled group, the idea must be presented to the group. The introduction of this idea takes the form of a main motion or resolution, and only one main motion (or resolution, which might include several parts) can be presented at any one time. However, if one main motion contains numerous independent parts or proposals, each of which can be adopted totally independent of the text of the others, a simple demand by one member forces the chair to put the question on them separately or to separate one or two parts from the whole to be debated and voted on separately.

All motions other than main motions are amendments to the main motion, motions used to the disposition of the main motion, or independent procedural motions (such as to recess or to adjourn).

Before discussing amendments and procedural motions, it is wise to discuss why such motions are essential or necessary.

Individuals present at a meeting are assumed to be members in good standing, who believe in the orderly transaction of business. The members know that they have rights, privileges, and responsibilities, and if a few seem to want to upset the success of the meeting, there must be some safeguards to protect the majority in its right to transact business. At the same time, the membership must be encouraged to think for itself and to participate in the deliberations.

When a main motion is made, many things can be done to it: one member may not want to consider the idea at all, but wishes to move on to some other business; another may want to defeat the motion; another may want to delay the vote on the motion; still another member may want to change the language in the motion so that it will be more acceptable to the member; others may want to refer the idea to a smaller group of members (a committee) for a more detailed study to be made of it before the assembly is asked to consider it or vote on it; others may want to stop talking and get on with the vote; and some may want to talk, but not for quite so long.

Obviously, when there are so many possible options and the members believe in participating, there must be some kind of order of precedence by which these options can be exercised. They are designated as amendments or procedural motions, and they have their own priorities or rank for consideration, that is, one takes precedence of consideration over another.

The generally accepted *ladder of motions* in the disposition of a main motion is as follows:

1. Adjourn.
2. Recess.
3. Table.
4. Close debate.
5. Limit debate or extend.
6. Postpone (amendable).
7. Refer to a committee (amendable).
8. Amend (amendable).
9. Main motion (amendable).

The above motions are listed in the order of their precedence; for example, a main motion, being at the bottom of the ladder of motions, is subordinate to all of the motions listed above it.

When a main motion is pending, all of the higher ranking motions may be offered if called up in the order of priority and must be disposed of if offered before voting on the main motion; all of them may be pending at the same time if called up in order of their priority even if no vote has been taken on any one of them.

As soon as a main motion is before the assembly, a motion to amend, if made, is in order, and becomes the immediate pending question. At that point, it becomes the only question open to discussion, and only after it is disposed of will the main motion, with or without amendments, recur as the immediate pending question.

When an amendment to the main motion is offered, being in the first degree it is open to amendment in one further degree. If an amendment to the amendment is called up for consideration, that becomes the immediate pending question, and the only question at that time open for debate.

While an amendment to the main motion is pending—or, an amendment to the amendment—a motion to refer the main motion to a committee is in order. If made, it becomes the immediate pending question and the only motion open to debate.

If no amendment is pending and a motion to refer is made, that motion becomes the immediate pending question. At this point, an amendment to the main motion is not in order until the motion to refer is disposed of; a motion to postpone the main motion is in order at that point. In other words, motions going up the ladder of motions are always in order if ranking above the immediate pending motion, but a motion on a rung of the ladder below a pending motion is not in order.

Once called up and pending, motions are voted on in the order coming down the ladder of motions. For example, if an amendment to the main motion is pending and a motion to refer is also pending, the first vote occurs on the motion to refer, and then the question recurs on the adoption of the amendment if the motion to refer is rejected; if the motion to refer is agreed to, taking the whole main motion away from the assembly for the time being, there is no further vote on the proposal until it is brought before the assembly again.

To summarize: All motions in the ladder of motions can be proposed to help resolve the main motion or the pending amendment, one at a time, going up the ladder. All motions are disposed of, one at a time, going down the ladder of motions, with the main motion the last to be disposed of. If an amendment to the main motion is offered, it becomes the immediately pending question or motion. If adopted, the main motion, now the pending motion, is under consideration as amended. If the amendment is rejected, the main motion is still the pending motion without the amendment unless some other amendments are proposed.

See also **Division of the Question.**

Procedural Motions

There are a number of procedural motions available, depending on the circumstances or situation at the time, which are used to accomplish certain ends or to correct improper procedures during the consideration of business. These motions may be proposed at any time, but must be disposed of before action on motions of less precedence or the pending main motion. Some of them require no vote but are taken care of by the chair.

There is no attempt to classify such motions, since their privilege is somewhat dependent on the circumstances of business before the assembly and the recognition or acknowledgment by the chair. These motions, discussed under their title, are:

- Adopt the agenda.
- Appeal the decision of the chair.
- Call a member to order.
- Change an adopted motion.
- Division of the assembly.
- Division of a question.
- Orders of the day (a call for the regular order).
- Parliamentary inquiry, including any point of information.
- Point of order.
- Question of consideration.
- Question of privilege.
- Reconsider.
- Regular Order.
- Rescind.
- Suspension of the rules.
- Withdrawal of proposal by author with unanimous consent or by motion.

N

NOMINATIONS

To nominate is to propose someone—presumably a well-qualified member—to fill a position for a particular office. Nominating is a serious responsibility. It requires thoughtful consideration to find the nominee best suited at that particular time, who will, if elected, keep the good name of the organization and promote its growth.

Nominations.   Nominations for office are made in several ways: by the president, by committee, from the floor, by ballot or petition, or by mail ballot. The documentary authority should contain the methods to be used for the offices to be filled and the eligibility requirements for the office. If no provision has been made, any member may move to adopt a method for nominations. Usually, the documentary authority prohibits the president from nominating candidates for office.

Who May Be Nominated.   Any voting member (a member in good standing) may be nominated, if eligible. Members may be nominated to more than one office if the documents of authority do not prohibit it. If bylaws prohibit serving in two offices and the member is nominated to more than one office, that person must choose which position to accept, and the other position is then open for further nominations. If the member is already serving as an officer, there is no need to resign from that office until the result of the election is announced. The member may then choose which office to fill. The resulting vacancy causes an imcomplete election, and nominations are then opened to fill the unfilled position. Members may be nominated whether present or not if previous consent to serve, if elected, has been obtained.

Nominations May Be Debated.   Members have the right to explain why they believe their candidate is best suited for any position. The debate is to promote the candidate, not to attack the opponent, as is done in political competition. Pitting personalities against each other has no place in ordinary organizations.

Nominations by Committee.   This is probably the best and most democratic way to provide nominees, but only if the committee has been selected with great care. Provisions for a nominating committee should be in the bylaws, and should include the size, the duties, the method of selection. It can be a standing committee which observes and notes the capabilities of possible candidates throughout the year or a special committee chosen at some specific time prior to election. This committee has the responsibility to protect the future of the society, making its selections carefully in an impartial and fair manner.

The committee can interview candidates, secure prior consent to serve if elected; investigate qualifications and provide for equitable representation. Its report represents the well-considered opinions of a selected group. A nominating committee report is always presented first before other nominations.

A nominating committee nominated and elected from the floor should reflect the wishes of the membership.

Committee members are not disqualified from accepting nominations for office and need not resign from the committee since their one vote is not the majority of the committee as long as the quorum is maintained. If a committee member has been nominated for the office of president, the member might feel that a resignation from committee was in order so as to refrain from the appearance of undue influence, but it is not required.

The *president* should not be a member of this committee, even as *ex officio*. The president may, as may any member, submit names to the committee, which holds its meetings in closed session. The committee may consider the names or ignore them. The president does not nominate, to preserve impartiality, but may have a friend place a particular nomination.

The nominating committee usually presents a single slate. That is all that is needed since there is the opportunity to present other names from the floor. The slate, as prepared by the committee, should be confidential until the stated date for its general announcement. Advance notice leaked to a certain few gives an unfair advantage.

The *report* of the committee is always presented at the designated meeting by the chairman of the committee, even if publicized in an earlier notice. When called upon by the chair, the chairman, without comment, presents the slate: "Your committee on nominations reports the following—for the office of president, Ms. A; for the office of first vice-president, Mr. B . . ." and so on until all names have been presented. The report is signed by all concurring members. It is handed to the president who rereads the report and declares the names placed in nomination.

There is no need for a minority report since any members who were not in the majority on the committee may nominate from the floor. After the report is presented, the committee ceases to exist, but may be reactivated should a need for more nominations arise. No action is taken on the report until election.

Nominations from the Floor.   After the report of the nominating committee, the chair calls for nominations from the floor, which are always in order unless the documents of authority provide otherwise. The chair may say, "Nominations are now in order for the office of . . . ," calling out each office to be filled. Any member, after recognition, may place a name in nomination. If a second is heard, it is merely to signify an endorsement; it is not required and is ignored unless the documentary authority supports seconding speeches.

Closing Nominations.   After the chair has called for all nominations and no one rises to present more names, the chair may declare the nominations closed. This may be done for each office as specified or after all the names have been presented for all the required offices. Nominations should not be closed too hastily. The chair can use some judgment if it appears that dilatory nominations are being made, where the nominee has no chance for support because of lack of qualifications or eligibility, or when too many names are being presented ever to achieve a majority vote. The chair may explain his or her reasons and, if there is no objection, close nominations.

Any member may, when no more names are presented, move to close nominations. This takes a majority vote, and is not debatable or amendable.

Nominations Reopened.   Nominations may be reopened by a motion and majority vote or by general consent.

No Nomination.   A member may cast a vote for any eligible candidate, even if that member was not nominated, by use of a write-in vote, when such votes are not prohibited in the documentary authority.

Nomination by Ballot.   Members place names of those they wish to see nominated on cards supplied by the organization. These are mailed to the nominating committee. The name of the nominator may be omitted if the provision is made that nominations be secret. Every name submitted is placed in nomination. There can be no nominations from the floor at a later time since every member has had an opportunity to nominate. This nominating list shows preferences only and does not elect.

Nomination by the Chair.   This is generally used in mass meetings when the chair may nominate for officers pro tem or committee members. The chair may nominate when bylaws require the chair to nominate members for a committee. The membership is then required to vote on accepting the nominations as the elected members of the committee. If any are rejected, the chair nominates other members. The membership, in this case, may not nominate.

Nomination by Petition.   This method, to be used, must be provided for in the bylaws, which should include specifics as to how this may be done—the number of signatures required, how many candidates can be endorsed, date and place for filing the petition, and how offices are to be designated. When compliance with the bylaws has been met, the names are placed on the voting ballot.

See also **Votes and Voting Methods, Write-in Vote.**

NOTICE OF MEETINGS

All members are entitled to notice of meetings and of matters requiring previous notice. Notices of meetings are given as stipulated in the bylaws or standing rules, in the announced call of the meeting, by mail provided the notice goes to every member, or is given orally at the previous meeting.

Provisions for meetings are usually contained in the bylaws, which set dates. The hour and place, which may need to be changed, belong in the standing rules.

Special meeting provisions are authorized in bylaws.

Notice of adjourned meetings are official in the motion moved and adopted to hold an adjourned meeting. Since it is a continuation of the same meeting, additional notice is not required, but it is not inappropriate to send out notices of time, place, and date.

See also **Previous Notice.**

O

OATH OF OFFICE

Most organizations hold a ceremony for installing newly elected officers into office. At the ceremony, the officers promise to fulfill their responsibilities of office and swear allegiance to the purposes of the organization. Installation ceremonies may be simple or elaborate according to the wishes of the society, but the actual induction should be serious and dignified.

Someone of importance to the society usually administers the oath. It may be administered individually or collectively.

Some organizations require the oath as a legal qualification to assume office.

An oath of office may also be administered to new members for induction into membership.

See also **Installations.**

OBTAINING RECOGNITION
See **Rights to Speak; Addressing the Chair.**

OFFICERS

Officers necessary for an organization to carry out its business are provided for in bylaws. The offices of president and secretary (or equivalent) are mandatory—the first to conduct the business and the second to record it.

Bylaws should specify the term of office, how succession to office is determined, the method for filling vacancies in office, how many offices a member may hold at one time, and if an officer may succeed himself in the same office. It should also state the qualifications for office and eligibility requirements for those who will hold office.

Since the society created its own bylaws, it has the right to add or abolish offices or terms of office, and to consolidate two or more offices by use of the amending process.

All officers are expected to assume the responsibilities implicit in the office they hold and to act accordingly.

An officer who has served more than half a term is considered to have served a full term.

If an ineligible member has been elected to office, that election is null and void. However, if that officer has begun to serve, any acts taken in that capacity during that time are considered legal.

If a term of office is specified as "for two years" or "until the end of a term" with no provision for an election prior to that time, the organization might find itself without leadership upon the expiration of the elected term. To protect the organization, the officers should be permitted to continue as de facto officers with full legal status until an election can be arranged. Bylaws should be written to protect the society from the lack of this continuity in office. If the rules for a term have added the phrase "or until a successor is elected," those officers may continue to hold office until a replacement is elected.

A vacancy in office is filled by the authority that created it. A vacancy in committee is filled by the appointing power.

Resignations from office are filled according to the bylaws, which usually require previous notice.

For removal from office, *see* **Discipline.**

President

The president has two roles to play—that of administrator and that of presiding officer. The president holds the seat of authority, which cannot be delegated. The influence spread from this office should prosper, not detract from, the organization.

As *administrator*, the president should use tact and discretion in human relations. He or she should see the organization as a sum of all its parts, and should be fair and impartial to all.

The president should lead, initiate, and have a purpose and a plan to implement it. The president usually supervises the work of committees in the execution of his or her plans, having won their allegiance by enthusiasm, common sense, and good judgment.

The president, as legal head of the society, speaks for it and represents it at all outside functions.

The president serves as chairman of the board, appoints committees, and performs other duties as the bylaws provide.

As *presiding officer*, the president should realize that principles are more important than rules, but should use good judgment to combine both.

The president should be firm and insistent on observance of rules as necessary, but adapt the formality of the meeting according to the size or complexity of the meeting. The president should always insure that motions are stated and put to vote, and that the results are announced correctly.

The president should preside in a dignified manner, assuring the rights of all members, preserving order, and regulating the assembly and its individuals. He should use the gavel sparingly, not in competition with noise or disturbance, to control the meeting. He or she should have a well-planned agenda and adhere to it, expediting procedures wherever possible and pacing the meeting.

The president should know that intelligent decision making requires identification of the problem and understanding of its purpose. For this, she or he should take care to explain and to clarify (always impartially). The president should know the mechanics of procedural rules and recognize the use of constructive strategy.

The president should not participate in debate while in the chair lest it inhibit impartiality. However, he or she should not hesitate to enter into debate from the floor, by leaving the chair, when his or her input would be valuable to the decisions to be made.

See also **Administrative Duties of the President; Agenda; Meeting Requirements; President; Presiding, Presiding Skills.**

President-Elect

This office is created for large organizations spread over wide geographical areas when members can rarely attend meetings and the duties of the president are so vast and so demanding that some plan for training a successor, thereby maintaining continuity in the office, is necessary. Organizations that can meet with reasonable frequency and with regular attendance have no need for this office; the disadvantages might often outweigh the advantages.

This office must be provided for in the bylaws, with the exact duties and limitations of the office, including the position held on the governing board, carefully established. Because of the enormous competition and the power the president shares with the president-elect, careful attention must be given to safeguards and controls. Bylaws should include the right of the president-elect to assume office or preside in the absence of the president, a method of filling such a vacancy in the office, and a provision for depriving a president-elect who neglects his duties or otherwise fails to satisfy the membership from continuing into office as president.

The president-elect is elected in the same way as other officers for the same term.

At the expiration of the incumbent president's term, the president-elect automatically becomes president for a full term.

Vice-President

The vice-president is an alter ego of the president. He should be chosen for possessing the same qualities of competence and leadership as the president.

The vice-president must be prepared to assume the duties of the president when the president is absent, or to complete an unexpired term upon request or need. The vice-president assumes the office of president automatically unless bylaws provide otherwise, or unless bylaws have provided for a president-elect whose position takes precedence.

While acting as president, the vice-president has all the powers and duties of the president except that he or she cannot:

1. Alter rulings of the president.
2. Fill vacancies during the absence of the president.
3. Appoint committee members when the president is so empowered in the bylaws.
4. Act as *ex officio* in place of the president.

During business meetings, the vice-president should pay close attention to proceedings in case called upon to preside on short notice.

The vice-president should be assigned specific duties of some importance, such as chairman of the program committee or bylaws committee. The vice-president should be the confidant of the president, as advisor when asked.

When bylaws provide for more than one vice-president, the first numbered succeeds to the presidency with the loss of the president. The second-numbered vice president then becomes the first vice-president, and so on. The vacancy occurs in the lowest ranking vice-presidency. Failure to designate the numerical order of the vice-presidents requires research into the minutes. The vice-president who had the most votes recorded then becomes the first vice-president.

Secretary

The secretary is an officer required to be present for a meeting to be legal. The qualifications for office are accuracy, orderliness, and the ability to prepare concise accurate records. The secretary should also be familiar with parliamentary procedures and the rules of the organization. As is also true for the corresponding secretary, the office requires a person with the ability to write well.

The secretary has many duties, which include those of a corresponding secretary if the organization has none.

Duties of the Secretary
See **Secretaries.**

Corresponding Secretary

If the organization is large, the office of a corresponding secretary may relieve the recording secretary of some responsibilities. Since a corresponding secretary provides the written public image of the organization, the position requires ability to write well, using good grammar, vocabulary, tact, and grace.

The corresponding secretary may send out notices for special meetings, invitations, and correspondence dealing with communication needs as specified in the bylaws.

Both Secretaries.   They should read correspondence, even if only the salient points, without interpreting the letters on their merits. Letters requesting action are better resolved under the appropriate item on the agenda or may be referred to the appropriate chairman.

Assistance from the President
See **Secretaries.**

Directors

These elected officers sit as members of the board. Their duty is to serve as the society's governing body between meetings of the general assembly, or as specified in the bylaws. Directors should be communicators, interpreting bylaws and rules, keeping in close contact with the members, finding their interests and needs. Directors should help to implement the purposes of the society and feel a strong commitment to it.

See also **Boards.**

Treasurer

The treasurer helps prepare the budget, acts as a comptroller of the organization's funds, protects its finances, and should be a member of the finance committee.

A treasurer must keep accurate, current records of all monies in complete book form, as supplied by the organization. That officer should receive and deposit all monies promptly in a bank of the society's choice, unless otherwise provided. The treasurer should pay all bills as directed—if accompanied by voucher, and obtain co-signature as required. All slips, receipts and vouchers are kept for audit, and the checkbook must balance. Financial statements, in totals, should be made at each meeting, giving the amount on hand at the previous meeting, receipts, disbursements, and the amount on hand at the current meeting. Courtesy requires that a written copy of this statement be given to the secretary for inclusion in the minutes.

All financial records must be submitted for annual audit.

A treasurer holds a position of trust. Eligibility for the office is competence with handling money and integrity.

A newly elected treasurer should start with a clean slate, with copies of the audit and other financial records, so that there is no responsibility for any previous errors. New treasurers should consult with the outgoing treasurer as to the necessary tax forms that will need to be prepared.

If a treasurer is to handle a great deal of money, he or she should be bonded as a protection to both the officer and to the society.

Treasurer's records are made available to members or committees on request.

Copies of financial reports may be included in the call of the meeting at the assembly's request.

Other Officers

More officers may be added in the society's bylaws as needed. The additions are optional. The duties of each office should accompany the creation of the office. There are such other officers as historian, sergeant-at-arms, doorkeeper, financial secretary, and executive director.

See also **Executive Secretary or Director.**

OPENING CEREMONIES

Opening ceremonies are not required except as standing rules may provide. The length and formality depends entirely upon the nature and size of the organization. If ceremonies are adopted, they are presented in the following order (some or all may become rituals to be observed):

Invocation—God before country.
National anthem and/or presentation of colors.
Pledge of allegiance to the flag of the United States of America (not "salute to the flag").
Welcome address by the mayor or other host official (if meeting is not held locally).
Introduction of honor guests.
Brief greetings from the presiding officer, which may be dignified, humorous, inspirational, or friendly, as the situation may require.
See also **Protocol.**

ORDER OF BUSINESS

The business of a meeting is the real reason for the organization's existence. Business is conducted systematically in a predicted sequence as provided for in the order of business of the adopted agenda, so that convenience and consistency are provided. After the meeting is called to order but before business begins, a society usually has some opening ceremonies according to custom or as listed in the agenda.

Business is brought before the assembly by a motion from the floor, from a committee report, or a resolution or communication, in the form of a substantive main motion. Such motions propose that the assembly take action, adopt an opinion, or support a policy. Only one piece of business at a time may be placed before the membership for consideration. Other motions are introduced to help dispose of the main motion or to aid procedures in the proper disposal of that motion. Even though an order of business has been adopted, there is opportunity for flexibility whereby the order may be changed, if there is no objection, or, if there is, by a motion to suspend the order so as to insert business not included in the agenda or to change the order of an item as scheduled to be presented. This requires a two-thirds vote, since it is a suspension of the rules. It is debatable but not amendable, and often done by general consent, but reasonable previous notice should be given.

See also **Agenda; Main Motion.**

ORDERS

Orders can mean a sequence of events, an item of business within a sequence of events, a directive, or proper decorum. An *order of business* refers to the established sequence of events as listed in the adopted document of authority or as adopted by the society's own rules. It can also refer to general types or categories of business such as are used in conventions.

General Orders

All the business items on the adopted agenda are the general orders, unless any item on it has been made a special order. These general orders are taken up in the order in which they appear on the agenda.

A motion may be made to make an item a general order (to enter business on the agenda) before the adoption of the agenda, by a majority vote that is debatable, amendable, and capable of being reconsidered. The time for entering the proposed item may be set for later on the same day or at a future meeting.

Adoption of a general order does not mean that its consideration may interfere with any pending business. The matter would be presented by the chair after the pending business has been disposed of or under new business. If business is pending, the chair directs the secretary to note the motion in the minutes to prevent overlooking its consideration. However, if business is pending when a general order is adopted, a motion to postpone the pending business until after the consideration of the general order would be in order.

See also **Postpone.**

Special Orders

Special orders provide that pending business be suspended in order to consider special business. A motion may be postponed or made a special order for a particular hour. When that time arrives pending business must be interrupted and the special order taken up immediately. Because of its power to interrupt, it takes a two-thirds vote to adopt, since, in effect, it suspends the regular order of the meeting.

The pending business may be postponed until after the special order has been acted upon. Special orders cannot suspend rules that relate to:

- Bylaws.
- Adjournment or recess.
- Question previously made special order.
- The priority of *the* special order.
- Questions of privilege.

A matter may be made *the* special order for a meeting for such business as amending or revising bylaws or considering dues and other business that might become lengthy or contentious. It then becomes the first order of business, if not the only order of business, for that meeting.

ORDERS OF THE DAY
(Call for the Regular Order)

An item of business can be made an order of the day by adoption of a motion for this purpose. It would be a general order if no time was specified. If a specific time is stated for its consideration, then it becomes a special order.

If business is not proceeding according to its proper order as scheduled in the adopted agenda, any member may rise, address the chair and say, "I call for the regular order," or, "I call for orders of the day."

This means that the member is calling attention to a departure from the regular order of business that should be in progress. Notice of such an infraction can also be reached by rising to a point of order.

If the member is correct, the chair will immediately call for a return to the regular order of business or proceed to the order scheduled for that hour.

This call is privileged on demand. No vote is taken on it.

ORGANIZING A PERMANENT SOCIETY

A small group meets to talk informally as to the need to band together for some desired purpose in which they are all agreed, interested in, and sympathetic to. Those who wish to establish an organization have an obvious need or specific reasons, but these reasons must be explicit and clearly identified. Joel David Welty says, "It is to find out if all are pulling together in the same direction, not after they get harnessed together." The group considers the kind of organization to be formed, whether it is to be for profit or nonprofit, incorporated or not, types of membership, and general methods of financing.

The group decides to call a mass meeting in order to interest others and to take steps to form a permanent organization. A permanent society is one intending to function over a considerable period of time, into perpetuity, or until dissolution. This "incubating coterie" group needs to be enthusiastic, willing to work hard and able to publicize effectively, to raise funds for immediate necessary expenses, and to make plans to carry out their intended purpose. They hire a meeting place and prepare and issue a call. The call puts the aims of the group in writing for the record, which is for those expected to be interested. The group then proceeds as in a mass meeting. The sponsoring group prepares a resolution in anticipation of its adoption, such as: "Resolved, that this assembly form a permanent society to be known as . . . , for the purpose . . . [as stated in the call]." There may be additional resolves, such as that a copy be sent to the local press.

Before the first mass meeting, the sponsoring group should have determined who is most competent to call the meeting to order, to serve as chairman and secretary pro tem, who shall nominate them, what rules of procedure (parliamentary authority) should be adopted, and who can best initiate and explain the purposes as stated in the call.

The meeting is called to order promptly at the appointed time. A sponsor then calls for the immediate nomination of a chairman pro tem, elected by voice vote. Once elected, the new chairman calls for nomination and election of a secretary pro tem, or one may be appointed by the chair if there is no objection. Adoption of a parliamentary authority should be next in order for use during the mass meeting.

The new secretary is then called upon to read the call, which serves as the bylaws of the meeting. The chair then calls upon a preselected person to explain the purpose of the meeting, to answer questions, and to urge support from those in attendance to join the group. The resolutions, as prepared, may then be read, or a committee may be appointed to write them. While it is doing so, additional information and persuasion may take place; or if there is no need, the meeting may recess, subject to the call of the chair.

When the resolution is ready, the chair reconvenes the meeting if it was in recess, and the resolution is read. The chair then states that the resolution is open for discussion. It may be amended, by adding to or striking out, or even with a substitute motion as long as the changes are germane and do not alter the intent of the call. These amendments are voted on until the resolution is perfected, after which the resolution, as amended, is put to vote for adoption by a majority (unless a previous agreement for a greater majority had been reached). Any motion proposed that is contrary to the purpose of the call may be ruled out of order.

Adoption of the resolution does not bring an organization into being. Further requirements are the adoption of bylaws and the enrollment of members. After the resolution is adopted, a motion is in order for the chairman pro tem to appoint a committee to draft bylaws, if a set has not already been prepared for submission to those in attendance. A parliamentarian should be consulted. If the group wishes to incorporate, an attorney must be engaged. The meeting is then adjourned after having set a date, place, and time for a second meeting.

At the second meeting, after the call to order, the chairman pro tem calls upon the pro tem secretary to read the minutes of the previous meeting, which are approved or approved as corrected. The chair then calls upon the chairman of the bylaws committee to read the proposed bylaws. Copies of these should have been distributed to all in attendance. Each article is read, one at a time, ad seriatim, and each article is open to amendment. After each article has been perfected, the chair once again offers an opportunity to amend or to add other articles. The chair then puts the entire set of bylaws to a vote, to be adopted by a majority vote, unless the promoters insist and agree upon a specified higher vote. Upon adoption, the bylaws take effect immediately unless a proviso for some other date has been specified and adopted. Only a negative vote may be reconsidered.

The chair then declares a recess in order for those present who wish to enroll to pay initiation fees, if any, and dues as specified in the new documentary authority at that time. Applications for joining should be prepared in advance. The new members sign a permanent record, which is placed on file with other articles of organization. These new members become charter members. After recess and reconvening, the chair calls upon the secretary to read the roll call of the now legally established membership.

The next business in order is for the nomination and election of officers, to be conducted according to the process as stipulated in the bylaws. At this time, only those who have paid dues and enrolled may vote. Any member is eligible for election. Usually, nominees have been selected in advance. The newly elected officers take office immediately unless a later time has been specified.

The new president, who may say a few words about the new administration or of appreciation, having taken the chair, now proceeds to the next business in order, which is the election of the board. Many times a third meeting is required to complete the business, particularly if the enrollment was large. Board members are nominated and elected according to the provisions of the documentary authority, or there may be a motion to recess to caucus on the selection of board members before placing names in nomination.

The next business in order is the appointment of standing committee chairmen as provided for in bylaws or by motion from the floor. These appointments are important at this time so that the organization may proceed while enthusiasm is at its peak. After elections and appointments, the new president may wish to thank all those who made the formation of the new organization possible and then may make any necessary announcements and adjourn the meeting. All subsequent meetings are held according to bylaw provisions or the charter.

The first meeting of the new board should be to arrange for filing and payment of articles of incorporation (if applicable), setting a budget and system of accounting, selecting a bank for the deposit of funds, developing plans for standing rules to be adopted at the first meeting of the organization, and developing plans for furthering the growth of the society.

See also **Mass Meeting Requirements; Proviso.**

P

PAIRING

Pairing is an established practice allowing absent members to register their attitude on a recorded vote by getting another member of the opposing view not to vote but to announce the agreement. This has the effect of canceling out two votes.

Pairing as a method of expressing the position of a member of an assembly on a vote has no standing if proxy voting is permitted, for each member could vote whether present or not. Legislatures, which do not utilize proxy voting, commonly use the practice of pairing. In the case of legislatures, when members report to the clerk or proper person that they will be absent for a vote and wish to pair with another, agreed-upon member who may or may not be present for the vote but wishes to pair their votes, one pro and one con, the clerk or proper person will see to it that the votes are so recorded; or the member who is present for the vote, when called upon to vote, announces that he or she is paired with another member, and if permitted to vote would vote yes or no, but states, "I withhold my vote." Thus the position of each member on that issue or question is established. This way, their votes cancel each other and the outcome of the voting is not affected, except that the member present does not actually vote.

In some organizations where delegates represent certain particular groups or interests, their bylaws include a provision that a specific alternate be paired with a specific delegate. Such practice is intended to pair both representatives, who will vote with like minds or opinions. However, this limits the availability of alternates, and if both were absent, a vote would be lost. In most instances, a delegate may be replaced by the first available alternate from that group.

PARLIAMENTARIAN

The primary responsibility of a parliamentarian is to interpret rules of procedure and the accompanying documents of authority. The parliamentarian should be qualified as an expert in parliamentary law and knowledge of the rules applying to a specific society so that his or her opinions, if accepted, will be highly regarded, even in court. A parliamentarian cannot serve properly unless fully trained for the job. He or she should know how to preside and should be familiar with one or more parliamentary authorities—that is, with books, such as this one, to be used by the organization as its guide for running a meeting.

A parliamentarian in whom great confidence can be placed should be appointed by the president. Some bylaws may require that the appointment be ratified by the board.

A parliamentarian serves as an advisor and takes no active part in business proceedings. If that person is a member of the organization, he or she should not participate in debate or vote unless the vote is by ballot so that his or her opinion will not influence other members. He or she should never serve on a committee or board—with the possible exception of a bylaws committee.

The main work of the parliamentarian—as an expert consultant on procedural rules—is done outside of meetings. He or she has no authority and cannot make a ruling, as by common law; that right is reserved only by the president or presiding officer. The parliamentarian may give advisory opinions, which cannot be appealed from as they are not rulings. Such opinions should be informed, impartial, tactful, and professional.

At times a parliamentarian should be flexible, but should take no position until forced to. Tradition should be respected. The parliamentarian who is employed on a yearly basis can become familiar with policies, problems, leaders, and pressure groups, enabling him or her to serve better than an *ad hoc* parliamentarian.

Every organization should have regulations defining the duties of the parliamentarian in its documents of authority. It also should have an adopted parliamentary authority from which the parliamentarians must work. A parliamentarian can help write bylaws that will coincide with the needs of the society in conjunction with those of their adopted authority.

Parliamentarians are a necessity for large meetings such as conventions, for which they have special responsibilities. They should know that their responsibility is to the organization that hires, that the will of the assembly must be protected from abuse by the presiding officer just as the presiding officer must be protected from a fractious assembly.

During meetings, the parliamentarian should sit near the presiding officer in order to assist the chair as needed. The parliamentarian should take an active role, but do so unobtrusively, not waiting for a bad situation to develop but anticipating problems. He should pay close attention to the proceedings and quietly call the chair's attention to procedural errors that might make a difference, before confusion develops, though he or she should not split hairs over minor infractions. The parliamentarian's role is to protect the presiding officer from embarrassment as well as to inform him or her of rules and to interpret them when necessary.

The parliamentarian has no authority to speak publicly except when asked to do so by the chair or by a member through the chair. The chair is not obligated to require the parliamentarian to give the requested information and may opt to do so from the chair. Not to do so, however, reveals a lack or confidence or lack of understanding in the role each plays.

Parliamentarian at Convention

The parliamentarian should be employed well in advance of the convention and should require, in writing, just what his or her duties and responsibilities will be. These may include explaining the procedures of a convention to new delegates, attending caucus and preboard meetings, giving a workshop on parliamentary procedure, and working with committees so as to assist with procedural advice and in writing bylaws or resolutions.

Once engaged, the parliamentarian should obtain copies of the documents of authority, minutes of the previous convention (if possible), and copies of any proposed bylaw amendments and resolutions (if any).

The parliamentarian should always attend the preconvention board meeting as a consultant. At this time, the parliamentarian can speak more freely as to what possible procedural conflicts might develop and call attention to errors or omissions. In fact, much of the parliamentarian's work might be done at this time. Care should be taken to offer only constructive criticism.

PARLIAMENTARY AUTHORITY
See **Documents of Authority.**

PARLIAMENTARY INQUIRY

A parliamentary inquiry or point of information is just exactly what the phrase implies—some member of an assembly in session seeks information from the chair as to procedural or parliamentary situations.

A genuine parliamentary inquiry should be a question directed to the chair as to the parliamentary or procedural status then prevailing in the assembly, the effect a proposed action would have on the procedure, the effect the action might have on subsequent or upcoming procedures, and how any of this would be in compliance or in conflict with the established procedures of the organization.

There is no reason for the use of both "parliamentary inquiry" and "point of information." Both are used for the same purpose, but "parliamentary inquiry" is more descriptive, and therefore should be used in preference to "point of information." In fact, "point of information" is misleading. If a member is seeking information on a pending motion, it should be sought from the proposer through the chair by asking if the member would yield for a question in order to obtain some information.

When answering a parliamentary inquiry, the chair should be limited under all circumstances to answering questions on procedural matters, parliamentary matters, or matters relating to the parliamentary situation, but should not answer questions on substantive matters. Therefore, questions submitted to the chair should always be designated a "parliamentary inquiry" instead of a "point of information," since this is the extent of answers the chair may render. The chair should not interpret the meaning of motions. A member could ask the chair, "What would be the effect of a motion if it were adopted?" The chair could reply as to the effect if adopted or if rejected, but could not support either action. A member could also ask to have a motion read again for one's own information, or ask through the chair if the chairman of a committee or any member present at the meeting could give the assembly information on a particular issue. A speaking member, however, may not ask another member a question unless such a request is made of the body and permission is granted. The speaking member may ask consent through the chair that he or she be permitted to ask the chairman, a committee member, or any other member certain information. If such a request is made through the chair, the procedure should be that the chair asks, "Is there any objection to the request of . . . ?" After a pause, if no one objects, the chair should state, "Without objection, it is so ordered."

To make a parliamentary inquiry, the member should either be recognized by the chair or be granted permission by the body with the consent of the speaking member to make such an inquiry. Otherwise, the member must be recognized in his or her own right. Unless otherwise prohibited by the documentary authority of the organization, a member, when recognized or otherwise permitted to make a parliamentary inquiry, should be allowed to make such an inquiry to inform himself or herself or the assembly as to the parliamentary status then existing.

The chair should not permit a parliamentary inquiry to interrupt the speaking member—unless unanimous consent is given—for the speaker may lose the train of thought. Besides, no action or vote can be taken until the speaking member has yielded or has concluded.

A member should always be permitted at the proper time to raise a genuine parliamentary inquiry before any action is taken, even if a motion to adjourn has been made. For example, the member may say, even though the motion to adjourn has been made, "Madam President (or Mr. Chairman), are we now voting on a motion to adjourn?", or "If this motion to adjourn is now adopted, when do we come back into session?"

The assembly is entitled to know what the parliamentary situation is, or else it cannot vote intelligently. This does not mean, however, that these inquiries can be used for the delay of the proceedings of the assembly. The chair should not permit such procedure.

PAST PRESIDENT

The immediate past president is the one who last served in that office, if duly elected, regardless of the time served—even if there never was an opportunity to serve. Bylaws should define the title and role of the immediate past president if there is to be one.

Unless bylaws designate a special assignment to a past president, no special privileges can be assumed.

A past president should be respected for the honor earned. The past president's role as advisor can be a rewarding one to the organization, when it is requested. A past president is assumed to have no axe to grind and can advise impartially.

PLURALITY VOTE

A plurality vote is the largest number of votes given to a nominee or to a proposition when there are more than two options.

Documents of authority may permit a plurality vote of less than a majority to be a winning vote, or a special rule to that effect may be adopted prior to taking the vote.

Election by plurality is used in the selection of committee members as a time-saving measure.

A plurality vote ought never elect general officers of an organization, since it permits a minority to control. Any candidate elected by a plurality may expect opposition from the majority.

A plurality vote is sometimes provided for in mail balloting to save the costs of a reballot as well as time.

POINT OF INFORMATION
See **Parliamentary Inquiries.**

POINT OF ORDER

When it appears that there has been some irregularity in the proceedings—an error, an omission, or a violation of rules—any member may interrupt by rising and stating, "I rise to a point of order." The interruption is permitted because the error must not continue. The point of order takes precedence over the pending question. The business that was interrupted proceeds immediately after the chair rules on the violation.

The point of order must be raised at the time the breach occurs. The chair will say, "State your point." The member will then reveal the discrepancy or infraction of rules. The chair may answer, "Your point is well taken," and correct the error immediately, or the chair may say, "Your point is not well taken," and continue with the business of the meeting—unless an appeal is taken, which is debatable. The chair may explain the reasons for the ruling. No vote is taken on the ruling unless the appeal is taken.

On a point of order, the chair is obliged to make a ruling, which is not debatable. The chair can rule the procedure out of order; for example, "The speaker's comment is not germane; kindly confine your remarks to the issue," or, "Will the member refrain from any criticism of the previous speaker." If the chair is in doubt, the decision must be submitted to the assembly, in which case it would be debatable. The chair then says, "The chair doubts the violation and asks the members to decide," such as, "A point of order has been raised on the action by the committee as beyond their jurisdiction." After any debate, the chair states, "All those who believe the committee acted rightfully, say aye; those who believe that the committee did not act rightfully, say no. The ayes appear to have it." (Pause.) "The ayes have it, and the action of the committee is sustained." Or, "The noes appear to have it." (Pause.) "The noes have it and the error will be corrected." There can be no appeal of decisions from the assembly.

POLICY STATEMENTS

An organization's policies are a "written contract of prudence or sagacity in the conduct of affairs, a course or plan of action, especially of self-interest as opposed to equity." So says *Funk and Wagnall's Dictionary*.

Policies relate to principles, aims, and customs of the society. Policies define beliefs, and philosophy, and are as binding on the organization as the bylaws that define its structure. Policies are adopted to determine consistent action in response to recurring problems. They are usually put into writing for reference and as a kind of protective insurance concerning the subject covered by the policy. Once adopted, policies set the standard for all further action that comes under its decisions.

Policies can be amended or rescinded according to procedural rules. A new policy can countermand an adopted old policy, or an old one that no longer is relevant may be rescinded. Policies should be carefully written, preserved, and reviewed periodically. Some organizations have a policy committee, often the executive committee, which reviews policies to keep them up-to-date.

Policy statements may be prepared by the board, the resolutions committee, or some other committee, and submitted to the membership for adoption. They are written much the same as resolutions except that *believing* replaces *whereas* and after the *resolved*, a statement of position is made: "Resolved, that [name of the organization] affirms [or assures, or condemns] certain stated beliefs or principles or positions."

Policy statements do not belong in the bylaws. They more readily belong in standing orders. They may be changed by the assembly by a majority vote, and therefore there is no reason for suspending them. Policy statements usually relate to positions taken on human rights, equal rights, professional codes, or standards for association operations.

On occasion, policies are unwritten but understood by the members. They are hidden because they relate to certain required admissions to membership, political biases, or preference for certain social classes. Since such policies have not been formally adopted, they can have no legal status. Ethical standards should be employed in the formulation of policies so that their existence is of pride and comfort, not embarrassment, to the organization.

See also **Documents of Authority**.

POLLS

To poll is to conduct a head count; it also means to vote, and to prepare a place where voting may take place.

Times to open and close the polls may be adopted in the rules of order or by motion from the floor. Tellers are responsible for providing adequate polling space, where voters may mark their ballots in private or where a voting machine has been prepared.

At the proper time, the chair declares the polls open, and if a quorum is present, members proceed to obtain ballots on which to mark their choices. Passing ballots along a row of seated voters can hardly be considered the proper way to conduct a secret ballot.

The ballots are marked, folded, and handed to the tellers, who deposit them in the ballot box in full view of the voter, or the voter may deposit the ballot in the ballot box in the presence of the tellers. This procedure is dependent upon the rules and practices of the organization.

At the time stipulated in the adopted rules for the polls to close, the chair will ask if all have voted who wish to vote, pause if a few are still casting ballots, and then declare the polls closed.

Polls may also be closed by a two-thirds vote, but may be reopened by a majority vote if it is discovered that some members have not yet voted who wish to do so.

If no time has been set for closing the polls, the chair will proceed to ask if all members have had an opportunity to vote, pause, and then declare the polls closed, with no objection, by general consent.

See also **Tellers and Balloting Procedures**.

POSTPONE

The motion to postpone merely defers any further consideration of the pending motion until the time specified in the adopted motion. The motions to postpone can include motions to "postpone to a time certain" and to "postpone indefinitely." Most parliamentary authorities give the two motions different ranks in the ladder of precedence, which only confuses. A better solution is to have only one motion to postpone and to place it on the ladder of precedence now given to the motion to postpone to a time certain. This motion to postpone is amendable and debatable, and amendments with a shorter time for postponement take precedence over those with longer times. For example, a motion to postpone until the next meeting would be given precedence over the motion to postpone indefinitely. To postpone indefinitely kills the proposition unless it is brought back some other way, such as reconsideration of the vote or a modified *de novo* motion complying with all necessary requirements. Under the procedure set forth here, the motion to table would in effect replace the motion to postpone indefinitely, since to table would kill the proposition, and it would not be debatable.

Unless the motion to postpone is amended to kill, it may not provide for putting the matter aside until some further nonexistent meeting or to a time too late for its further consideration (such as to postpone a motion to hold a Memorial Day parade until after the June meeting).

Motions that are postponed to a time certain and not reached at the time of adjournment become unfinished business at the next regular meeting. This motion may be used in several ways. A motion may be made to postpone to a time certain to some time later in the meeting, or to the next regular meeting, or to be made a special order at the next meeting. It may also be used to put aside to an unspecified time, such as after certain reports have been made or until expert consultation has been obtained.

A majority vote adopts. The motion can be reconsidered.

PRECEDENTS

Any deliberative assembly transacting business establishes precedents when it officially takes a procedural action, be it a new procedure or the affirmation of an old one.

A precedent is established when the chair on its own initiative calls a member to order for conducting himself or herself contrary to the established procedure of that assembly. If no appeal is taken from the chair's verdict, that sets a precedent for the future conduct of business by that assembly.

Any time a member of an assembly makes a point of order against the procedure in the transaction of the assembly's business, the chair has the responsibility to rule immediately on that point of order or to refer that point of order to the membership for decision. The chair may entertain debate for its own edification, but usually, on the advice of the parliamentarian, makes a ruling as soon as the point of order has been made. If, for various reasons, the chair decides that it would be better for the assembly to make the decision in the first instance, it is the chair's prerogative to submit the question to the assembly, in which case the point of order is debatable. The vote of the assembly is the final verdict, and that establishes a precedent and becomes the established procedure.

If the chair makes the ruling or renders a decision, it is subject to appeal; if no appeal is taken from the decision of the chair, the decision becomes a precedent for the conduct of the assembly's business. If an appeal is taken, whether the chair is reversed or not, the verdict of the assembly becomes a precedent for the future. These guidelines are very important in the proper conduct of business of the organization concerned.

All such decisions by the chair or the assembly may be reversed at any subsequent date—by the chair ruling differently or by the assembly majority voting differently. However, instability is not good procedure and is certainly not recommended. Decisions should be carefully weighed before they are handed down and should not be changed unless a change really is merited.

Precedents of an organization should be compiled and alpha-betized so they will be readily available to the membership of the assembly at all times. They should be prepared properly and at-tached to the documentary authority as guidelines for the organi-zation to follow.

See also **Documents of Authority.**

PREFERENTIAL BALLOTING

Preferential ballot voting refers to a number of voting methods by which, on a single ballot, when there are more than two choices available, the second, third (or more) choices may be accounted for if no majority was reached on the first ballot. In preferential voting, the second, and third (or more) choices of voters are counted toward obtaining a majority vote.

In one method, the voter indicates his choice in numerical order: first choice as *1*, second choice as *2*, and so on. In counting the votes, they are arranged in piles according to first choices, which are counted and recorded. If no one receives a majority vote, the ballots are redistributed according to second choices, and so on.

Another method drops the names of those with the lowest count, and the second and third choices are added to the first choices in the hope of attaining a majority.

Another method drops all but the two leading nominees. Then all who are dropped are divided, according to choices, to the two remaining nominees.

It is a complicated, time-consuming system susceptible to mis-calculation—actually, a mathematical game. Tellers should be fully instructed in the selected voting method.

There is no reason to use preferential voting except in a mail ballot, where it is expensive and impractical to reballot.

Preferential voting may only be used if authorized in the bylaws, accompanied with detailed instructions for the method to be used.

PRESIDENT

The president, by common usage, is the chief representative of an organization, but holds no more powers than any other member except those assigned to him in the bylaws and by custom.

The president has the responsibility to serve as administrator, presiding officer, and inspirational leader.

Although the president is often elected because of popularity—having the ability to "win friends and influence people"—such a criterion is insufficient. A good president must know the rules of parliamentary law and how to use them; how to preside well, fairly and firmly, with dignity; how to control decorum of debate; how to expedite business; and how to make decisions promptly and impartially. A good president should be able to plan, to implement those plans, and to work with the members with tact and good humor. The president needs to possess the High *C*s: Competence, Character, Charisma, Clout, and Courtesy.

See also **Chairman; Officers.**

President's Vote

If the presiding officer is a member, he or she has the same right to vote as any other member, but usually refrains from voting so as to preserve the appearance of impartiality.

The president usually casts a vote when the vote is by ballot or roll call (his or her name called last—when the vote will not influence observers).

The president may opt to vote or not when the decision could affect the result, for example, to break a tie vote or to create or destroy a two-thirds vote. In such cases, the chair votes as conscience dictates. Such a deciding vote is sometimes called a "casting" vote.

PRESIDING

Presiding includes conducting the adopted agenda with each item of business in order: (1) call to order; (2) assigning the floor; (3) ruling on all points of order, parliamentary inquiry, and appeal; (4) observing the decorum of debate, maintaining control and order; (5) announcing each item of business in order; (6) processing all motions to their disposal, taking the vote, and announcing the result properly; and (7) adjourning the meeting promptly.

Good judgment tells the presiding officer when to stand and when to sit while presiding.

A president should preside at all meetings of the organization unless documents of authority say otherwise.

See also **Agenda.**

Presiding Skills

Any president or presiding officer, to preside well, should be familiar with the bylaws, rules and regulations of the organization, and adopted parliamentary authority, and should know the precedence of motions and how to conduct a meeting. The president should come to a meeting early to check that all is in readiness: comfort of the room, microphone in working order, presence of a quorum, readiness of the secretary, necessary papers and books at hand, and list of all committees and chairmen.

At the appointed time, the president (or presiding officer) should stand before the lectern, tap the gavel once, call the meeting to order, and wait for quiet. The presiding officer should look at the members, making face-to-face contact. The manner of the presiding officer should be relaxed, friendly, dignified, and calm. Standing erect and animated, his or her voice should be enthusiastic and projected so as to be audible in the rear of the room. The full authority to conduct the meeting is the presiding officer's responsibility and must be used without hesitation.

The floor should be assigned impartially. Debate should be encouraged, but firm control must be maintained. The chair should insure that debate is germane and courteous, and that no illegal interruptions are permitted.

The president may suggest proper ways to word a motion, clarifying and explaining when necessary, knowing that intelligent decision making is not possible without understanding the problem and its purpose. The presiding officer does not participate in debate unless the chair is vacated. The vote is taken accurately and unhurriedly, and announced clearly. The presiding officer does not split hairs over the mechanics of procedures, as substance is more important. The chair should not preside solely "by the book," knowing that to do so is not the complete answer to good presiding.

The presiding officer should watch the members' reactions and pay attention to debate. If the members seem restless, the presiding officer should expedite, and if they seem confused, the presiding officer should back up and explain. The chair should use the gavel to call the meeting to order, to adjourn, and to maintain order, not to drown out disorder.

When recognizing members, the chair uses last names and refrains from the familiarity of first names except in small groups, to preserve formality and impartiality. The chair should always protect the minority.

See also **Agenda.**

PRESIDING BY OTHERS THAN THE PRESIDENT

No unauthorized person has a legal right to preside. Courts have ruled that the elected officials must exercise their rights in that capacity. If a nonmember presides, even when the president is present, the meeting cannot be valid. Only the elected member, one delegated to take the president's place as specified in the bylaws, has the authority to make rulings.

If a nonmember is to preside, provisions for this must be provided for in the documentary authority.

There are occasions when the elected chairman or president is unable to preside. Bylaws should provide for such a contingency and generally do so by stating who shall then take temporary rights to the chair.

If the president leaves the chair temporarily, the vice-presidents, in succession (the president-elect, if there is one) will be called upon to preside until the president's return.

If the president expects to be absent, a chairman pro tem for that meeting only will be appointed with the approval of the membership, in the event that the vice-presidents will be absent also. Or, the assembly, by motion, may decide to elect their own chairman pro tem by majority vote.

If the president and vice-presidents are absent, the secretary, after waiting no more than ten minutes, may call the meeting to order and conduct an election of a chairman pro tem by voice vote. A temporary chairman must relinquish this position when the legally elected officer arrives. A temporary chairman has no authority to appoint committees or a chairman, to serve as *ex officio*, speak for the society, or make rulings other than for procedural rules. He or she may not assume any powers particularly granted to the president in the documents of authority.

In the absence of a secretary, the presiding officer may appoint a secretary pro tem, who will take minutes and sign them as pro tem secretary if there is no objection. If there is an objection, the members may elect a secretary pro tem. The presiding officer may fill any other absent office in the same way if there is a need to do so, for a single meeting. If the vacancy is to become permanent, the vacancy in office is filled in accordance with the bylaw provisions.

No one may preside at any meeting not properly called, even with a quorum present.

See also **Vacancy in Office.**

PREVIOUS NOTICE

Previous notice is a safeguard for many parliamentary procedures. It should be provided for in bylaws or standing rules. It protects the absentees and other members as well.

Previous notice may be inserted in the call to meeting, in the house bulletin, or other mailings as required, so that the information will be given in adequate time for all members to receive notice in the mail. The notice should contain the exact contents of the proposals to be introduced. In the event of a series of notices, the complete text is not required, but an accurate purport must be submitted.

A notice may be given orally at the preceding meeting if the organization meets as often as quarterly. The notice should be made when no business is pending. A member may not interrupt a speaker, but may rise, address the chair, and, after recognition, state that the purpose of the interruption is to offer a previous notice. The chair will then state the previous notice as presented and direct the secretary to make a note of the fact in the minutes for the record.

Previous notice of intent to rescind, reconsider, or to propose new business may be made.

At the next meeting, the member is given preference in recognition to call up the reconsideration or motion to rescind under unfinished business or to state the motion under new business. Previous notice that applies to new business must indicate the motion exactly as it is to be proposed, since any change or amendment to it that exceeds that of the announced notice is invalid. All previous notices are entered in the minutes.

Previous notice may be withdrawn at the same meeting and requires no vote, but it cannot be withdrawn when it is too late to notify members or when the motion it affects cannot be proposed by another member.

Motions that affect the basic rights of members should require previous notice, such as amendments to change bylaws and adopted motions.

It is in order to propose a previous notice until adjournment is declared.

PRIVILEGED BUSINESS

Privileged business is the business of an assembly that falls in a category of preferential consideration over all other business to be transacted by the assembly. Its precedence has been determined from the experience over the years because of the kind and nature of the business, be it substantive or procedural motions. It is placed in the privileged category because of customs and traditions founded on the needs for transacting business, and of protecting the organization and its membership.

To illustrate: If a member rises to a question of personal privilege, which is a privileged procedural motion, and is duly recognized by the chair, that person may then also offer a motion to censure another member, and that motion becomes privileged business for the immediate consideration of the assembly.

The rank on the ladder of precedence, whether for a substantive motion or resolution, or a procedural motion, is dependent upon the charter, the bylaws, the standing rules of procedure of the organization concerned, the parliamentary authority of the organization, or the generally accepted parliamentary procedure.

Privileged procedural motions of most organizations include: to adjourn, to recess, questions of privilege and call for the regular order as well as points of order and appeals from the decision of the chair. Such motions are so highly privileged that they are permitted to interrupt, set aside temporarily, or have the effect of postponing the pending business until a subsequent time. The precedence of motions in all categories sets the pattern and order for the disposition of business coming before the assembly concerned.

See also **Motions, Precedence of Motions; Questions of Privilege.**

PRIVILEGED MOTIONS

Privileged motions are given the highest order of precedence. They are of such importance that they may be moved and disposed of immediately before any other motions of less precedence are acted on. These motions do not deal with the substance of a main motion.

Privileged motions may be submitted at any time and may interrupt the pending business—but not the speaker unless the matter is urgent.

There are five privileged motions (listed in order of precedence):

Adjourn: Adjourn permits the society to close its meeting at will, even if business is pending. It is not debatable or amendable.

Adjourn to a time certain: This motion sets a time for an adjourned meeting, enabling the organization to continue its business on another day before the regular meeting as scheduled. The motion is not debatable, but may be amended as to time only.

Recess: Recess provides temporary respite from business, for whatever reason. It is not debatable, but is amendable as to time only.

Question of privilege: This motion provides for immediate attention to matters considered urgent enough to preempt the business of the meeting.

Regular order or orders of the day: This motion protects orderly procedure, allowing a "traffic control" of business when it has departed from its regular order.

The privileged motions to adjourn, adjourn to a time certain, or to recess may, when no other business is pending, become the main motion, subject to applicable rules.

PROCEDURAL MOTIONS

Procedural motions that do not relate directly to the business under discussion must be resolved before action can be taken on the pending main motion or amendment and are termed incidental motions by some parliamentary authorities. They are proposed as the need arises and must be disposed of immediately before consideration of the substantive business can continue. Most of them are decided by the presiding officer and are not true motions, but are requests for which no vote is required.

Most parliamentary authorities classify motions into various categories such as incidental and subsidiary. Such categories have no value in the development of procedure for the transaction of business. Therefore, no effort has been made to classify these motions. The purpose of this book is to present these motions as to their privileged status so the user (the mover) may know when each type of motion is in order.

Three motions generally classified as procedural by parliamentary authorities and that may be raised while a question is pending are points of order, call for the regular order or the orders of the day, and point of information. *Point of order* calls the chair's attention to a departure from the authorized rules of procedure. A member may, without recognition, "rise to a point of order that . . ." The chair then either sustains the point and proceeds to correct it or denies that it is valid and orders the business to resume. A member may appeal from the ruling of the chair. *Call for the regular order or the orders of the day* is not recommended in this volume as a point of order since a call for the regular order accomplishes the same end and is more expressive. *Point of information* or *Parliamentary inquiry* is used to solicit information from the chair on the parliamentary situation.

PROCESSING A MAIN MOTION

When a member wishes to present a main motion properly:

1. The member rises after the floor has been cleared, addresses the chair by title, and waits to be recognized. Sometimes rules require that the member state his or her name or unit of representation.

2. The chair recognizes the member by stating his name or using some other designation of identification, such as, "The chair recognizes the speaker at microphone number three."

3. The member then states the motion, beginning with, "I move that . . . ," giving the precise text of the motion.

4. If there is no objection, the chair states the motion, repeating it in the exact words of the maker, preferably with a copy of the motion in his hand. The chair may ask for a copy in writing. If the member has difficulty in stating the motion clearly, the chair may offer assistance, with the maker's permission, but may not alter the intent of the motion. The motion as stated by the member through the chair is the legal motion to be inserted in the minutes.

5. Any member may raise a question of consideration at this point—or at any time after the motion is before the assembly but before the assembly has taken action on it.

6. If no one raises the question of consideration, the motion is now open for debate. The maker of the motion has the first opportunity to speak to the motion if he or she desires. The maker should not speak against the motion but may vote against it, unless it is amended so that it is no longer his or her idea. At this stage, amendments to the main motion are in order.

7. As they are recognized by the chair, members may take turns debating the motion pro and con. All debate must relate to the question (be germane). Any remarks are addressed to the chair. Use of names or attacks on motive or personalities should be ruled out of order by the chair.

8. When debate ceases, no one rises to speak further, or the motion to close debate has been ordered, the chair puts the motion to a vote as stated or as amended. The chair takes the vote, both pro and con, by stating, "All those in favor of . . . say aye; all those opposed to . . . say no." "The ayes appear to have it." (Pause.) "The ayes have it, and the motion to . . . is adopted." The chair may then instruct who is to implement any required action on the motion. Or, the

chair may say, "The noes appear to have it." (Pause.) "The noes have it and the motion to . . . is lost." If the vote was counted, the chair always announces the count first before announcing the result, declaring which side won or lost.

If a two-thirds vote or division was required, the chair takes a standing vote if the group is large. A show of hands is sufficient in a smaller group. The chair then states, "The affirmative has it, and the motion to . . . is adopted," or, "The negative has it, and the motion to . . . is defeated (or lost)."

If a member is dissatisfied with the result of a voice vote, he calls for "division," but this must be done before the final result of the vote has been announced by the chair. Division is a demand for retaking the vote, and the chair will oblige. The chair may decide to retake the vote without a demand from the assembly when the vote seems to be close and the result unsure.

The chair may call for a counted vote, or a member may move for a counted vote. This method is used mainly when a two-thirds vote is required. The motion must be made and adopted to take a counted vote unless the chair orders it.

9. The adopted main motion remains in effect, unless executed, rescinded, or reconsidered.
10. The chair is responsible to see that the adopted motion will be implemented (who is to act on it or who is to be informed). When applicable, the chair then announces the next business, in order.

See also **Division of Assembly; Question of Consideration.**

PROTOCOL

Protocol involves courtesy and consideration. Observance of protocol is always in order: It contributes to the esteem of an organization. It also involves attention to the rank of the persons involved as past presidents and honored members.

A protocol committee insures that honored guests are seated in the right pecking order. In conventions, this committee should work with the president, who may appoint the committee chairman. It provides for the clergy to present invocations and benedictions as required. If opening ceremonies are planned, this committee may arrange for a leader to the pledge of allegiance to the flag, and for any flag ceremonies, music, chorus, and the like. It works closely with the general convention coordinator to provide welcoming ceremonies for any local officials.

In seating arrangements, the president is always in the center, the first ranking guest is seated on the right of the president, and the second ranking guest, on the left. This alternating pattern continues until the platform or banquet table is filled.

When introducing guests, the highest ranking offical is presented first; other introductions proceed down the scale. However, if the guests are expected to say a few words, begin with the lowest rank, since the highest ranking official should be given prominence and the most time to address the group.

On occasion, a second table is placed below the head table or to one side. This table is usually occupied by past-presidents or members of the press. When presenting past-presidents, always include the year of their administration.

Special or honored guests should be invited in advance and should be informed as to place, the hour they are expected to be presented, the length of time alloted for their speech, and if they are expected to answer questions. Necessary arrangements should be made for transportation to and from airports, hotel reservations, and payment of fees or an honorarium, if any. Honored guests should be informed of seating arrangements and escorted to their assigned places by members of the protocol committee, one of whom should greet them at the door and introduce them to the president and other officers if they have not already met.

Receiving lines should always be as short as possible. Honored guests should never have to stand in line for refreshments. Thank-you notes should be sent from the secretary on behalf of the organization.

PROVISO

A proviso, which is generally introduced by the word *provided*, contains a phrase or clause placing a condition, limitation, qualification, or contingency; it usually is found in statutes, written agreements, contracts, grants, or the documentary authority of an organization (bylaws, standing rules, or standing orders).

A proviso basically modifies the application of that part of a document. The effect is to declare that something shall not operate except as stipulated.

Bouvier's Law Dictionary states that "proviso differs from an exception. An exception *exempts,* absolutely, from the operation of an engagement or an enactment; a proviso defeats their operation *conditionally.* An exception takes out of an engagement or enactment something that would otherwise be part of the subject-matter of it; a proviso avoids them by way of defeasance or excuse."

Provisos are sometimes used to set forth the effective date of bylaws or amendments to bylaws; otherwise, bylaws and their amendments become effective immediately upon adoption. A proviso is sometimes used in bylaws to stipulate the date of elections of officers who will not take office until some later date.

Example of a proviso: "The bylaws may be amended after a thirty-day notice, *provided,* a two-thirds vote of those present and voting, a quorum being present, vote in the affirmative."

Provisos, when needed, can serve a good purpose, though too many might encumber the bylaws and complicate their interpretation and execution.

PROXY VOTING

Proxy voting gives the power of attorney to a member to cast the votes for another legal vote holder. It provides for an exception to the rule that voters must be present at a meeting in order to cast a vote.

Proxy voting does not belong in ordinary societies unless specifically provided for in the bylaws. The method of using such votes must be carefully spelled out to include the validity of the member to grant the proxy, who is entitled to the vote, how many votes the proxy holder may cast, and on which issues or candidates the proxy vote may be used. A proxy holder must show proof of authority to use the vote on a properly authenticated ballot. State, province, and federal laws should be consulted to ascertain if proxy voting is permitted.

Proxy voting properly belongs in incorporated organizations that deal with stocks or real estate, and in certain political organizations. If a state empowers an incorporated organization to use proxy voting, that right cannot be denied in bylaws.

If proxy voting is permitted, the president or credentials committee decides upon the validity of the appointed proxies. The decision is binding. Proxy holders must have signed proof of the transfer of voting power to them, which must be from duly qualified members.

Proxies are good for only one meeting or session, or otherwise as stipulated in the documentary authority. Proxy votes are nontransferable, containing the name of the member transferring the proxy, the person to whom the proxy is granted, and the name of the person for whom he wishes the vote to be cast or the opinion desired by the transferring member. The member holding proxies is also entitled to cast one vote as a qualified voting member in addition to the proxies.

Voting for officers should be done by ballot. (How can votes be authenticated by a member calling out, "I cast seventeen votes for Mr. X"?) In proxy voting, decisions are determined by a majority of votes cast, members present or not present.

Proxy votes may not be counted to make a quorum unless so authorized in the documentary authority.

Proxy voting is not recommended for ordinary use. It can discourage attendance, and transfers an inalienable right to another without positive assurance that the vote has not been manipulated.

Sample Proxy

   (Name of organization)

I,   (Name of member, unit of representation, if any)

do hereby appoint   (Name of proxy)   to be my true and lawful attorney in fact for me in my name and stead to vote at   (Name and date of meeting)   for   (Name of candidate selected)   for the office of President (or other candidates as have been nominated) (or for yes or no on a particular issue).

   (Written signature of member)

Date   _____

PUTTING THE QUESTION

When it appears that an assembly is ready to vote on any issue, the chair puts the question, and the assembly proceeds to vote unless before the vote begins someone seeks recognition to offer an amendment, to debate, or to make a point of order.

Whenever a speaking member yields the floor and no one seeks recognition, the chair should always state the pending question, and after a pause, if no one seeks recognition, the chair should put the question to a vote. The silence of the assembly when the chair states the pending question is evidence that the membership is, in fact, ready to vote. It appears to be an insult to an intelligent membership for the chair to continue by asking the assembly, "Are you ready for the question?" or, "Is there any further debate?" Every time there is a hiatus, a good presiding officer will alert the membership to the question by stating, for example: "The question is on agreeing to the amendment by . . . to the main motion [telling the assembly the substance of what the motion is]." If no one then seeks recognition after a pause to give everyone a chance, the chair should put the question, saying: "All in favor of the amendment to the main motion say Aye." (Pause.) "Those opposed say No." (Pause.) "The ayes (or noes) appear to have it." (Pause.) "The ayes (or noes) have it, and the amendment is agreed to." This procedure is emphasized because, after the pause following the chair's statement that "the ayes (or noes) have it and the amendment is agreed to or not agreed to," it is too late to call for another type of vote.

The chair, on its own, could back up and reopen debate—or allow a new vote because something had been overlooked, as, for example, if a member calls to his or her attention that another member had sought recognition unsuccessfully. Also, a member could move to reconsider the vote. If the motion is agreed to, the pending question would again be brought before the assembly for renewed action; then the member could even call for a different type of vote.

The chair should never recognize the words, "Question, question." There are those in most organizations who feel that to call out such words requires the chair to put the question on the issue immediately. If this were true, the member who calls out could control the meeting and cut off debate.

Members can always take the initiative to get a vote on the pending question by saying, "I move that we close debate on . . . ," or by requesting that debate be limited. The chair brings this motion to a vote immediately simply because the motion to close or limit debate is not debatable. The motion requires a two-thirds vote for adoption.

Motions to close debate should be used with great caution. Much good time can be wasted by this procedure. If the debate and amending procedure are proceeding smoothly, the purpose of a deliberative assembly is being accomplished. Shortcuts can be expensive when propositions and their solutions are not sufficiently considered. Closing debate too soon can abuse minority rights.

Q

QUESTION OF CONSIDERATION

A question of consideration—whether an assembly will consider a main motion at that time—as distinguished from procedural motions, is significant and deserves the attention of the entire membership in attendance at a meeting. It involves their rights.

When a main motion is made, any member, without recognition, has a right to address the chair and say, "Mr. President, I rise to question the consideration of this motion." The fact that the chair has stated the question or that discussion has begun does not prevent a member from raising a question of consideration. This right is retained until some action has been taken. If the assembly has considered the matter long enough to take any action on it, or to adopt an amendment or take some other action on the motion, it would then be too late to raise a question of consideration. The assembly has then taken jurisdiction of the motion.

When the question of consideration is raised by a member, even if debate has begun, allowance is made for the assembly to decide immediately if it wishes to consider the motion further, without debate, by a majority vote. The motion has a high priority ranking with making a point of order.

When a member raises a question of consideration, the chair must put it to a vote immediately, by stating, "Is it the will of the assembly to consider this motion at this time?" or, "Shall the motion be now considered?"

The rationale for this motion is that no three persons (one, the maker; two, the seconder; and three, the chair who states it) have the right to impose their will on a majority of the assembled voters, as has been traditional. Why should any three members at a meeting of 100 or more be empowered to determine what the membership should take time to discuss?

If the main motion has been made and no one rises to question its consideration, obviously the members agree to its consideration and debate on it will continue until the motion is disposed of in some other way.

Under present orthodox procedure as defined in books of parliamentary authorities, in the case of objection to consideration, it takes a two-thirds vote to block consideration of a main motion even before debate on it has begun. This does not appear to be good procedure and this book does not recommend it. How is the membership to learn what is involved in a proposal until there has been some discussion of it? There should always be a procedure by which a majority of the voters may decide if they wish to consider a matter or to avoid consideration of a sensitive, controversial, or critical issue even though the discussion has begun. This volume proposes to determine that question of consideration by a majority vote, even after some discussion.

Procedural rules allow motions to a pending main motion, such as to postpone, table, close debate, or commit, before the final vote is taken, which will stop debate at that time; but there should be a procedure to block the consideration by a majority vote. Time would have been wasted if the majority did not want to consider the matter in the first instance. This is particularly important since a second to a main motion under orthodox procedure has little significance. In any assembly, some member can nearly always be found to second any motion. The procedure proposed here allows the membership, not just three members, to determine the use of their time. It also repudiates any reason for a second to a main motion being requested.

Motions denied consideration may be renewed at the proper time after recognition from the chair, when the chair determines the renewal is not dilatory.

See also **Dilatory Motions.**

QUESTIONS OF PRIVILEGE

Questions of privilege involve matters relating to the rights and privileges of the assembly or its members; assembly rights take precedence over individual rights.

Questions of privilege can be divided into two categories. The first relates to matters concerned with the integrity, credibility, functioning, and very being of the organization. The second relates to matters that reflect on the character or integrity of the individual members of the assembly. Both may be concerned with the rights, the safety, or the comfort of all members of the assembly collectively or of any individual member.

Any member of an assembly may rise to a question of privilege falling within the first category, in defense of the institution as such. When a member addresses the chair, stating, "Mr. President [or Madam Chairman], I rise to a question of privilege," the chair responds by asking the member to state the "privilege affecting the assembly," or to state the "personal privilege" as the case might be.

A member recognized for a question of privilege may proceed to state why he or she arose. For example, a newspaper may have published derogatory remarks against the institution. In such a case, a motion is in order to demand an apology from the newspaper or to set in motion a libel suit.

Questions coming under the second category are generally referred to as "questions of personal privilege." Members seek recognition on such questions when doubt has been cast on their ability or integrity for some reason. (Any member might also, in the name of personal privilege, make a point of order against another member in debate for undue reflection on another member, unless the documentary authority of that organization makes such a procedure out of order.) The member being abused merely needs to rise, address the chair, and say: "I make a point of order that . . . ," or, "I call for the regular order," or, "I call the member to order for unduly reflecting on me and ask that that person be required to take his seat."

A member being abused may interrupt the speaker for a question of personal privilege. The chair, if it does not deny the member the charge or privilege on grounds that no personal privilege is involved, then takes over and admonishes the member for improper conduct, or orders the member to take his or her seat, if the rules so allow. However, after recognition the abused member could offer a privileged motion to settle the matter before discussing the issue.

In both categories the procedure is highly privileged when a member is recognized by the chair for that purpose. Once recognized, the member must speak to the subject, pointing out the grievances or making a motion involving them. Such motions generally involve privileged business.

The above procedure could result in a motion to censure or expel a member, or to sue a person or a publication for slander or libel.

After a member raises a question of privilege and states the purpose for seeking recognition, the chair either may recognize the person for that purpose or may refuse recognition on the grounds that no privilege is involved in the member's citation. This decision, of course, is subject to appeal.

A member rising to a question of privilege may not interrupt the speaking member without consent, unless that member is the person against whom the question of personal privilege is being raised, or unless, of course, the rules provide for the same. Once a question of privilege is recognized by the chair, the procedure becomes privileged until disposed of.

Once recognized, a member must limit all remarks to the question of privilege; such recognition may not be utilized to waste time or to discuss extraneous matters.

The privilege given to this business is granted in order to correct or remedy a situation without delay. When no motion is made, it is not debatable or amendable, and no vote is taken on it. The chair determines if the question of privilege is serious enough to require immediate attention, or can wait until the speaker has completed his or her remarks, or if the question is, indeed, asking for a legitimate privilege.

If the question of privilege is as simple as a request that the speaker use the microphone or that the air conditioner be turned off, the chair should take care of it immediately, as it affects the rights and comfort of the members. If the chair determines that the request is not germane or is not privileged, that ruling may be appealed.

Members should use restraint and good judgment when rising to a question of privilege and not interrupt a speaker except for urgent matters.

See also **Discipline.**

Privileged Business

Privileged business or privileged motions are made privileged by the rules of procedure or the documentary authority of the assembly or organization. Questions of privilege and questions of personal privilege (which involve matters relating to the rights and privileges of an assembly and its members), particularly when reduced to the form of a main motion or resolution, usually become privileged business.

Privileged business or privileged motions normally include motions to adjourn and to recess, questions of privilege, and orders of the day (calls for regular order). Such motions are so highly privileged that they are permitted to interrupt, set aside temporarily, or have the effect of postponing the pending business until the privileged business is disposed of. The precedence of motions—in all categories—sets the pattern and order for the disposition of business.

QUORUM

Quorum is the Latin word meaning "of whom," that is, the number of members, "of whom" you will be one. Quorum has been defined as the number of members who must be present at a properly called meeting in order for action taken by the assembly to be valid. This prevents the too few from making decisions for the many. The number of members required to be present to constitute a quorum is usually specified in the bylaws. If no quorum is stipulated, the quorum is assumed to be a majority of the entire membership.

A quorum should be realistic, not so large that a representative group cannot be obtained under poor conditions, but not so small that action taken does not adequately express the wishes of the majority of members. A quorum may be computed as a specific number of members or as a percentage of the entire membership (usually somewhere between 5 and 25 percent) depending on the nature of the organization.

In boards and committees, a quorum is the majority of its membership unless otherwise provided in the bylaws.

A quorum at a mass meeting or any group where membership is not accurately accounted for is the number of members present at the meeting.

A quorum at a convention is a majority of the delegates registered whether present in the assembly hall or not.

The president, as a member, is counted in the quorum of the board and of the assembly but is not counted as an *ex officio* member of a committee. In the former cases, the president has the obligation to attend; as *ex officio*, the president has the privilege of attending but not the obligation. Nonmembers are not counted nor are members who have been disqualified in some way. Less than a quorum vote does not determine the absence of a quorum. Even if some members do not vote, with the presence of a quorum, the motion is adopted by the majority of those who do vote. Members who abstain from voting may be counted to determine the presence of a quorum.

It is the chair's responsibility to check that a quorum is present before calling a meeting to order. This fact is often stated by the chair so that the secretary may include it in the minutes. It protects the assembly as proof that action taken was valid in the event of a later lawsuit. This statement is not required; a quorum is always assumed to be present unless challenged by any member or declared not present by the chair. If a quorum is doubted, this must be done at the time of doubt unless, in the case of a past meeting, facts can be produced to prove the quorum's absence.

A quorum should be maintained throughout the meeting. If the chair doubts the presence of the quorum, a count will be ordered. If a member questions the lack of a quorum, that member may rise to a "point of no quorum" or say, "I ask for a quorum count." The chair will then comply. Interruption of business (as opposed to a speech) is permissible, since without a quorum there is no need to continue—any further business or action taken would be invalid.

If no quorum is present the meeting may recess to take steps to obtain one, move for an adjourned meeting, or move to adjourn. Should business be so urgent that it cannot wait until another meeting, the assembly may, of necessity, informally consider action, but any decisions made must be ratified at a meeting where a quorum is present before they become binding. If the action taken is not ratified, those who took action are liable.

On occasion, an organization finds that its quorum has become too large for the expected average attendance. Because the quorum is stated in the bylaws, every legal measure should be invoked to reduce the size of the quorum, by obtaining a quorum present to validate a bylaw amendment. All members can be contacted by mail or telephone urging their attendance, if only long enough to provide a quorum and to vote, or a vote could be conducted by mail ballot. The amendment to the bylaws would strike out the old quorum requirement and insert a new number. This way the action can be accomplished in one motion.

If the minutes fail to state that a quorum was present, the presumption is that it was. Since the continuance of the organization should have priority over any one of its rules, as a last resort, a notice could be sent to all members that those in attendance at the next regular meeting will be assumed to be a quorum and that action to reduce the quorum will be taken. At the next meeting, with the new quorum, that action should be ratified.

A quorum of two or more is legal if bylaws should provide such authority and the members were actually present at a duly convened meeting.

Proxy votes may not be counted to achieve a quorum unless authorized in the documents of authority. Members are usually required to be physically present to be counted in a quorum.

R

RATIFY

To ratify is to validate action taken at a previous meeting, where there was the absence of a quorum, in order to legalize that action. It is necessary to ratify when (1) no quorum was present and the assembly took an invalid action, (2) when officers or the board acted beyond the scope of their responsibilities as defined in the bylaws, or (3) when the parent body took action beyond the scope of its bylaws in anticipation of approval from the constituent units.

On occasion, action must be taken where the required decision is so urgent it cannot wait for a regular meeting. Members, at their own risk, may take such action in the belief that it will be ratified (confirmed) at the next regular meeting.

Any member may move to ratify. It is a main motion, debatable, and amendable only as to what part of the action is to be ratified. It requires a majority vote, and the affirmative vote may not be reconsidered.

No action can be ratified that is not within the authority of the bylaws.

READING PAPERS

Members may not arbitrarily usurp the time of the assembly by reading extensively from papers, books, or documents.

Brief excerpts are allowed, with no objection, to prove a point during debate, but for longer reading, consent must be obtained from the membership. The member who wishes to read requests consent, which may be granted by general consent, or, upon objection, by a vote of a majority, with no debate, no amendment.

Minutes, papers requiring action such as resolutions, amendments to bylaws, and the like are read orally in entirety if copies are not distributed to each member. Reading of papers should not be repeated just to accommodate temporarily absent members.

RECESS

Recess is an intermission during a meeting, a time out between business activities, on motion by a majority vote or by general consent. After the recess, business resumes at the point of interruption.

Recess is called for various reasons, such as to ballot, to count ballots, to caucus, to enroll new members when organizing a new society, to improve the comfort of the members during a meeting, and when no quorum is present but there is an effort to obtain one.

If recess time has been preestablished, the chair declares the meeting in recess when that time arrives. If the chair fails to do so, any member may call for the regular order even if a motion is pending.

Recess takes precedence over a special order of business unless the recess time is postponed by sanction of the assembly.

During a convention, at the end of each meeting except the last, the chair declares the meeting in recess until the next meeting. The next meeting begins with some necessary announcements, such as the report of the credentials committee if there is any change in enrollment. Business is resumed where it was interrupted.

To Move to Recess.   This motion is privileged. The maker of the motion to recess should state the duration of the recess. Unless the assembly recesses subject to the call of the chair, the chair will call the meeting to order at the proper time. In a recess to ballot, the report of the vote should be made as soon as the vote has been counted. The motion to recess is not debatable, is amendable only as to time, cannot be reconsidered, and may not interrupt a speaker. It may be renewed after a reasonable time or after the transaction of further business.

RECOGNITION
See **Debate.**

RECOMMENDATIONS

Committees and boards may submit reports to the assembly with recommendations that the assembly take certain action: to authorize a contract, express an opinion, or vote to adopt a program or a policy. It may also recommend defeat of a proposition.

Such recommendations are usually placed at the end of the report. The reporting member reads the recommendation and then presents it in the form of a motion for its adoption.

The purpose of putting the recommendation in motion form is to permit the assembly to act directly on the recommendation, which is debatable and amendable. All procedural motions may be applied to it. If more than one recommendation is presented, all of them should be read before action is taken on each one in the order presented.

RECONSIDER

This motion enables the assembly to consider once again a motion which it has already adopted. Sometimes a motion has been decided upon too hastily, or new information has developed that could necessitate a new decision. The motion to reconsider opens discussion as if the decision had never been made.

The motion to reconsider is American in origin, first used in the House of Representatives, circa 1802.

Any member may move to reconsider. No member should be penalized for the way she or he votes.

The motion to reconsider can be applied to a vote on almost any motion. A member may enter the motion without moving to vote on it immediately. This protects the mover from losing the right to get a vote on reconsideration at the same or next meeting, where it may be called up.

The motion is debatable if the motion which is to be reconsidered is debatable. Debate opens discussion on the motion to be reconsidered. It requires a majority vote and is not amendable. If the motion to reconsider is lost, it cannot be reconsidered except by unanimous consent.

The motion to reconsider has some unusual aspects: It is subject to time limits; it may be made only on the same or next meeting day as specified in the adopted authority or bylaws; it takes precedence over the main motion and yields to none; its adoption suspends action taken on the main motion immediately if the motion has not already been implemented; and it has two forms—one form is to move to reconsider and the other to call up the motion to be reconsidered.

Upon adoption of the motion to reconsider a question, the chair declares the matter open for consideration and amendment or for readoption as the case might require.

If business is pending and a motion to reconsider is entered, the chair directs the secretary to make note of the motion and continues with the pending business. As soon as that is disposed of, it is the duty of the chair to remind the members of the motion to reconsider. The chair may, by general consent, take up the motion to reconsider.

If the chair does not do so, any member, on the same or next meeting day, may move to call up the motion to reconsider. If the motion is called up on the same day, those who have exhausted their turn to speak on the motion have full rights of debate restored when the motion is called up on the next day. Debate may go into the merits of the main question and any of its amendments.

If the result of the vote is negative, no further action is taken. If the result of the vote is affirmative on the motion to reconsider, another vote is required to adopt the motion that has been reconsidered together with any amendments that have been applied to it. Thus, an affirmative action on the motion to reconsider requires at least two votes—one to reconsider and one to decide on the disposition of the main motion.

In committee, there is no limit on the number of times a motion may be reconsidered and no time limit on when the motion may be proposed. If the motion has been amended by a separate vote, after the vote to reconsider the main motion has been adopted, another vote would have to be taken to reconsider the vote on the adopted amendment.

REFERENCE COMMITTEES

Many large organizations make excellent use of reference committees when they have so many departments, branches, or subdivisions that it would become impossible for each constituent part to bring full discussion of its problems before the convention body and then devote the necessary time to resolve them. Each committee may act as an independent reference source devoted to researching its own particular subject. The objective of the reference committee is to hold hearings to obtain as much information on the assigned subject as possible.

Reference committees may consist of regular standing committees plus additional special committees assigned to some particular area of research or work. Such committees may be appointed by the president or be composed of members selected from a specific group, since the committee's composition should be representative members from the particular field of concern.

Most committees are small in number, although any interested member may attend its hearings. Hearings of the committee should be scheduled to avoid conflict so that members may attend more than one, particularly if at a convention or annual meeting. On occasion, the concerns of some committees may overlap and a joint hearing may be arranged, although each committee is free to submit its own recommendations to the general assembly.

The members of the committee usually sit in front during a hearing. A chairman is appointed to preside over the conduct of the hearing, to assign the floor, to see that only one member is speaking at a time, and to see that no one monopolizes the floor, which is usually done in advance by setting a limit to the number or length of speeches.

The committee then listens carefully to comments, opinions, and suggestions from all concerned members. Committee members answer questions, clarify comments, explain purposes. No motions, debate, or votes are permitted at this time. The committee may call upon certain experts, officers, staff, or others to assist in giving information. Such consideration allows all members more opportunity to be heard and to express their views than can be permitted in the general assembly. In this way, much of the groundwork—the details—of the proposition are presented and reviewed.

After the members have left the hearing, the committee, in closed session, evaluates what it has heard and prepares its recommendation for presentation to the general assembly. This is adopted by majority vote. A minority opinion may be prepared.

It is possible for the committee to move adoption of its recommendation, to offer an amendment to a proposition referred to it, to submit a resolution of its own, or to recommend adoption, rejection, amendment, further referral, or some other solution.

All reference committees must bring in some recommendation to the voting body on each proposal referred to it. The committee has no power to adopt or reject an assignment on its own.

Delegates should be given, in advance of the convention, a list of place and time for each committee hearing.

Written reference proposals often must be submitted to the resolutions committee in advance of convention, for further processing on the convention floor. Frequently, proposals coming from members, officers, or constituent groups are referred to the reference committees.

Recommendations issuing from reference committees carry great influence because of the in-depth study given to a proposition by the committees, the information obtained from experts, and the time and effort expended to arrive at a viable advocacy.

In many cases, the resolutions committee serves as the reference committee, particularly when the organization is not very large.

See **Conventions, Convention Resolutions Committee; Hearings.**

REGULAR ORDER
See **Orders of the Day.**

RENEWAL OF A MOTION

Motions that failed to be adopted may be renewed at another meeting but may not be reintroduced at the same meeting. No assembly is obliged to repeat consideration of business a second time on the same day except by use of such motions as reconsider and rescind.

If a motion has been altered enough to become a substantially different question, it may be renewed at the same meeting—unless a specific rule, for example that no motion may be renewed as long as the vote on it can be reconsidered, prevents such action.

Certain procedural motions such as to suspend the rules may be renewed at the same meeting if sufficient change has been made to justify a second time around—for example, sufficient substantive change in the language, so as to make it a new question. Various procedural motions, as adjourn, recess, and the like may be renewed when not dilatory.

REPORT OF TELLERS
See **Tellers and Balloting Procedures.**

REPORTS

Reports should require thoughtful preparation. In general:

- Write the report in advance of its presentation. Anything worth doing is worth doing well.
- Use words that are familiar to the writer. Look up words in the dictionary, if necessary. Maintain a standard of quality that will reflect well on the writer.
- Write the report in the third person. Space the lines. If typing, use triple spacing, and leave ample margins at the top, bottom, and both sides of each page. If not, write legibly.
- Present positive, provable statements.
- Use background material as briefly as needed.
- Reread the report and eliminate unnecessary words. Rewrite if needed.
- Read the report aloud, time it, and delete where necessary.
- Date the report and sign with the writer's name and title.

Reports of officers and boards may:

- Include a statement of the objectives of the administration, citing cases of the work done toward achieving its goals.
- Include any unique features developed during the administration.

Committee Reports

The preparing of reports by committees should be agreed to by a majority of the committee, all members having been notified of its preparation. The report is usually written by the chairman with or without the assistance of other members of the committee.

Consideration of the proposed report permits amendments, even substitution, if necessary. A committee member may note disapproval of any part of the report, stating that part. After the majority of committee members approve the report, it is signed by all concurring members, with the chairman's name first or with the chairman alone designating his or her name as chairman. The report, when signed, becomes the official report of the committee.

Sometimes a report such as a presentation for information, a partial report of progress, or a simple statement of fact is so brief that it is given orally. No action should be taken on any report unless motions are made to adopt its recommendations. If adopted, they are included in the minutes. Copies of committee reports should be handed to the secretary to place on file or, by adopted motion, to be attached to or "spread on" the minutes. Reports are dated the day of filing in the assembly.

Committee reports may not be amended by nonmembers of the committee except to correct facts. The report itself should not be adopted, as the assembly would become responsible for every word contained in the report. The recommendations contained in the report are acted upon by the assembly.

The reporting member or chairman should be given preferential recognition to make any motions to approve the recommendations contained in the report and to speak first in support of them.

Special Committee Report.   The report of a special committee should contain its name, if it has one, or identify itself by the motion to create it. It should state its assignment, the facts uncovered, the findings or work acted upon, any conclusions or decisions made, and recommendations for approval or disapproval of the motion referred to it, together with any other recommendations or suggestions for the disposition of the assignment.

Standing Committee Report.   Standing committee reports should contain the name of the committee and a report of the activities pursuant to the committee's documentary responsibilities, together with recommendations for any desired action in regard to its duties.

Executive Board Report.   This report may be prepared by the executive director, the president, the secretary, or any combination of the three. The report is presented at annual meetings or conventions, and must be agreed to by a majority of the board members. It is given for information on the administrative duties of the board, as required in the bylaws.

Executive Director's or Secretary's Report.   The executive secretary's report relates to the duties of his or her office as defined in the bylaws and by direction of the executive board and the president, regarding the administrative duties of office, management, and personnel.

Minority Report.
See **Minority Report.**

Report of the President

A president's report is made for the entire organization—the members, the committees, and the board. It becomes the official statement of the condition of the organization. The report should be a synopsis of facts and information of the work done during the administration of the reporting president. Its purpose is to communicate by written record the "state of the organization." It should not represent factional or minority action or opinions, nor should it preempt the committee chairmen's reports.

Treasurer's Report

The treasurer's statement is presented at each regular meeting. Since it is given in totals only, it is brief and may be given orally. A written copy should be submitted to the secretary to insure accurate inclusion in the minutes. Such a statement presents the balance on hand at the previous meeting, receipts and disbursements, and balance on hand at the current meeting. No action is taken on this statement since it has not been verified. Questions may be permitted briefly.

The treasurer's report, as presented at annual meetings or convention, is a full financial report and should be audited. It may be presented in the same form as monthly statements but with more detail. Reported balances should be dated. The treasurer reads the report if copies have not been distributed, in which case comment on any particular items may be made. At the conclusion of this report, the auditor's report is read. Approval of this report carries with it the report of the treasurer.

The chair assumes the motion to adopt the report of the auditors and immediately puts the question on the adoption of the auditor's report.

When an organization's financial record involves considerable funds, the auditor may be called upon to give the report on any or all items. Large organizations usually employ a CPA to audit bank books and all financial records.

If the report has not been audited, a motion is in order to refer it to an audit committee to be appointed.

Without an audit, the treasurer is personally responsible for any errors in the bank balance. With an adopted audit, the society assumes the responsibility for any errors except where fraudulence is proven.

See also **Auditor; Minority Report.**

Report on Finances

This report is prepared by the chairman of the finance committee with the assistance of the treasurer. The form used should be that as required by the organization. Details of the report are reserved for the executive board to study and question unless a written report is to be distributed. It is presented for information, but questions are permitted on any particular items. The report, when completed, is referred to the auditors.

Reports of Other Officers

Officers generally report only at the annual meeting, usually in regard to their stewardship of their office, or on some special responsibility assigned to them in the bylaws. They are called upon to report in the order of rank as listed in the bylaws. At convention, they may report immediately following the adoption of the credentials, rules, and program committees. Reports are received and filed.

On occasion, an officer may have an interim progress report to present.

REQUESTS—INQUIRIES

Members frequently require information not directly related to the pending motion in order to evaluate the motion and come to a considered opinion. They may wish to achieve some action that is not directly in accordance with the organization's policies or procedures. A member may rise, address the chair, and ask permission to proceed. On recognition, the member may request information from other members. Such inquiries may be made to permit a member to read a pertinent news article, to ask that a nonmember be permitted to speak as an expert or that a contentious speaker be excused from continuing his or her address, to interrupt a member in debate to correct a misstatement, or to clarify a remark. This of course should be done only with the consent of the assembly. Reservations or objections to such requests may be entertained and the requests may be modified.

Members may request to be excused from duty temporarily. If the intent is to be excused permanently, a resignation is usually in order. Such a motion applies only to duties obligated in the bylaws. If the duty is not compulsory, no excuse is necessary.

See also **Reading Papers; Resignations.**

RESCIND

The purpose of the motion to rescind is to strike out, cancel, or abolish a previous action. It applies to any motion adopted or action taken at a previous meeting regardless of the time passed. It may be applied only to a previous decision or that part which has not already been implemented. It may not be applied to signed contracts or election of officers who have been notified of their election. This motion is frequently used in conjunction with the motion to expunge as two motions in one action—to rescind and expunge.

The motion is not in order if the matter is still eligible for reconsideration.

Any member may move to rescind. The motion is debatable, amendable, and requires a majority vote or the same vote as required to adopt.

Provisions of bylaws may not be rescinded except in accordance with bylaw provisions. Procedural motions may be applied to the motion to rescind. Adoption of the motion to rescind restores the original status, just as though the original motion or action had never been approved.

Members should give previous notice of intent to move to rescind at the next meeting, but while considerate or advisable, it is not absolutely required unless the documentary authority so provides. Previous notice does not prevent other action being taken on a previous decision, such as is the case with the motion to reconsider. If the member who gave previous notice fails to move to rescind, any member may do so. The motion is made when no business is pending. After recognition, the member may say, "I move to rescind the motion that we pay for all expenses of delegates to the New York convention," or, "I call up my motion as stated in the previous notice, to rescind the . . ." Debate can be closed or limited on such motions. The motion to rescind can be renewed or withdrawn.

See also **Changing Previous Decisions.**

RESIGNATIONS

Members have the right to resign at any time. A resignation may be made orally unless bylaws provide some other method. A resignation is not offical until it has been accepted by the members or a committee as specified in the bylaws.

Acceptance of a resignation signifies that the member left the organization without further charges against him, financial or otherwise, and was not under suspension.

If the member was liable for dues or other fees or if charges have been brought, the member is dropped from the rolls in bad standing, unless the resignation should be withheld to allow action against that person as a member. The member may be sued or expelled and the member's name expunged from the roster. Usually, such a member is merely dropped, as the better way to solve a bad bargain.

Some resignations contain a proviso that the resignation will take effect at a future date. Until that date, the member remains in the organization with full rights.

Officers may resign from office, which does not always include a resignation from membership. Officers who resign with a later effective date remain in office until that date arrives.

If an effective date is included in the resignation, the resignation previous to that date can be withdrawn.

A member of a committee addresses the resignation to the appointing power.

RESOLUTIONS

Resolutions, when moved, become main motions—amendable, debatable, and requiring a majority vote (unless the documentary authority stipulates otherwise), and the vote may be reconsidered.

Resolutions may differ from main motions by being more complex, more important, usually longer, and requiring more formality. They also may differ by including a preamble giving the reasons and background for the resolution.

Preambles are often referred to as "whereas clauses" and take the form shown in the sample resolution below. A preamble (the whereas) is the explanatory clause. *Whereas* is a ceremonial expression. *Since* could well be a substitute word.

A preamble is not required. A resolution could begin with the resolve, sometimes stated as "ordered" (for example, "Ordered, that the executive director shall receive a bonus of five hundred dollars at the annual meeting for his work in preparing and cataloguing our organization books, papers, and historical files").

There may be one or many whereases in a preamble. It should not be necessary to read preambles, especially when there are many resolutions to be presented or copies have been distributed.

Since preambles have no legal importance, amendments to them are not in order until the resolution is adopted. Any modification to the preamble can then be brought into conformity with the adopted resolution.

Resolutions are usually prepared by a committee, but not necessarily so.

Resolutions take the following form:

Whereas, (underlined, set apart) the *W* in *Whereas* is capitalized, followed by a comma. The first word after *Whereas* is also capitalized. Each Whereas is a separate paragraph. There is no period after the preamble.

Resolved, (underlined, set apart) followed by a comma. The first word after *Resolved* is also capitalized. Each Resolve is a separate paragraph.

The Resolve is the enacting clause, stating the action, position, or opinion desired, or the decision that must be made. There can be one or more resolves.

The Further Resolved clause, not necessarily prefaced with "further," is the effecting clause. Usually, this additional Resolved is required to state who is to implement the adopted resolution or who is to be informed.

If the resolution is printed, the words *Whereas* and *Resolved* are italicized.

The words *and, be it, therefore be it* are seldom necessary. If used, they are not followed with any punctuation.

If there is a series of resolutions to be presented, a request may be made to adopt them all en bloc. Or there may be a call for division of the question, in which case the resolutions are considered seriatim. Any particular resolution may be singled out for separate consideration.

Usually, noncontroversial resolutions are acted upon without debate, often adopted by tapping the gavel—with no objection.

If resolutions are considered en bloc, any member can offer an amendment to strike out any one of them or to get a separate vote on any one.

If unanimous consent for consideration en bloc is denied, each resolution must be considered separately. Two or more resolutions of the same nature may be consolidated into one resolution.

Sample Resolution

Re: supporting the restoration of the Statue of Liberty and Ellis Island.

Whereas,   Preliminary studies undertaken by the National Park Service indicate deterioration of both the statue and the island;

Whereas,   The Statue of Liberty has structural problems in addition to a need for repair work on elevators and stairways;

Whereas,   The National Park survey showed the need for realistic preservation on Unit One, including Great Hall, and other buildings;

Whereas,   Construction must be looked upon in terms of future development as a major living memorial;

Whereas,   All Americans are being counted on to raise an estimated 230 million dollars for the cost of restoration in addition to funding provided through corporate and individual gifts; therefore

Resolved,   That the Staten Island Community Clubs, Inc., in convention assembled this 18th day of May 1984, urges its members to support, by financing in part, the restoration of the Statue of Liberty and Ellis Island by sending contributions to
The Statue of Liberty-Ellis Island Foundation, Inc.
P.O. Box 1986
New York, N.Y. 10018

REVOTE

To revote means trying a second method of voting on the same question. This must occur before the chair announces the final vote, stating whether the question is adopted or rejected. It then is too late for a member to request that the vote be taken in a different form; that announcement stands unless the vote is reconsidered. Any member voting may move to reconsider the vote and if adopted then may request a vote by any method of his or her own choice that is also in accordance with the rules.

What most parliamentarians refer to as a "revote" is really nothing more than getting another chance at the same vote by another method. This is often done when some member fears that the result of the vote in progress would be unfavorable. For example, if a member doubts the result of a voice vote, before the chair finally announces the results, that member may ask for a division.

A roll call vote or vote by ballot depending upon the provisions of the documentary authority, can be ordered even after trying to vote by other methods, if the final results have not been announced by the chair.

See also **Ballot; Division of Assembly; Reconsider; Votes and Voting Methods, Revote or Recount; Votes and Voting Methods, Roll Call Voting.**

RIGHTS OF AN ORGANIZATION

An organization of itself has certain rights, which are determined by vote and contained in its bylaws and rules. It has the right to:

1. Incorporate, merge, consolidate, or dissolve.
2. Promote its objectives or change them.
3. Exercise authority as granted by law.
4. Determine rights, duties, obligations, and eligibility for membership of members, officers, committees, and the board (when not in conflict with federal or state laws).
5. Delegate powers and limitations to all members and employees within its legal authority.
6. Choose its officers, directors, and committees, and remove them from office in accordance with the documentary authority.
7. Discipline members, within bylaws and the law.
8. Own property and litigate, if incorporated.
9. Protect the convenience of the assembly versus a member.
10. Refuse to entertain undesirable motions.

The procedure of an organization should conform to the adopted rules, but infractions per se do not invalidate any action taken.

RIGHTS TO SPEAK

Every member is entitled to speak in debate and to propose motions. The presiding officer must recognize any member who desires to speak if that member seeks this right in the proper manner.

When no one has the floor, the member rises, addresses the chair by the proper title, and waits to be recognized. In a small group, the chair will recognize the member with a nod or state the member's name. In a larger group, the chair might recognize the member by stating, "The chair recognizes the delegate at microphone number three," or, "The chair recognizes the member at the aisle seat." The member may then state a motion, beginning with "I move that . . ." The maker of the motion should have the first right to speak to the motion after it has been restated by the chair.

If the chair is in doubt as to who should be recognized, the chair may seek assistance from the assembly. If a member believes the chair mistakenly selected the wrong member, a point of order could be made, and the chair's ruling appealed. The chair has full authority to recognize members, usually choosing those who rose and addressed the chair first, those who have not yet had a turn, those who seldom seek the floor, those who are known to be expert in the field that relates to the motion, or those who seek to speak against the motion.

Once a member has been assigned the floor, that member is entitled to be heard without interruption as long as no rules are violated. Certain interruptions may be legally made, but should not be made unless the matter is urgent.

To preserve order as well as fair play, the following principles apply:

Only one member may speak at a time.

When recognized, members should identify themselves.

No member may have a second turn until every member who desires a first turn has had an opportunity to speak.

Each member must speak within the established time limit, which is ten minutes unless other limits have been imposed.

All discussion must be kept germane.

The chair should not recognize members solely because they stand while another has the floor, who call out without recognition to preempt the right to speak (such impropriety should be ignored), who seek to debate an undebatable question, or who seek to offer a motion (unless that motion takes precedence over the pending question).

During debate, the president always speaks of himself or herself in the third person as "the chair" or "your president."

See also **Interruptions to Debate.**

RULES OF ORDER

Organizations are free to adopt written rules which are binding on it. These are standing rules of order that the organization uses for its procedures.

An adopted parliamentary authority provides rules of order for use by groups that do not have rules of their own sufficient to cover every eventuality. Rules of order provide procedure for the transaction of business.

Adoption of a parliamentary authority book provides an organization with rules that can be applied without confusion or misunderstanding. This permits smoothly functioning procedures. The procedure in the parliamentary authority book is subordinate to procedures set forth in the organization's documents of authority.

See also **Agenda; Order of Business.**

S

SECRETARIES

Recording Secretary

The recording secretary is an officer required, together with the president, for a meeting to be legal. The recording secretary should be accurate and orderly, possess the ability to take proper notes and decipher them, and know procedural rules.

The recording secretary is the curator responsible to preserve all official records. There are many duties for this office. The recording secretary:

1. Prepares, for the president, a roster of committees, with names of chairmen and their assignments; a copy of all motions postponed until the next meeting; a memo of any unfinished business interrupted by adjournment; and an advance copy of the current minutes for the president's perusal and corrections, if any. He or she assists the president in watching the presence of a quorum.

2. Keeps available copies of bylaws, amendments, rules, the adopted parliamentary authority, and a roster of members in good standing; is prepared to read the roll call whenever requested; records addresses and telephone numbers.
3. Keeps original bylaws up-to-date and in proper order. Records bylaw amendments correctly or revisions with dates in both minutes and bylaw record.
4. Records concisely and authentically the minutes of each meeting in separate books, one for the assembly, one for the board. Takes the minutes for both groups.
5. Is custodian for all records which are open to inspection by committees and members at any time convenient to the secretary.
6. Notifies officers, committee members, and delegates of their appointments and prepares credentials for delegates.
7. Frequently handles the personal correspondence of the president in relation to the organization's business, and for the organization or board, and sends out all the notices.
8. In the absence of the president or other qualified officers, calls the meeting to order and presides over the election of a president pro tem.
9. Occasionally assists the president with preparation of an agenda.
10. As a member, may make motions, debate, and vote, but is frequently too busy to participate in this manner.

The president may assist the secretary in the taking of minutes by:

1. Making sure the secretary has a copy of all written material that will be used during the meeting.
2. Possibly reviewing the agenda with the secretary, explaining what questions may arise, indicating possible trends in the discussion.
3. Explaining how to take minutes, if necessary.
4. Identifying members who speak so that the secretary may get their names or affiliations correctly.
5. Stating each motion clearly and accurately and each business in order.
6. Stating clearly the final decision and disposition of the problem.
7. Being prepared to appoint someone capable to serve as secretary pro tem should the secretary be obliged to leave early.

Corresponding Secretary

If the organization is large, the office of corresponding secretary may be valuable, to relieve the recording secretary of some of the work. Since a corresponding secretary provides the written public image of the organization, the requirements for the position are for a person who can write well, with tact and grace, using good grammar and vocabulary.

The corresponding secretary may send out all notices for special meetings or any other called meetings; conducts the correspondence for the society; keeps its stationery; may read aloud any correspondence addressed to the organization (usually stating only salient points), and remembering it is not the right of the secretary to interpret the merits of a letter. To expedite matters, it is often wise to resolve correspondence at one time rather than take up that mail which calls for action under new business. Letters requesting action are usually given to the appropriate committee chairman. Those letters that are resolved under new business, whose postponement could not affect the action or that are unimportant may be saved for last, when the agenda is crowded. The mail is read by the corresponding secretary. Mail addressed to the president should be read by the recording secretary.

See also **Minutes; Officers, Secretary.**

SERGEANT-AT-ARMS

A sergeant-at-arms, or an equivalent aide, in ordinary societies has the responsibility to assist the presiding officer and the members in maintaining order.

The chair may direct the sergeant-at-arms to evict an offending nonmember or a member as ordered by the assembly. In either case, witnesses should always be assigned to attest that no undue force was used in the event of a later suit by the offender. The sergeant-at-arms may be assigned other duties that pertain to the convenience or comfort of the members, or as a personal aide to the presiding officer. If the group is large, as in a convention, he may be assigned assistants. These members may serve as ushers for the proper seating of delegates or for escorting visiting dignitaries to the platform.

SERIATIM

To consider seriatim means that each set of resolutions, bylaws, propositions, or whatever that has many parts can be considered one at a time, article by article, or paragraph by paragraph. To order seriatim consideration, a request or a motion to that effect must be made unless rules provide for it. The motion is not debatable, is amendable, and may be adopted by general consent or majority vote. It may be reconsidered.

When adopted, a member has the right to debate each item of business as it comes before the body without exhausting the right to debate the other parts of the issue. Each paragraph is read. The chair then asks for discussion or amendment. No vote is taken on that part as amended. The chair moves to the next part for consideration and amendment. When all parts have been considered, the chair asks if there are any further amendments. When debate has been completed, the chair puts the entire proposition to a vote as amended.

See also **Division of the Question.**

SESSION

A single meeting or a series of meetings may be called a *session*; the terms are frequently used interchangeably. However, a session is usually considered to be a series of consecutive meetings.

A session, as in the case of a convention, usually consists of one or more distinct meetings separated by recess and lasting for one or more days.

In parliamentary law, a meeting is understood to be a continuous assembly during which members are not separated except for a brief recess. Even adjournment or recess from day to day, which terminates a meeting, does not terminate a session.

SOCIAL HOUR

Organizations should not underestimate the value of a social hour after or before meetings, and should schedule some time for this. At this time, much committee groundwork is laid, and members are sifted out as to their interests and abilities. Officers and chairmen can meet informally with the members on issues of concern. Many good suggestions develop during such informal talks. Members who feel disgruntled because their motion was defeated may have these feelings harmlessly diverted if they can let off steam within the "family."

SLATE

Candidates chosen by the nominating committee for each distinct office compose the slate of nominees. The best qualified at the time are then selected. If the members are dissatisfied, they may nominate from the floor.

Most organizations require the committee to present at least a single nominee for each office. There is a disadvantage in requiring the committee to present a multiple slate. One nominee may obviously be less qualified; or with two equally qualified nominees, one is sure to lose, which is unnecessarily hurtful to one nominee, who may withdraw from future competition. When the committee nominates two nominees for the same post, it makes it easier for a minority group to elect its candidate.

See also **Nominations.**

SPECIAL COMMITTEES
See **Committees,** *Ad Hoc* **or Special Committees.**

SPECIAL MEETINGS

Special meetings provide for transaction of business between regular meetings. Bylaws should establish provisions for calling such meetings: who may call them, usually the president, the executive board, or, by written request, a designated number of officers or members. The bylaw provisions for special meetings should include the number of days of advance notice required and a specific statement of business to be considered. Only such business may be conducted as specified in the call. Time and place of meeting and how the notice will be given should also be in bylaw requirements, as well as the required signatures for calling the meeting.

The special meeting is called to order by the presiding officer. Minutes of the regular meeting are not read, but the minutes of the special meeting are read first for approval at the next regular meeting. Minutes of a special meeting may be read and approved at any subsequent adjourned special meeting.

The call of meeting is read as the first order of business of the meeting as stated in the call. The purpose of the call is then under consideration; when it is completed, the meeting is adjourned. If the business is not completed at the special meeting, a motion to hold an adjourned special meeting may be adopted, provided it does not interfere with the regular meeting. The quorum for a special meeting is the same as that for a regular meeting.

If business is so urgent that action must be taken for which no notice was given, that action must be ratified at the next regular meeting. On occasion, a call to a special meeting may contain a proviso to include other business by stating "and for such other business as may properly come before the assembly."

See also **Meeting Requirements; Proviso; Ratify.**

STANDING ORDERS

Standing orders of an organization are a part of its documentary authority and usually relate to its policies, customs, and administrative details.

For further explanation, see **Documents of Authority,** *and* **Standing Orders.**

STANDING RULES

Standing rules are concerned with the procedural rules by which a meeting is conducted. They can be adopted or changed at will by a majority vote, preferably with previous notice. Most of these rules develop through the life of the organization when and as the need arises. The authority of the organization to develop such rules is continuous. Like special rules or standing orders, they are kept separate from bylaws but are filed with them.

Standing rules are adopted main motions that continue in force until amended or rescinded. A standing rule may be suspended by a two-thirds vote for the duration of the meeting or for a specified time within that meeting, but no longer. It is not in order to move to suspend all standing rules at the same time. Notice to suspend a rule should specify the part to be suspended and the purpose of the suspension.

Standing rules may not conflict with bylaws, but they override the rules of the adopted parliamentary authority.

A sample of matters that may well be included in the standing rules for conducting business follows.

The standing rules shall govern the proceedings of meetings of the general membership unless suspended in a particular case by a two-thirds vote or by general consent, preferably after proper notice. A proposed format for standing rules of procedure is set forth below.

1. The presiding officer having called the meeting to order, the order of business of the general membership of . . . shall be as follows:

- Reports and recommendations, if any, of officers:
  - President
  - Vice-president
  - Secretary
  - Treasurer, including audit report
  - Executive director
  - Others
- Reports and recommendations, if any, from board of directors
- Reports and recommendations, if any, from standing committees in the order listed in the bylaws. For example:
  - Finance
  - Long-range planning
  - Membership
  - Nominations
  - Public relations
  - Research
  - Others as stipulated in bylaws
- Reports of special or *ad hoc* committees
- Special orders, if any, such as nominations and elections
- Unfinished business and general orders
- New business

2. When a main motion is pending before the assembly, the ladder of motions may be set forth as below and shall have precedence as they stand arranged as follows (from highest priority to lowest):

    Adjourn
    Recess
    Raise a question of privilege
    Call for the regular order (call for the orders of the day)
    Table
    Close debate
    Limit or extend limits of debate
    Postpone, amendable
    Commit or refer
    Amend
    Main motion

3. Committee rules:
   A. The membership of the standing committees shall be appointed annually by the board of directors and

shall serve until their successors are appointed. Each committee shall have jurisdiction, respectively, over the subject matters falling within the scope of the committee. Each committee shall take jurisdiction over matters referred to it by the assembly, and such other details as specified.

   B.   Each chairman must name a vice-chairman from among the membership of the committee.

   C.   Each committee shall submit a report on its activities with any recommendations at each annual session, and to the board, with such other details as specified by the board.

4.   The officers listed in the bylaws shall be nominated and elected by the assembly.

5.   The election of directors shall be by the assembly by plurality ballot at the annual session.

6.   Voting on any pending question, not specified in the bylaws or standing rules of procedure, may be by the chair stating "without objection" if there is no objection; by voice vote; by division vote (by show of hands or by standing), with or without tellers; or by ballot. Any member may demand any method listed above except by ballot, which may be done on motion by majority vote.

7.   The rules contained in the adopted parliamentary authority shall govern in all cases to which they are applicable and in which they are not inconsistent with the bylaws and any standing rules of procedure.

Convention or annual session standing rules are often referred to as rules of procedure, but they should utilize the same standing rules as adopted for the conduct of their business meetings. If any changes in any particular existing standing rule are needed for the convention, such as setting a time limit for speeches, they could be adopted at the beginning of the session. Some samples are:

1.   Hats may not be worn on the assembly floor.

2.   Smokers must sit in the section assigned for smoking.

3.   Speeches for and against motions shall be limited to five minutes.

STOPPING THE CLOCK

When legislatures have provided in their constitutions or laws of federal and state governments that their legislature is to be adjourned by a specified date or after a certain number of days, legislators often find that certain proposals that need enactment have not yet been passed. To accomplish this, they have been known to "stop the clock" before that designated hour. The official clock is stopped by agreement of the "powers that be" without any motion or announcement one minute before the designated hour. This has been done by the Senate of the United States to gain time to complete its business before a seasonal recess. Courts have decreed that action taken after the designated true hour is void. Clocks in the assembly hall must agree with clocks on the outside.

Stop the clock procedure has no place in ordinary assemblies.

SUNSHINE LAWS

Sunshine Laws of various states are designed to make information on government activity more available to the public. Here is how one state defines the right to know: "All power residing in and being derived from the people, all officers of government as their substitutes and agents are at all times accountable to them." Therefore, the public's right to access to government proceedings and records shall not be unreasonably restricted. This has been interpreted to mean that officials must reveal their decisions, but are not obliged to make public their deliberations. The right to know, at the present time, does not include the right to know by what process officials reach a decision.

To correct this, "sunshine" laws have been created to protect the public's right to know what paid officials or elected leaders are deciding and how they arrive at these decisions.

A meeting, open to the public, however, does not include the right of the public to participate, unless invited. Sunshine laws rarely apply to voluntary deliberative bodies. They are intended to apply to public bodies such as legislatures and quasi-judicial groups such as boards of education.

Sunshine laws vary from state to state; thus, organizations, in particular those that are incorporated, should be acquainted with the provisions of such laws within their respective state. Matters of sensitive nature, such as those affecting security, dealing with personnel or property, or preferring charges may be considered in closed session to protect the welfare of the organization and its membership.

Sunset Clause

Sunset clauses, laws, or rules ordain the death of any existing laws, rules or regulations after a specified period, unless they are renewed or extended. Few nongovernmental organizations attach any importance to a sunset rule. A long-standing policy or program that has outlived its usefulness can be brought to a conclusion by the motion to rescind.

SUSPEND THE RULES

On occasion, an assembly desires to take up consideration of a matter which the already adopted standing rules would prevent. The motion to suspend the rules may be moved when no business is pending, but usually requires a notice of such intention. A two-thirds vote is required; the motion is debatable but not usually amendable. The purpose of this motion is to suspend the rule only temporarily until the business for which the suspension was requested has been considered. The motion permits the assembly to take up consideration of business out of the regular adopted order, such as to consider a motion before the time set by a postponement or to suspend the rules in order to present a special guest.

To move to suspend the rules for any reason, when adopted, requires that the maker of the motion be immediately recognized by the chair to propose the motion for which the suspension was adopted. Bylaws cannot be suspended unless they contain provisions for their suspension.

T

TABLE

The motion to table ranks very high in the precedence of motions. It is outranked by the motion to adjourn and the motion to recess. This means one can move to table any motion or question below that rank which is pending before the assembly. To rise to a question of personal privilege or call for the orders of the day is ranked higher in the precedence of motions by the orthodox parliamentarians of America, but any motion or resolution under consideration resulting from these procedures could be laid on the table. Thus, the motion to table would take precedence over voting on a motion or a resolution resulting from a motion. The motion to table

TABLE   189

as described here has the effect of killing whatever it is applied to, when adopted; it does not mean to lay the matter aside until it is taken up from the table again at a later time by the adoption—by majority vote without debate—of a motion. To table literally means to kill a proposal unless the vote to table is reconsidered; when the right to reconsider is lost, the action is final.

In these years of speed and limited time for group action, there must be a procedure available to the members of an assembly to dispose of a pending matter negatively by an affirmative majority vote and without debate. This, in final analysis, deprives no one of a right. It might delay positive action on the proposal, but it also gives time for further study of that proposal, which could be renewed at a subsequent meeting. If it were a positive action to adopt a program without debate, that would present a different problem; that could take away rights of individual members. It presents a question of which might be the least harmful to all concerned: action or inaction.

A vote that tabled a proposition may be reconsidered within the proper time, and reversed by a majority vote. A motion to reconsider the vote tabling a motion to reconsider is not in order, but a motion to reconsider the vote by which an amendment to a motion was tabled is in order.

The adoption of a motion to table a main motion takes with it not only the main motion and any adopted amendment, but all other pending matters thereto; i.e., any pending amendments or any pending procedural motions not yet disposed of. Briefly put, a main motion or resolution, if tabled, takes with it all amendments, motions, or propositions, even any already agreed to or still pending. The motion to table a pending amendment or pending motion to a main motion, if agreed to, does not take with it the main motion.

Also, if a first-degree amendment (primary), to which an amendment is pending, is tabled, it takes with it the amendment to the amendment (the second-degree or secondary amendment). An amendment to an amendment (second degree) may be tabled without affecting the first-degree or primary amendment to which it was offered.

Any member may move to table any motion under consideration by the assembly before the final vote on it has been taken.

A motion to table an amendment that has a secondary amendment applied to it takes both amendments with it as being tabled.

A motion to recess or adjourn takes precedence over the motion to table. All other motions on the ladder of precedence below *table* may be tabled.

The motion is not debatable or amendable and takes a majority vote.

TAPE RECORDINGS

The use of tape recording or other electronic recording devices in deliberative societies does not come under the "right of free speech." Permission to use recording devices should be granted by the speaker.

Recordings taken on tapes or by a stenotypist should not qualify as valid minutes. Tapes may be tampered with, cut, or spliced. Also, both forms of recordings include every word of discussion and much immaterial data that would need to be excised in selecting the necessary information for the minutes. However, minutes may be written from recordings, and recordings have value when a review of debate is desired, as in a study or research group.

See also **Minutes.**

TELECONFERENCES

Teleconferences for committee or board meetings are designed to save time, money, and effort. Many organizations, in particular those whose membership is widely scattered geographically, permit the use of conference by telephone.

If the organization is incorporated, such conferences are set up as provided in the articles of incorporation for that state. For such conference decisions to be legal, at least a quorum should have responded and participate in the conference (the quorum is the majority of the members, the same as in a regular committee meeting). All members should have been notified of the date and time of the teleconference. All decisions should be taken by voice just as in a roll call vote, unless general consent is permitted.

TELLERS AND BALLOTING PROCEDURES

Tellers compose a committee to conduct election procedure. They are usually appointed by the president as persons of ability and integrity and should be representative of each candidate or from each faction. The number needed depends on the size of the meeting and the voting method being used. Paper balloting requires that there be enough tellers to insure a rapid, efficient vote counting.

When a paper ballot is used, one of the tellers is appointed chairman. Prior to voting, he may explain to the voters the proper way to mark ballots with an X, the space for write-in votes, how to fold the ballot, or any other necessary voting directions.

Tellers are responsible for providing a ballot box, a polling place, and the preparation of ballots.

As soon as the chair or the adopted rules declare the polls open, tellers distribute ballots to eligible voters. They check with the credentials committee for validity of any proxy votes. Tellers watch the balloting to prevent fraud. In larger elections, inspectors representing each faction may also be appointed to keep watch.

Once the polls are closed, the tellers may retire to a closed session (with inspectors, if any, who may not participate but may watch) and proceed to count the ballots and prepare the report.

Recording Ballots

Unbroken ballots (the slate as presented) are counted first, then broken ballots where voters have mixed their choices. As the chairman reads the names from the ballots for each office, the tellers mark a line after each name. After all ballots have been accounted for, the tellers check to see if their counts match. If not, the tally is repeated until the error is accounted for. When completed, the report is prepared.

Blanks and illegal ballots are to be ignored. Two or more ballots folded together are illegal. Two folded together, one blank, are counted as one vote.

More than the required number of votes cast in a series voids the ballot since it cannot be determined which candidates were to receive the votes.

If there are too few votes in a series, count those cast as legal.

Votes cast for those ineligible to hold office are counted to determine a majority.

Unintelligible votes are illegal, but are counted to compute a majority.

Misspelling does not make a vote illegal if the intent is clear.

If any doubtful votes can affect the result, they are submitted to the assembly for a decision.

Reporting

The chairman of the tellers signals to the president when the report is ready. The president then calls upon the chairman to read the report. The reporter never declares who is elected or what has been adopted or lost.

The report of the tellers includes:

- number of votes cast.
- number of illegal votes (if any).
- number of votes for those ineligible to serve (if any).
- number of votes necessary for election.

For the office of president, for example, the report also includes:

Ms. A.   . . . votes.
Mr. B.   . . . votes.

Each office is listed in turn.

The report is signed by the tellers. After the chairman reads the report, it is handed to the chair, who rereads it, repeating the vote, and declares who is elected, thus announcing and verifying the result of the ballot. The teller's complete report is entered in the minutes.

In the case of counting votes on a proposition, the counting proceeds the same as for elections except the votes cast in the affirmative and in the negative are recorded separately.

When a two-thirds vote or a counted division has been called for, tellers may count from different assigned sections of the assembly, tabulate their counts, and prepare the result. This is then handed to the president, who announces the result.

If the result of the vote has not been challenged, the chair may order, with no objection, the ballots to be detroyed. If the vote has been close or emotional, it is wise to order the ballots held by the secretary for a short period of time (about thirty days), after which they may be destroyed. On motion from the floor, ballots may be ordered destroyed.

See also **Voting Irregularities, Challenging a Vote.**

TERMS OF OFFICE

Bylaws should define (1) the term of office, (2) when office is assumed, (3) if there can be succession to office, (4) if a member can hold more than one office at a time, (5) how vacancies are filled, and (6) eligibility for office.

Parliamentary law provides for officers to assume office upon the announcement of their election. Most bylaws, to avoid confusion, provide for new officers to assume office at the close of the annual meeting or convention; the bylaws may provide otherwise.

The outgoing president may conclude the business of the administration, then present the new president, who may wish to speak briefly to the members, outlining future plans and announcing the new committee chairmen (if ready to do so). After this, the meeting is adjourned. Committees may be appointed later when so authorized.

The length of unexpired terms that must be filled or computations of eligibility for reelection are determined by the length of time in office. If an officer serves more than half a term, it is assumed that it has been a full term.

When bylaws require that an officer serve a specified number of years on the board before being eligible for a particular office, that service must be consecutive and immediately prior to the election year.

See also **Vacancy in Office.**

TRIAL AND EXPULSION OF MEMBERS

In the rare event that infractions of an organization's laws or required conduct become serious, whether within a meeting or outside the meeting, charges may be brought against such members to consider their expulsion from membership or some other punishment.

Every organization has the right to protect itself from abuses of membership and to insist upon and enforce compliance to its rules. Infractions may range from damaging the good name of the organization, causing embarrassment to its members, or hindering its work, all the way to drug abuse, committing a criminal offense, or malfeasance in office.

A formal complaint must be made by a member or a committee. Sufficient charges should be preferred in writing. A motion is then made to create a committee to investigate the charges. This is done in strict confidence. The accused may be interviewed. Others may also be interviewed. Since legal proof of facts is often difficult to obtain, hearsay is permitted. Witnesses are not sworn in.

The committee reports its findings and recommendations to the assembly in closed session. If the committee recommends a trial, a resolution must be carefully prepared. Sometimes the committee prepares an exoneration.

The accused has a right to be informed of the charges in adequate time to prepare a defense and to have the presence of an attorney at the trial. Since attorneys will surely be present if the charges are severe, the trial will be conducted in a judicial manner and under the strict observance of procedural rules and the organization's documents of authority. Any deciding vote must be by ballot, and a two-thirds vote should be required for expulsion and so stipulated in the documentary authority.

An easier and confidential solution is for the committee to confront the accused privately with the evidence against him or her and give that person the opportunity to resign quietly.

If the charges can be proved, the committee usually is able to obtain a resignation, which resolves the problem without notoriety. The reasons for a decision to dismiss from membership must never be revealed since this provides grounds for libel. Great care should be taken when charges are preferred, since a wrongful charge may result in a suit for damages. Guilt, as established, is not as in a court of law, but as to fitness to retain membership.

Indecorum at a meeting does not invalidate any decisions made unless the votes themselves were illegal.

Minutes should contain all action taken prior to a vote for censure or expulsion, but none of the discussion. The minutes may be essential if court action is taken.

See also **Discipline.**

U

UNANIMOUS CONSENT PROCEDURE

Unanimous or general consent procedure is the easiest and most expeditious way any group or assembly can transact its business, as long as there is unanimity of opinion.

Unanimous consent procedure may be divided into two general classes: (1) the disposition of substantive or procedural business by unanimous consent, and (2) the determination of a procedure for the disposition of business by a unanimous consent agreement.

In the first class, if a main motion is pending and there appears to be no one seeking recognition to debate it further, the chair may state, "Without objection, the motion is agreed to." If there is no objection to the chair's statement, the matter is disposed of. In addition, a member of the assembly may submit a resolution (or motion) and, after some discussion, ask unanimous consent that the resolution (or motion) be adopted. The chair then states, "Is there objection?" (Pause.) "The chair hears none, and the resolution is agreed to."

At any particular time during the session of an assembly when there is need for a recess, the chair may state, "Without objection, the assembly will recess for ten minutes." Any member of the assembly may also ask unanimous consent that the assembly recess for ten minutes, in which case the chair would state, "Without objection, it is so ordered, and the assembly will stand in recess for ten minutes." Of course, if there is objection, a motion to recess would have to be made and carried to become effective.

There are endless possibilities for an assembly to transact its business by unanimous consent. When there is no opposition, the assembly or group meeting can save time and energy by resorting to unanimous consent or general consent procedure.

In the second class, if the business before the meeting is controversial, reasonable members of the organization might be willing to enter into a unanimous consent agreement, providing the procedure for the disposition of the controversial business.

Any such proposed unanimous consent agreement should be properly drafted, so that when it is presented, it is unmistakably clear and precise; it should avoid any ambiguous language leading to misinterpretation of intent. To present such an agreement, any member may submit it in writing or submit it orally. In the former case the chair may read it or have it read by the secretary. After it has been read or submitted orally, the chair asks if there are any objections to the agreement. Members may reserve the right to object in order to have various aspects of the agreement explained, as long as no one calls for the regular order. Finally, the chair puts the question if there is objection to the unanimous consent agreement, and if none is heard, the assembly enters into such an agreement. The form and scope of such an agreement would be dependent upon the needs of the occasion. The agreement could propose the time to begin the consideration of a proposition, how long it would be considered or debated, and how the time for debate would be divided. The agreement might contain provisions, such as if any amendments would be in order; if certain procedural motions, as reference, would be in order; and the like. Thus, if an assembly is willing to enter into such a unanimous consent agreement, individuals might give up some of their rights under general parliamentary law to offer amendments or to make motions.

See also **General Consent.**

UNDEBATABLE MOTIONS AND PROCEDURES

Undebatable motions and procedures are:

adjourn.
appeal, when it applies to indecorum or an undebatable motion.

amend, to an undebatable motion.
call for a separate vote.
call up a motion to reconsider.
close debate.
close session.
division of a question.
division of assembly.
limit or extend debate.
parliamentary inquiry.
permission to speak after a reprimand.
point of order.
question of consideration.
reconsider an undebatable motion.
requests.

UNFINISHED BUSINESS

Unfinished business comes near the end of the order of business. At that time, motions that were postponed at the previous meeting, business that was scheduled for the previous meeting but was not reached at the time of adjournment, and pending business that was not completed at the time of adjournment are announced by the chair in the order they are to be considered.

Unfinished business comes immediately before the introduction of new business. Items that were discussed but not entered on the agenda do not come up as unfinished business and must be introduced as new business. Items referred to committee do not come up as unfinished business.

V

VACANCY IN OFFICE

An office is not vacant as long as the incumbent officer is performing the responsibilities of the office. An office is vacant when no member has the responsibility or the authority to serve in that capacity.

Bylaws should specify rules governing vacancies. Vacancies occur at death, resignation, expulsion, or departure out of the district for the unexpired term of office.

If an elected officer has been discovered to be ineligible to serve, has flagrantly neglected or been unable to perform the required duties, or has failed to attend meetings, members may declare the office vacant as an implied resignation. They may then proceed to fill the vacancy according to bylaw regulations.

An officer who is functioning in office, however poorly, may not be removed from office merely by declaring a vacancy.

Vacancies should be filled promptly. Any information of an impending vacancy may not be withheld.

Vacancies are filled by the authority that elected or appointed to office. Sometimes they are filled by the board and sometimes by the membership. With previous notice, a special election may be called to fill the vacancy. Vacancies are filled only for the unexpired term.

It should be out of order for a member to accept election to office for the sole purpose of resigning to create a vacancy and permit a subsequent appointment.

See also **Discipline.**

VERIFICATION OF A VOTE
See **Division of Assembly.**

VICE-PRESIDENT
See **Officers, Vice-President.**

VOTES AND VOTING METHODS

Votes are required to validate decisions. It is the legal duty or obligation for members to vote and express their choice. Those who do not vote are legally bound by the decisions of those who do vote. Votes cast by legal voters determine the will of the assembly.

See also **Abstention.**

Method

There are many ways to take a vote, each serving a specific purpose. Choosing the method may be determined by the documentary authority. Presiding officers for votes in regular meetings on substantive or other motions use voice vote, show of hands, or a rising vote—the most commonly used methods.

If no method has been provided for, any member may move to adopt a method of voting. This requires a majority vote and is amendable and debatable only if no motion is pending.

Requirements

Most votes are adopted with the approval of a majority of legal votes cast by those legally entitled to vote who were present at a properly called meeting, a quorum being present. Documents of authority and parliamentary rules may provide other requirements under specific circumstances.

Voting Entitlements

Bylaws define who may vote. They may include such statements as: "All who are members may vote. Exceptions must be stated in bylaws." "Members are not required to vote and may abstain." "Members in arrears for dues may vote unless bylaws provide otherwise." "Members who shall receive personal direct benefits or profit should not vote unless other members are also included."

Honorary members may speak but may not vote unless bylaws so provide. Members may vote for themselves when qualified to hold office. Members may change their vote until the chair announces the results, except when ballot voting is used. Members may not debate after voting has begun to explain a vote. Once voting has begun, the presiding officer should not permit interruptions unless there is an emergency.

The assembly has the final decision in determining all voting processes or results of votes that have been questioned, such as entitlement to vote or to determine results of a vote.

Absentee Voting

The right to vote is generally limited to those present at the meeting. The only votes absent members may use are proxy voting and mail balloting. Neither method may be used unless provided for in the documents of authority.

Ballot Voting

This method of voting is the most democratic since it provides for secrecy. A member need not reveal how he or she votes. A ballot *is* a secret vote.

Usually, bylaws or documents of authority provide when and how a ballot shall be taken. Balloting is most commonly used for elections, to prefer charges or determine punishment of members, or whenever members wish to vote without revealing their sentiments or position, knowledge of which might be used to their disadvantage.

If bylaws require a ballot vote, this rule cannot be suspended, even by a unanimous vote. Any member may move to vote by ballot.

The presiding officer may not order a ballot vote, but if the proposition has been emotionally argued or contentious, the chair may ask that if there is no objection, a vote be taken by ballot.

Balloting may be conducted on paper, by machine, or by computer.

All ballots should be accurately prepared well in advance. Paper ballots should be printed. Also, a provision should be made that voters may mark their ballots in private. Ballots should provide that:

1. All nominees are listed for each office in the order as predetermined in the bylaws or by assembly. An adequate space should be left for write-in votes.
2. All issues should be clearly stated with adequate space to check the yes or no, or the selection if it is a multiple choice. Clear and definite instructions for balloting should be explained by the chairman of tellers or printed on the ballot itself in a conspicuous place.

In some organizations, members leave the room to ballot while the business of the assembly continues. Sometimes a recess is declared, and in other cases, opportunity for voting is provided between meetings.

See also **Polls; Tellers and Balloting Procedures; Votes and Voting Methods, Method.**

Bullet Vote

This is a vote cast for only one nominee from among a list where more than one person may be chosen. The other possible votes are ignored. While the one vote strengthens the voter's choice, the voter loses the opportunity to select others.

Computer Voting

This vote is more familiarly known as button or electronic voting. It provides immediate results. The method is used in legislatures, large political conventions, and other large organizations where many delegates attend.

Consensus

This is not really a vote. It means that after thorough discussion, a compromise has been reached that is acceptable to all.

Cumulative Voting

This vote is used when more than one nominee of equal rank may be voted for, in elections for such positions as directors, delegates, or committee members. The vote may also apply to an issue where there are several choices, such as in filling blanks. Each voter may cast as many votes as entitled—the voter's own ballot plus the proxies held. All votes may be concentrated on one nominee, or distributed as the voter chooses or has been instructed. Less than the number of votes cast of the assigned votes are accredited, but more than the number voids the ballot. This method may only be used when specifically provided for in the bylaws.

General Consent

When there is no objection it means that most members are obviously in favor of the proposition or candidate; therefore, there is no need to take a vote. If there is one objection, however, a vote must be taken.

See also **Unanimous Consent Procedure.**

Machine Voting

Voting machines are used for public voting and in large conventions, so the vote tally can be accurate and rapid. Use of this method requires personnel trained to set up the machine with the slate of candidates or issues accurately and properly listed, and who can instruct voters unfamiliar with their use. Inspectors should be assigned to observe the voting to prevent tampering with the machine.

Mail Ballot

This form of voting must be authorized in bylaws. It is used where the membership is widespread geographically or where issues to be decided upon are so important that a majority vote of the entire membership is required. The mailing list must correspond exactly with the certified roll of voting members. If no secrecy is required, the ballot is mailed to the member together with instructions, sometimes with explanatory information, and the time when the ballot is to be in the hands of the tellers. The ballot is signed by the voter, and the signature is checked against the roll to insure that no one else has voted in the member's name. If the ballot is to be secret, each member is sent a ballot together with careful instructions as to processing it. The ballot is to be cast, folded according to instructions, and deposited and sealed in a plain envelope as provided. This envelope is then inserted in a return envelope on which the voter writes his signature. The secretary or the tellers mark the name on the voting roll as having voted. The return envelope is opened, the sealed envelope is removed and opened, and the ballot, kept folded, is deposited in the ballot box. At the appointed time, the tellers remove and unfold the ballots and proceed with the count.

See also **Mail Balloting.**

Plurality Vote
See **Plurality Vote.**

Preferential Voting

Preferential voting refers to a number of voting methods by which, on a single ballot, when there are more than two choices available, the second, third, or other choice may be accounted for also if no majority is reached on the first ballot.

It is a complicated, time-consuming system, actually a mathematical process susceptible to miscalculation. There is no reason to use such a method except in a mail ballot where it is expensive and impractical to reballot.

Preferential voting may only be used if the bylaws authorize it and provide detailed instructions for the method to be used. In preferential voting, the first, second, third, and other choices are counted toward obtaining a majority.

Briefly, in one method the voter indicates his choice in numerical order, first choice as 1, second choice as 2, and so on. The votes are arranged in piles according to first choice; they are counted and recorded. If no choice receives a majority, the ballots are redistributed according to second choice and so on.

Another system drops the choices with the lowest count, and the second and third choices of those votes are added to the first choices, in the hope of obtaining a majority.

Another method drops all but the two leading nominees. Then all who were dropped have their votes divided, according to choice, between the two remaining nominees.

When no candidate obtains a majority, instead of reballoting, a quota vote, a form of transferable votes, provides that some one candidate reaches a majority. Tellers must be skilled in this method's use.

See also **Preferential Balloting**.

Proxy Voting
See **Proxy Voting.**

Revote or Recount

When no majority has been reached in an election, a revote is required in continuum until one has been achieved. Candidates having fewer than a majority may not be dropped from the list unless prior arrangement has been adopted.

If a member believes the result of the count in a ballot vote is inaccurate, the count may be challenged if this is done at the time of the vote. If a member believes the outcome of a voice vote will be close, that member may call for a division of assembly. The chair may also order a recount or take a revote.

See also **Division of Assembly; Voting Irregularities, Challenging a Vote.**

Rising or Standing Vote

This method of taking a vote is used whenever a two-thirds vote is required; if, as a result of noisy debate, the chair decides that a rising vote will safeguard the announcement of the result or on a call for division of assembly.

See also **Voting Requirements, Two-Thirds Vote.**

Roll Call Voting

This form of voting is often called yea and nay voting. Roll call voting may be adopted in bylaws or by motion from the floor. The motion is not debatable or amendable and requires a majority vote. It can be reconsidered.

Roll call has infrequent use in ordinary organizations. Its main use is in legislatures and governing or political bodies where the voters represent others who believe that the right to know should include knowing how their representative voted. Roll call places each member's vote on record.

The secretary calls each member's name in order alphabetically. The name of the presiding officer, who usually votes only if it can affect the result, is called last.

Members respond to their names with aye or no, or, if they wish to abstain, with "present" or "here."

The secretary repeats each vote to verify it as it is recorded next to the voter's name in one of three columns: for aye, no, and abstain. This provides for rapid, easy tally.

Roll call votes are entered in the minutes after each name, together with the results, as are all counted votes. Members who wish to change their vote may do so until the chair announces the result of the vote. Those who entered the polling place after their names were called have an opportunity to vote, as do those who abstained on the first call of the voters' names.

In the event that not enough votes are cast to prove the presence of a quorum, the chair will direct the secretary to record enough names of those present who responded as abstaining to prove that a quorum is present.

Secretary Casting One Vote

If bylaws require a ballot vote, even if there is but one nominee, the bylaws may not be suspended even by a unanimous vote to do so. If there is no such requirement, the motion to have the secretary cast one ballot, as a majority of one vote cast, is in order, but not recommended. The secretary must actually cast the ballot. The chair must announce the result.

Show of Hands

A show of hands is more accurate than a voice vote. The chair may determine which method to use. It is not a counted vote unless a count has been called for, in which case hands may be counted instead of taking a rising vote—when the group is small enough that hands may be seen by all the assembly. Show of hands is usually used when a two-thirds vote is required and the group is small. The chair always explains how the vote is to proceed. The chair states, "All those in favor of . . . , raise you right hand; lower." "All those opposed to . . . , raise your right hand; lower." After this, the chair announces the result.

Telephone Vote

Many corporations allow voting of boards or committees to be conducted by telephone. This method may only be used if the charter or bylaws permit. The voting procedure must be carefully specified and conducted strictly according to regulations: all notified, a quorum responding. Calls to individual members, even though each has been contacted, is not a legitimate substitute for a telephone or teleconference call as described in the documentary authority.

See also **Teleconferences.**

Tie Vote

Whenever a vote results in a tie, the motion or election is lost as there was not a majority to adopt or elect. The chair, if it has not already voted, may opt to break the tie, or if the vote resulted in a majority of one, opt to make a tie. Unless the chair feels strong sentiment about the issue, the chair will usually refrain from voting since, in either case, half the voters will be in opposition to the outcome. Unless the vote was by ballot, the partiality of the chair has been revealed. (Some organizations grant a bylaw permission for the chair to have a second or "casting" vote in case of a tie.)

See also **President, President's Vote.**

Unanimous Vote

A unanimous vote means that every voter is in agreement, not that some are assumed to be in agreement because they have not voted. Some may decide that their vote in opposition will not prevail and thus refrain from voicing opposition. That does not constitute a unanimous vote but one of general consent, where it is understood that some may feel opposed but are indifferent to registering opposition.

A requirement of a unanimous vote is not good since one dissenting member—a minority—has the power to destroy the vote of the majority of all other voters. It is good procedure to have a unanimous vote if there is no objection. If there is objection a motion would be in order, determined by a majority.

No motion is in order to make a vote unanimous when it was not. It would deprive voters of their rightful vote, and to vote against it would reveal how an objector voted, thus denying the right to privacy.

Unit Rule

Unit rule permits delegates at convention to cast all votes of the area they represent as one vote as the majority of the delegates decide. This method may only be used if authorized in bylaws or charter.

Voice Vote

This method is the most regularly used method for any motion that does not require more than a majority vote. It is simple and quick, but not accurate. The chair decides the outcome of a voice vote. This method should not be used when it appears that the result of the vote will be close and determining a majority will be difficult, especially when one side, usually the minority, outshouts the majority. The chair may decide to use a show of hands, a rising vote, or a division vote.

Write-in Vote

This method is always in order when the vote is by ballot unless the bylaws prohibit it. It provides an opportunity for the election of a candidate who has not been nominated. This is not always to the advantage or best interests of a society. Any dissident group, without knowledge of the rest of the membership, may carry a "dark horse" into office. But, in cases where a group of officers have provided for self-perpetuation, such a method for using write-in votes might have some justification.

VOTING IRREGULARITIES

Challenging a Vote

The validity of a vote may be challenged by any member as to the results of the tally or the right of another member to vote, to use proxies, or to vote on an issue for personal gain. The chair may rule on such a challenge, ask the credentials committee to submit data, consult the tellers, or ask the assembly to decide. There can be no appeal from the decision of the assembly. A challenge must be made before the vote is to be taken on it or immediately after the result has been announced. The challenge may interrupt a speaker.

Counting Illegal Votes

All votes cast by illegal voters are not counted in determining results. All illegal votes cast by legal voters are not counted. Illegal votes are of little concern unless they can affect the result. They are not counted except to determine the presence of a quorum.

See also **Illegal Votes and Votes Not Counted.**

Voting Frauds

Fraudulent votes should be of concern to voters. They violate the will of the assembly and of the people. Fraudulent abuses are easily achieved where the voting monitors and tellers lack integrity and ability. If the votes are illegal or discovered to be illegal and declared void, they are of no consequence unless they can affect the result of the vote. Some abuses are as follows:

1. Names inserted in registration books of those who have died, who are transients, or are in mental hospitals. A matching signature should be required in an official permanent register book.

2. Paper ballots that are easy to change, erase, or stuff. "It ain't how the ballots go in that counts, it's how they come out." The voter should be sure his or her ballot has been properly deposited.

3. Assistance frauds at voting machines. Such wrongdoers may show the voter how to vote while casting several votes. The handle of the curtain should be closed all the way. All levers on the party emblem sign (voting a straight ticket) should be all the way down and not pushed back up.

4. Voting machines may have wedges inserted to prevent the lever from going down all the way. Labels may be switched. Clocks may be changed to permit fraudulent voters an early vote before voting hours begin.

5. Setting the machine at a higher figure than zero for a party or an issue.

6. Absentee ballots not delivered in time, miscounted, or otherwise tampered with. Ballots should be carefully sealed.

7. Voters have a right to inspect rolls before or after the voting to check if anyone voted in their name, or if any phony names were added.

VOTING REQUIREMENTS

Majority Vote

A majority vote is defined as over half of the legal votes cast by members legally entitled to vote. Documents of authority must define precisely what a majority shall be: a majority of those present and voting, of those present, of the entire membership, of a quorum, or of members in good standing.

See also **Majority Vote.**

Two-Thirds Vote

Any vote requirement that is greater than a majority is inconsistent with the concept that a majority decides. Such a requirement can work in reverse to the desired effect of obtaining a large majority since one-third plus one, a minority, can control the voting result. The same goes for any other proportion designated, such as four-fifths, nine-tenths, or even unanimity.   .

Any requirements for two-thirds votes should be set forth in the bylaws or in the standing rules.

All two-thirds votes should be taken by division, which includes a show of hands, a standing vote, or a roll call. When the outcome of a vote is obviously one-sided, a careful count is unnecessary. The chair may announce the result as adopted or rejected without taking a count. A rapid count may be taken by a count-off (serpentine vote). The chair asks those in favor of the motion to stand, to count off, and to be seated. Then the chair asks those who are opposed to the motion to stand, count off, and be seated. The chair must then announce the result of each count and the vote and declare which side won. Another way to count, used when attendance is large, is with tellers appointed by the chair. When sections of the assembly are asked to rise in favor or in opposition, the tellers count off the votes, tally them, and hand the result to the chair for announcement.

An easy calculation for tallying a two-thirds vote is to double the number of no votes. If it exceeds the number of yes votes, a two-thirds vote was not obtained.

See also **Division of Assembly.**

Vote to Elect Committee Membership

This method is used in small groups when electing committee members where more than the required number for the committee have been named. The chair calls each name in the order of nomination. Hands are counted. Those nominees who first receive a majority vote are declared elected. The rest of the names are ignored. This vote can also be taken by a rising vote.

VOTING RIGHTS AND RULES

1. A member in arrears for dues may vote unless bylaws say otherwise, or the member has been formally dropped from the rolls.
2. A member can abstain from voting even though voting is a duty. No one should be compelled to vote.
3. All members have the freedom to vote as they choose except under a unit vote rule.
4. A member may vote for himself or herself for office, when qualified.
5. Members may change their votes until the announcement of the result, except in ballot voting. After the announcement, the change can be made only by permission of the assembly.
6. Members do not have the right to explain their votes before the announcement of the results. This would be equivalent to debate.
7. No member should vote when there is a conflict of interest, wherein the member stands to gain personally.
8. No member under suspension may vote.
9. In a counted vote, the affirmative is counted first, then the negative. During this time, no member should enter or leave the room.
10. Whenever questions arise as to the propriety or order of voting procedures, they are referred to the assembly for a decision.
11. Once voting has begun, the chair should not permit any interruptions except in emergency.
12. *Ex officio* members usually may vote; honorary members may not vote unless the documentary authority states otherwise.

WITHDRAWAL OF A MOTION

A member making a motion, including an amendment, may withdraw it at any time before the assembly takes an action on it. Action by the assembly on a motion, or any pending matter offered to it, includes any unanimous consent agreement providing for a disposition of the matter, adoption of a motion to limit or close debate on it, agreeing to an amendment to it, referring the issue to a committee, or the adoption of a motion to postpone the proposal, along with a long list of actual actions that might be taken on any proposal.

If any action is taken by the assembly on a motion or proposal, then the maker of any of the respective parts of the whole on which any action has been taken loses the right to withdraw it: It is no longer the property of the mover; the assembly possesses it. For example, if an amendment to the main motion has been agreed to, the main motion may not be withdrawn by the maker except by consent of the assembly. If another amendment is then offered to the main motion but no action on it has been taken, the person offering the amendment may withdraw it and does not need the consent of the assembly.

If the proposer of a main motion does properly withdraw it, then any amendment, motion, or whatever that has been called up and is pending but on which action has not been taken by the assembly falls with the withdrawal of the main motion.

After the assembly has taken action on a pending matter—not including its actual adoption or rejection—even though the right to withdraw it is lost, it may be withdrawn by general consent. The proposer of the pending matter merely asks general consent of the assembly to withdraw it. The chair states, "If there are no objections, the motion is withdrawn." If there is objection to the request, a motion would be in order, such as "I move to table the motion," or "I move to withdraw the motion." In either case, a majority vote is required to take such action. Withdrawn motions are not entered in the minutes if no action has been taken thereon. If action was taken, such as granting permission to withdraw, it is entered in the minutes.

Index

Absentee, 1
Absentee voting, 1, 2, 198
Abstention, 2
Accepting a report, 2
Acclamation, 3
Addressing the Chair (*see also* Recognition), 3
Ad hoc committee, 48
Adjourn. *See* Adjournment.
Adjournment, 4–6
  Adjourn, motion to, 4–6
    Amendments to, 4
    Precedence of, 4
    Privileged, 150
    Session, impact on, 182
    Sine die, 5, 6
    Time certain, 4, 5, 150
  Board, sine die, 29, 30
  Stopping the clock, 186, 187
Administrative duties of president, 6
Administrative manager. *See* Executive Secretary.
Adopting a report, 2, 3
Agenda (*see also* Order of Business), 7–12
  Adopting, 8
  Amendments to, 7
  Announcements, 11, 21
  Business:
    New, 31
    Unfinished, 30, 31
  Convention business, 68, 69
  General orders, 131
  "Good of the order" provision, 97, 98
  Orders of the day, 135, 151
  Regular order, 132, 151
  Rules of order, 179
  Sample, 9–11
  Social hour, 182

Unanimous consent procedure, 56
Unfinished business, 196
Agreeing to a report, 2, 3
Alternates, 81
Amendments and amending process, 12–20
  Advantages of, 12
  Agenda, 7
  Bylaws, 33
    Previously adopted, 36, 37
  Charter of organization, 44
  Division of the question, 20
  First degree, 15–19
  Friendly, 12, 13
  Germaneness of, 12, 97
  Improper, 20
  Illustration of, 15–19
  Motions
    Amendable, 117
    Assumed or implied, 24
  Mover's control of (*see also* Friendly Amendments), 12, 13
  Perfecting, 13–15
  Precedence of, 13, 14
  Previously adopted decisions, 41–43
  Process, illustration of, 16
    Chart 1, 16
    Chart 2, 16
  Second degree, 16–19
  Substitute, 13–15
Announcements, 11, 21
Annual meeting, 21, 22
Annual session, 22
Appeal from ruling of the Chair, 22, 23
Appreciation resolution. *See* Courtesy Resolution.
Articles of bylaws. *See* Bylaws.

Articles of incorporation, 43, 44
Assembly. *See* Deliberative
    Assemblies.
Associate membership, 24
Assumed motions, 24
Attendance, 1
Attorney, 24, 25, 43, 44
Auditor, 25, 26
Authority, parliamentary (*see also*
    Rules of order), 179

Ballots (*see also* Voting and Voting
    Methods), 26, 27
  Casting one vote, 203
  Election by, of committee
      members, 51
  Illegal votes, 100, 101
  Mail, 103, 104, 140, 200, 201
  Nomination by, 123
  Polls, 142, 143
  Preferential, 145, 201
  Recording of, 191
  Report of tellers, 191, 192
  Secretary casting one vote, 203
  Tellers, duties of, 190–92
  Votes not counted, 100, 101
  Voting procedures, 190–92, 198,
      199
  Write-in vote, 205
Boards, 27–30
  Adjournment of, sine die, 29, 30
  Authority, 27
  Committee membership,
      appointment of, by, 51
  Composition, 28
  Corporate, 28
  Directors, 128, 129
  Ex officio members, 94
  Executive, reports of, 170
  Executive committee, 28
  Executive secretary, duties of, 94
  Functions of, 28
  Meetings of, 28
    Minutes, 28
    Procedure of business, 28, 29
  Quorum, 162
  Reports to membership, 29

Responsibilities of, 29
Sine die adjournment, 29, 30
Teleconferences, 30, 190
Tenure, 30
Unincorporated, 28
Vacancies on, 30
Budget, Finance commitee
    responsibilities, 96
Bullet vote, 199
Business (*see also* Agenda; Order of
    Business), 30, 31
  Convention agenda, 68, 69
  Main motion, 104, 105
  New, 31
  Unanimous consent procedure,
      194, 195
  Unfinished, 196
Button voting. *See* Computer
    Voting.
Bylaws (*see also* Constitution;
    Documents of Authority),
    31–38, 89, 90
  Absentee members, protection of,
      in, 1
  Adoption of, 33, 34
  Amendments, 33, 36, 37
  Articles of, 33
  Constitution, function of, in
      deliberative assemblies, 58
  Construction of, 32
  Contents, guidelines for, 34–36
  Convention
    Applicability to, 60, 67
    Provision for, 60
  Duties, delegation of, 81
  Effective date, 33
  Emergency situations, provisions
      for, 93
  Executive committee, composition
      and duties of, 93
  Form, 33
  Interpretation of, 38
  Membership
    Honorary, 99, 100
    Qualifications for, 110
  Officers
    Installation of, 101

Provisions for, 124, 125
Past president, specifying title and
    role of, in, 140
President-elect, specifying duties
    and limitations in, 126, 127
Provisions, suspension of certain,
    89, 90
Provisos to, 154, 155
Revision of, 37, 38
Rights of organization, specifying
    in, 177
Suspension of, 188
Terms of office, definition of, in,
    192
Vacancies, provisions for, 196
Voting entitlement, provision for,
    198
Writing of, 32

Call to convention. *See* Convention.
Call of the House. *See* Votes and
    Voting Methods.
Call meeting to order, 38, 39
Call to a meeting, 107, 108, 183,
    184
Call for regular orders. *See* Orders
    of the Day.
Candidate, 39
Caucus, screening by, of, 39
Nominating committee, review
    by, of, 121, 122
Nonnominated, write-in votes for,
    123
Write-in votes for, 39
Cards, color, use of in conventions,
    66, 67
Caucus, 39, 40
Censure, 40, 86
Chair (*see also* Presiding Officer):
Addressing, 3
Ruling of, appeal from, 22, 23
Chairman (*see also* Presiding
    Officer), 40, 41
Co-chairman, 41
Vice-chairman, 41
Challenging a vote, 205

Changing a previous decision, 41–
    43
Charter:
Attorney, function of, 24, 25
Certificate of incorporation, 43,
    44
Constitution, subordination of, to,
    58
Dissolution, 86, 87
Merger of corporate societies, 11,
    112
Sunshine laws, impact of State,
    187
Teleconferences, use of, for
    meetings, 190
Charter members, 44
Close debate, 44, 45
Closed session, 45, 46
Closing nominations, 122, 123
Color cards, 66, 67
Co-chairman, 41
Commit, 46–48
Committees, 48–55
Act, directing to, 49
Bylaws, to prepare, 32
Chairman, 40, 41, 52
Conduct in, 52, 53
Creation of, 49, 50
Discharge, 83
Duties, delegation of, 81
Ex officio members, 94
Executive, 93, 94
Finance, 95, 96
Hearings, 99
Informal consideration by, 53
Investigate, duties of, to, 49, 193
Limitation on, 53
Membership
    By appointment, 50
    By ballot, 51
    Ex officio, 94
    Nomination, 50
    President as ex officio, 6
    Qualifications of, 51
    Resignation, 174
    Vote to elect, 54, 207
Minutes, 54

Committees (*continued*)
  Sample, 55
  Motions to commit, recommit,
    and refer to, 46–48
  Nominating, 121, 122, 183
  Of one, 54
  Permanent society, establishing
    for, 133, 134
  Preconvention, 61, 62
  Protocol, 153, 154
  Powers of, 53, 54
  Quorum, 162
  Reconsider, 167
  Reference to, 167, 168
  Reports
    Executive board, 170
    Minority, 112
    Nominating, 122
    Preparation of, 169
    Special committee, 170
    Standing committee, 170
  Special, 48, 170
  Standing, 48, 49, 170
  Standing rules, matters included
    in, 185, 186
  Subcommittees, 53
  Teleconferences, use of, 190
  Tellers as, 190
  Vote to elect membership, 54,
    207
Computer voting, 199
Conduct in committee, 52, 53
Conflict of interest, abstention from
  vote, 2
Consensus, 56, 199
  Informal consideration to reach,
    56, 57
Consent. *See* General Consent;
    Unanimous Consent.
Consent agenda, 56
Consider informally, 56, 57
  Conduct in small committees, 53
Consideration (*see also* Debate;
    Question of Consideration):
  Creating a blank, 70
  Discharging a committee from, 83

En bloc, 93, 175, 176
Informal, 56, 57
Inquiries during, 172, 173
Main motion, processing of, 152,
  153
Objection to, 158, 159
Putting the question, 156, 157
Question of, 158, 159
Requests during, 172, 173
Resolutions, 174–76
Seriatim, 182
Unanimous consent procedure,
  194, 195
Consolidation (*see also* Merger), 57
Constitution (*see also* Bylaws), 31,
  58, 89
Consultant, 58
Conventions, 58–70
  Agenda, business, 68, 69
    Sample, 68, 69
  Alternates, 81
  Aspects of, 59
  Business agenda, 68, 69
  Call to, components of, 62
  Color cards, use of, 66, 67
  Committees
    Credentials, 64
    Minutes, 67, 68
    Preconvention, 61, 62
    Program, 65, 66
    Reference, 168
    Resolutions or platforms, 62, 63
    Rules, 65
  Components of, 59
  Co-ordinator, duties of, 60
  Courtesy resolution, 69, 70
  Delegates, 59, 79–81
    Alternates, 81
    Duties, 80
    Instructed, 80
    New, 80
    Qualifications, 79
    Reports of, 80, 81
  Executive board report, 170
  Microphones, floor, use of, 66, 67
  Minutes, 67, 68

Opening ceremonies, 63
Parliamentarian, duties and
    responsibilities, 138
Preconvention
    Committees, 61, 62
    Preparation, 60, 61
Professional bureau, services of,
    61, 62
Quorum, 162
Registrar's duties, 60, 61
Standing rules for, 186
Treasurer's duties, 60, 61
Unit rule, 204
Corporate boards, functions of, 28
Corresponding secretary, 180, 181
Counsel. *See* Attorney.
Counting of illegal votes, 205
Courtesy resolution, 69, 70
Creating a blank, 70
Credentials committee, convention,
    64
Customs (*see also* Precedents), 70

Debate, 71–79
    Close, 44, 45
    Control, 76
    Decorum, rules of, 72–74
    Extending limit, 103
    Floor privileges, 96, 97
    Germaneness, 97
    Informal consideration during,
        56, 57
    Inquiries during, 172, 173
    Interruptions to, 76, 102
    Limit, 102, 103
        Motion to extend beyond, 102,
        103
    Main motion, 104, 105
    Members' responsibilities, 71, 72
    Nominations, 121
    Parliamentary inquiry, 138–40
    Point of order, 76, 77, 140, 141
    Presiding officer, role of, during,
        74, 75
    Questions of privilege, 77, 159–
        61

Questions to a speaking member,
    77
    Reading of papers during, 164
    Regular order, 76
    Responsibilities
        Member, 71, 72
        Presiding officer, 74, 75
    Requests during, 172, 173
    Rights to speak, 178, 179
    Rules of decorum, 72–74
    Speaking member, questions to,
        77
    Strategy for
        General, 77, 78
        Presiding officer, 79
    Techniques, 78
    Termination, methods for, 75, 76
    Undebatable motions, 195, 196
    Yielding for questions, 77
Decisions, changing previous, 41–43
Decorations committee, 61
Decorum:
        Presiding officer's duty to
            maintain, 83–85
        Rules of, during debate, 72–74
        Sergeant at Arms, duties of,
            181
Delegates to conventions, 59, 79–81
Delegating duties, 81
Deliberative assemblies, 81, 82
    Dissolution, 86, 87
    Division, 87, 88
    Legal requirements, 82
    Purpose, 81, 82
    Questions of privilege, 159–61
    Rights of organization, 177
    Sunshine laws, impact of State,
        187
Dilatory motions, 82
Director, executive. *See* Executive
    Director.
Directors. *See* Boards.
Discharge a committee, 83
Discipline, 83–85
    Censure, 40
    Members' responsibilities, 79

Discipline (*continued*)
  Interrupt a speaker
    Motions that may not, 77
    Yielding, 77
  Question of privilege, 159–61
  Responsibilities
    Members, 85
    Presiding officer, 83–85
  Rules of decorum during debate,
    72–74
  Trial and expulsion of members,
    193, 194
Dissolutions, 86, 87
Division of assembly, 87, 88, 207
Division of a question, 20, 88
Documents of authority, 89–92
  Articles of incorporation, 43, 44
  Bylaws, 31–38, 89, 90
  Charter certificate of
    incorporation, 43, 44
  Constitution, 58, 89
  Consultants, knowledge of, by, 58
  Emergency situations, provisions
    for, 93
  Ex officio membership, provision
    for, 94
  Executive secretary, provision for,
    94
  Nominations, provisions for, 120,
    121
  Parliamentarian, duties and
    responsibilities, 137
  Parliamentary authority, 179
  Policy statements, 142
  Precedents and practices, 91, 144,
    145
  Privileged business, 161
  Provisos to, 154, 155
  Rights of organization, 177
  Rules of order, 179
  Standing orders, 90, 91, 184
  Standing rules of procedure, 90,
    184–86
  Voting requirements, 197, 198

Elections (*see also* Nominations), 92,
  93

Acclamation, 3
Ballot voting, 26, 27, 190–92
Bullet vote, 199
By ballot, committee membership,
  51
Candidates, 39
Cumulative voting, 200
Emergency situations, provisions
  for, 93
Ineligible member, 125
Nomination procedures, 120–
  23
Plurality vote, 140
Rules, general, 92, 93
Special, to fill vacancy, 197
Tellers, duties of, 190–92
Write-in vote, 205
Electronic voting. *See* Computer
  Voting.
Emergency situations, 93
En bloc consideration, 93, 175,
  176
En grosse. *See* En bloc.
Eviction of member, 84
Ex officio, 94
Exception, 154, 155
Executive board. *See* Boards.
Executive committee, 28, 93, 94
Executive director. *See* Executive
  Secretary.
Executive secretary, 94, 171
Executive session. *See* Closed
  Session.
Expulsion of member, 193, 194
Expunge, 94, 95
Extend debate or limitation of. *See*
  Debate.

Filling blanks. *See* Creating a Blank.
Finance committee, 95, 96, 172
Floor microphones. *See*
  Microphones.
Floor privileges, 96, 97
Fraudulent votes, 206
Friendly amendments, 12, 13

General consent (*see also* Consensus; Unanimous Consent), 56, 97, 194, 195, 200

General orders, 131

Germaneness, requirement for, 12, 97

"Good of the order", 97, 98

Guest Speakers, 3, 98, 99, 154

Hearings, 99

Honorary membership, 99, 100

Hospitality committee, 61

Illegal votes, 100, 101, 205

Implied motions, 24

Improper amendments, 20

Improper motions, 116

Incorporation. *See* Charter.

Indecorum. *See* Debate; Disciplines; Rights to Speak.

Informal consideration, 56, 57

Information, point of. *See* Parliamentary Inquiry; Point of Information.

Inquiries (*see also* Requests), 172, 173

Inquiry, parliamentary. *See* Parliamentary Inquiry.

Installations, 101, 124

Interpretation of bylaws. *See* Bylaws.

Interruptions to debate, 76, 77, 102
  Motion, privileged, which may not, 77
  Yielding, 77

Ladder of motions, 118
  Privileged motions, 150, 151
  Standing rules, specifications in, 185

Legal interruptions to debate, 76, 102
  Point of order, 140, 141

Legal requirements for deliberative assemblies, 82

Limiting debate, 102, 103
  Extending time, 103

Limitations on committees, 53

Machine voting, 103, 200

Mail balloting, 103, 104, 140, 200, 201

Main motion, 104, 105, 130
  Amendments to, 15–19
  Decisions, changing previous, 41–43
  Preparation of, 105
  Processing of, 152, 153
  Putting the question, 156, 157
  Question of consideration, 158, 159
  Resolutions, 174

Majority vote, 2, 106, 206, 207

Mass meetings, 106–8
  Permanent society, formation of, 132
  Quorum, 162
  Sine die adjournment, 6

Meetings:
  Annual, 21, 22
  Board, 28
  Call to order, 38, 39
  Closed sessions, 45, 46
  Conventions, 58–70
  Mass, requirements for, 106–8
  Notice, 124
  Previous notice, 149
  Quorum, 109
  Requirements, 108, 109
  Rights of membership, 111
  Sessions, closed, 45, 46
  Special, 183, 184

Membership, 109–11
  Absentee, rights of, 1
  Alternates, 81
  Associate, 24
  Censure, 40
  Classes of, 110
  Charter, 44
  Committees
    Appointment of, by, 50
    Chairman, 52
    Election of, by ballot, 51
    Nomination of, 50
    Qualifications of, 51
    Vote to elect, 54, 207

Membership (*continued*)
  Conduct requiring disciplinary
    action, 84
  Consultants, 58
  Debate, responsibilities during,
    71, 72, 79
  Delegates, *See* Conventions.
  Discipline, 83–85
    Members' responsibilities, 85
    Presiding officer's
      responsibilities, 83–85
  Ex officio, 94
  Expulsion, 193, 194
  Honorary, 99, 100
  Obligations of, 110
  Questions of personal privilege,
    159–61
  Quorum, 161–63
  Resignation from, 110, 174
  Rights of, at meetings, 111
  Rights to speak, 178
  Trial and expulsion for
    misconduct, 85, 193, 194
  Voting entitlement, 198
Merger (*see also* Consolidation), 111,
    112
Microphones, floor, use of in
    conventions, 66, 67
Minority report, 112
Minutes, 113–116
  Board meetings, 28
  Committee, 54
    Investigating formal complaint
      against member, 193
    Sample, 55
  Contents, 114, 115
  Convention, 67, 68
  Expunge, 94, 95
  Reading of, 164
  Roll call vote, recording of, 203
  Sample, 55, 115
  Special, 183
  Tape recordings, use of, 190
Misconduct
    Member, 84
    Presiding officer, 85, 86
Motions, 116–20

Adjourn, 4
Adjourn sine die, 5
Adjourn to time certain, 4, 5
Adopt agenda, 8
Adopt report, 2, 3
Adopted, changing previously,
    41–43
Agenda, adopt, 8
Agree to report, 2, 3
Amendable, 117
Assumed, 24
Close debate, 44, 45
Close nominations, 122, 123
Close session, 45, 46
Commit, 46–48
Consent, general, 97
Consider informally, 57
Create a committee, 49, 50
Debate
  Control of, through, 76
  Extending limit, 103
  Interruption of, for certain, 102
  Limit, 102, 103
Dilatory, 82
Discharge a committee, 83
Division of assembly, 87, 88
Expunge, 94, 95
"Good of the order", 97, 98
Implied, 24
Improper, 116
In order, 116
Informal consideration, providing
    for, 56, 57
Interruption of debate for
    certain, 102
Ladder of, 118
Limit debate, 102, 103
  Extending time, 103
Main, 104, 105, 130
  Preparation of, 105
  Processing of, 152,153
  Putting the question, 156, 157
Mover's control of (*see also*
    Friendly Amendments), 12,
    13
Order of business, affecting, 8, 9
Postpone, 143, 144

Precedence, 117–19
  Privileged, 150, 151
  Privileged business, 149, 150
  Standing rules specifying, 185
  Previous notice for certain, 149
Privilege, question of, 77
Privileged, 150, 151
  Interrupting a speaker, 77
Privileged business, 150
Procedural, 119, 120, 151
Questions of privilege, 77
Ratify, 163, 164
Recess, 165
Recommendations, to act on, 165
Recommit, 46–48
Reconsider, 165–67
Refer, 46–48
Renewal of, 168, 169
Reopen nominations, 123
Rescind, 173, 174
Rights to speak, 178
"Second" (*see also* Question of
    Consideration), 158, 159
Seriatim, 182
Sessions, to close, 45, 46
Suspend the rules, 188
Suspension of regular order, for
    special orders, 131
Table, 188–90
Undebatable, 195, 196
Vote by ballot, 26
Vote of confidence, 85
Withdrawal, 208, 209
Mover of motions, control of (*see
    also* Friendly Amendments),
    12, 13

New business, 31
Nominations (*see also* Elections),
    120–23
  Candidate, 39
  Closing, 122, 123
  Debate, 121
  Eligibility, 121
  Methods for making, 120–23
  Ballot, 123
  Chair, 123

  Committee, 121, 122, 183
  Floor, 122
  Petition, 123
Nominating committee, 121, 122,
    183
Nonnominated candidate, voting
    for, 123
Reopening, 123
Slate, requirements of, 183
Write-in votes, 123
Notice of meetings, 124

Oath of office, 124
Obtaining recognition. *See*
    Addressing the Chair;
    Recognition; Rights to Speak.
Officers, 124–30
  Absentee, nominated, elected or
    appointed as, 1
  Bylaws, provisions in, related to,
    124, 125
  Candidates, 39
  Censure, 40
  Corresponding secretary, 128
  Directors, 128, 129
  Duties
    Delegation of, 81
    In absence of presiding officer,
      147, 148
  Election
    Ineligible member, 125
    Plurality voting, 140
  Executive board reports, 170
  Installation of, 101
  Meeting, requirements for
    presence of certain, 109
  Nominations for, 120–23
  Oath, 124
  Organizing permanent society,
    function of, 133, 134
  Other, 129, 130
  President, 6, 126, 127, 145, 146,
    180
  President-elect, 126, 127
  Presiding officer, duties of others,
    in absence of, 147, 148
  Reports

Officers (*continued*)
  Executive director or secretary, 171
  Other, 172
  President, 171
  Treasurer, 171, 172
  Resignation, 174
  Secretary
    Assistance from president, 180
    Corresponding, 128, 181
    Duties, 128
    Recording, 179, 180
  Terms of office, 192, 193
  Treasurer, 129
    Audit of reports of, 25, 26
  Vacancies, 196, 197
  Vice-president, 127, 128
Opening ceremonies, 63, 130
Order, point of. *See* Point of Order.
Order of business (*see also* Agenda), 130–32
  Agenda, 7, 9–11
  General orders, 9, 131
  Mass meetings, 108
  Motions
    Affecting, 8, 9
    Dilatory, 82
  New business, 31
  Orders, 131
  Orders of the day, 132
  Privileged business, 149, 150
  Regular order, 8, 132
  Rules of order, 179
  Sample, 9–11
  Special orders, 9, 131
  Unfinished business, 30, 31, 196
Orders of the day (*see also* Agenda; Order of Business), 132, 151
  Call for, as procedural motion, 151
Organization (*see also* Deliberative Assemblies), dissolution of, 86, 87
Organizing a permanent society. *See* Permanent Society.

Pairing (*see also* Voting and Voting Methods), 135, 136
Papers, reading of, 164
Parliamentarian, 136–38
Parliamentary authority, 179
Parliamentary inquiry, 138–40, 151
Past president, 140
Pending question, division of, 88
Permanent society, organizing of, 133
  Mass meetings, 106–8
  Merger of, 111, 112
Place, Lucille, xii, xiii
Platform committee, 62, 63
Plurality vote, 140
Point of information (*see also* Parliamentary Inquiry), 138–40, 151
Point of order, 140, 141, 151
  Debate, during, 76, 77
  Precedents established through, 91, 144
  Ruling of the Chair, appeal from, 22, 23
Policy statements, 141, 142
Polls, 142, 143
Postpone, 143, 144
  Indefinitely, 143
  Time certain, 143, 144
Powers of committees, 53, 54
Practices and precedents, 91
Preambles, 175
Precedence of motions, 117–19
Precedents (*see also* Customs), 70, 91, 144, 145
Preconvention committees, 61, 62
Preconvention preparation. *See* Conventions.
Preferential balloting, 145
President, 145, 146
  Committee membership
    Appointment of, by, 50
    Nomination of, by, 50
  Functions of, 125, 126
  Past, 140
  Reports by, 171
  Secretary, assistance to, 180

Voting procedures, 146
President-elect, 126, 127
Presiding, 146–148
Presiding Officer (*see also* President):
  Absence of, duties of others in,
    147, 148
  Call meeting to order, 38, 39
  Censure of, for misconduct, 86
  Chairman as, 40, 41
  Debate, 74–76
  Discipline, responsibilities, 83–85
  Duties and responsibilities, 146,
    147
  Meetings, requirement for
    presence of, 109
  Misconduct, 85, 86
  Motions, dilatory, rulings on, 82
  Strategies during debate, 79
  Suspension of, for misconduct,
    85, 86
Previous notice, 148, 149
  Adjourn to time certain, 5
  Bylaw amendments, 36, 37
  Bylaw revision, 37, 38
  Changing previous decisions, 42
  Discharge a committee, 83
  Expunge, 95
  Mass meetings, 106
  Meetings, requirement for, 109
  Rescind, 173, 174
  Special election, 197
Privilege, question of. *See* Questions
  of Privilege.
Privileged business, 149, 150
Privileged motions, 150, 151
Procedural motions, 119, 120, 151
  Undebatable, 195, 196
Program committee, at convention,
  65, 66
Protocol, 153, 154
  Committee, 61
  Guest speakers, 98, 99
  Opening ceremonies, 130
Proviso, 154, 155
Proxy voting, 155, 156, 198
  Absentee, 1, 2
  Pairing, in lieu of, 135, 136

Sample, 156
Public relations committee, 61
Putting the question, 156, 157

Question. *See* Pending Question.
Question, putting the. *See* Putting
  the Question.
Question of consideration, 158, 159
Questions of privilege, 77, 102, 150,
  159–61
Quorum, 161–63
  Absentees, 1
  Abstention, 2
  Committees, 53
  Ex officio members, 94
  Majority vote, 106
  Mass meeting, 107
  Meeting, requirement for
    presence of, 109

Ratify, 163, 164
Reading papers, 164
  Inquiries and requests, 172, 173
Recess, 150, 164, 165
  Informal consideration, 56, 57
  Session, impact on, 182
  v. Adjourn to time certain, 4
Recognition:
  Addressing the Chair, 3
  Color cards, use of in convention,
    66, 67
  Floor privileges, 96, 97
  Microphones, use of floor, in
    convention, 66, 67
  Presiding officer, role during
    debate, 74
  Privileged motions, interrupting a
    speaker for, 77
  Rights to speak, 178, 179
  Rules of decorum during debate,
    72–74
Recommendations, 165
  Reference committee, by, 168
Recommit, 46–48
Reconsider, 165–67
Recording ballots, 191
Recording secretary, 179, 180

Recording secretary (*continued*)
   Assistance from president, 180
   Minutes by, 113–15
Recount, 202
Refer, 46–48
Reference committee, 167, 168
Registrar, duties of at convention, 60, 61
Regular order. *See* Orders of the Day.
Renewal of a motion, 168, 169
Reopening nominations, 123
Reports, 169–72
   Accept, adopt, or agree to, 2, 3
   Board, 29
   Executive director or secretary, 171
   Finance committee, 172
   Minority, 112, 113
   Nominating committee, 122
   Preparation of, 169
   President, 171
   Recommendations, 165
   Tellers, 191, 192
   Treasurer, 171, 172
Requests, 172, 173
Rescind, 173, 174
   v. Sunset clause, 188
Resignation of members, 110, 174
Resolutions, 174–76
   Courtesy, 69, 70
   Dissolution of organization, 86, 87
   En bloc consideration, 175, 176
   Policy statements, 141, 142
   Sample, 176
Resolutions committee, 62, 63
Responsibilities. *See* Debate; Membership.
Revision of bylaws. *See* Bylaws.
Revote, 176, 177, 202
Rights of an organization, 177
Rights to speak, 96, 97, 178, 179
Rising vote, 202
Roll call voting, 202, 203
Rules committee, at convention, 65

Rules of order (*see also* Parliamentary Authority), 179

"Second" (*see also* Question of Consideration), 158, 159
Secretaries, 179–81
   Assistance from the president, 180
   Casting of one vote, 203
   Corresponding, 180, 181
   Duties, 128
   Meeting, requirement for presence of, 109
   Minutes, 113, 114
   Recording, 179, 180
Secretary, executive, report of, 171
Seriatim consideration, 182
Sergeant at Arms, 181
Sessions, 182
   Annual, 22
   Closed, 45, 46
Show of hands, 203
Sine die adjournment, 5, 6, 29, 30
Slate, composition of, 183
Social hour, 182
Speaker, guest. *See* Guest Speakers.
Special committees, 48, 170
Special elections, 197
Special meetings, 183, 184
Special orders, 131
Standing committees, 48–50, 170
Standing orders, 90, 91, 184
   Policy statements, 142
Standing rules of procedure, 90, 184–86
   Format of, 184–86
   Parliamentary authority, 179
   Rights of organization, 177
   Rules of order, 179
   Suspension of, 188
Standing vote, 202
Stopping the clock, 186, 187
Strategy for debate, 77–79
Strike-out-and-insert amendments, 14

Subsidary Motions, 118
Sunset clause, 188
Sunshine laws, 45, 46, 187
Suspend the rules, 188

Table, 188–90
Tape recordings, 190
Techniques in debate, 78
Teleconferences, 30, 190
Telephone vote, 203, 204
Tellers and balloting procedures,
    190–92
  Polls, 142, 143
  Preferential voting, 201
  Procedures, 190–92
  Recording ballots, 191
  Report of tellers, 191, 192
Tenure of boards, 30
Term of office, 192, 193
Termination of debate, 75, 76
Tie vote, 204
Time certain, adjourn to, 4, 5
Treasurer, 129
  Conventions, duties of, 60
  Reports, 171, 172
    Audit of, 25, 26
Trial and expulsion of members,
    25, 193, 194
Two-thirds vote, 207

Unanimous consent, 194, 195
  Agenda items, procedure for, 56
  Agreement, formulation of, 195
  Implied (acclamation), 3
  Procedure, 194, 195
  Reading of certain papers, 164
Unanimous vote, 204
Undebatable motions and
    procedures, 195, 196
Unfinished business, 30, 31, 196
Unincorporated boards, functions
    of, 28

Vacancies in offices, 196, 197
  Board member, 30
  Duties of officers, in absence of
    presiding officer, 147, 148

Verification of vote. See Division of
    Assembly.
Vice-President, 127, 128
Voice vote, 205
Votes not counted, 100, 101
Voting irregularities. See Voting and
    Voting Methods.
Voting rights and rules. See Voting
    and Voting Methods.
Voting and voting methods, 197–
    205
  Absentee, 1, 2, 198
  Abstention from, 2
  Balloting procedures, 190–92
  Ballots, 26, 27, 51, 198, 199
  Bullet vote, 199
  Call of the House (roll call), 202,
    203
  Casting of one vote, 203
  Committee membership, vote to
    elect, 54, 207
  Computer voting, 199
  Consensus, 56, 199
  Cumulative voting, 200
  Division of assembly, 87, 88
  Elections, rules, general, 92, 93
  En bloc, 93
  Entitlements, 198
  General consent, 200
  Illegal votes, 100, 101
  Irregularities
    Challenging a vote, 205
    Fraud, 206
    Illegal votes, counting of, 205
  Machine, 103, 200
  Mail ballots, 103, 104, 140, 200,
    201
  Majority vote, 106, 206, 207
  Method, selection of, 197
  Nominations, write-in, 123
  Pairing, 135, 136
  Plurality vote, 140
  Polls, 142, 143
  Preferential balloting, 145, 201
  President's vote, 146
  Presiding officer, role of, 75

Voting and voting
   methods (*continued*)
  Proxy, 155, 156, 198
    Sample, 156
  Putting the question, 156, 157
  Reconsider, 165–67
  Recount, 202
  Requirements, 197, 198
  Revote, 176, 177, 202
  Rights, 208
  Rising vote, 202
  Roll call vote, 202, 203
  Rules, 208
  Secretary casting one vote, 203
  Show of hands, 203
  Standing rules, 186
  Standing vote, 202
  Telephone vote, 203, 204
  Tellers, 190–92
  Tie vote, 204
  Two-thirds vote, 207
  Unanimous vote, 204
  Unit rule, 204
  Voice vote, 205
  Vote count, verification by
    division of assembly, 87, 88
  Vote to elect committee
    membership, 207
  Votes not counted, 100, 101
  Write-in vote, 205
Voting requirements. *See* Voting
  and Voting Methods.

Whereas clause. *See* Preambles.
Withdrawal of a motion, 208, 209
Write-in vote, 205

Yea and nay voting. *See* Roll Call
  Voting.
Yielding for interruption, 77